John Farman

The very Bloody History of History of Britain

(Without the boring bits!)

THE LAST BIT!

RED FOX

A Red Fox Book

Published by Random House Children's Books
61–63 Uxbridge Road, London W5 5SA

A RANDOM HOUSE GROUP COMPANY
London Melbourne Sydney Auckland
Johannesburg and agencies throughout the world

Copyright © John Farman 1994, 1997, 2001

5 7 9 10 8 6

Original edition first published in Great Britain by
The Bodley Head Children's Books, 1994

This updated Red Fox edition 2001

Printed and bound in Great Britain by
Antony Rowe Ltd, Chippenham, Wiltshire

Papers used by The Random House Group Ltd are natural, recyclable products
made from wood grown in sustainable forests. The manufacturing processes conform
to the environmental regulations of the country of origin.

THE RANDOM HOUSE GROUP Limited Reg. No. 954009
www.**kids**at**randomhouse**.co.uk

ISBN 9780099417781

Contents

Introduction iv

1945 1

1946 5

1947 10

1948 14

1949 18

1950 22

1951 28

1952 33

1953 37

1954 42

1955 46

1956 51

1957 57

1958 61

1959 66

1960 71

1961 75

1962 79

1963 84

1964 89

1965 93

1966 99

1967 105

1968 110

1969 115

1970 120

1971 125

1972 129

1973 135

1974 140

1975 145

1976 149

1977 155

1978 160

1979 165

1980 170

1981 175

1982 181

1983 186

1984 191

1985 196

1986 202

1987 207

1988 213

1989 219

1990 224

1991 230

1992 237

1993 243

1994 249

1995 257

1996 263

1997 270

1998 275

1999 278

2000 281

Introduction

If you were one of the three people (excluding my mother) who struggled through my last mighty work, you will have discovered that, as a historian, I would have made a very good baker. You might remember that I found history, as it was taught at the half school, half prison camp that I 'attended', just a string of obscure dates that seemed to have as much relevance to my little life as a book on etiquette to a professional wrestler.

Part I of my Very Bloody History of Britain (without the boring bits) covered everything from when your great, great (× 600) grandparents grovelled around in the primeval slime waiting for something to happen, to our finest hour when we showed

When are you going to evolve?

the horrid Hun (in their worstest hour) where to get off in World War 2. This book will drag you through the last fifty years to the present when, with a bit of luck, our future will one day merge into someone else's history.

So where do we start and what will we cover?

After the horrors of war, Britain looked optimistically (if a bit apprehensively) to the road ahead. Our young chaps, fed up with Kraut crushing, took a break from wondering if they were ever going to live beyond their teens, and girls, having shown what they could do in the war, began to anticipate something approaching equal opportunities (and more men to choose from).

In some ways, however, wartime had been quite straightforward, both for humble peasants (like what I am) who, let's face it, only had to worry about coming out of it in one piece, and their leaders who, for once, could forget party politics and just get on with the job of flattening foes.

Peacetime, unfortunately, just ain't that easy, as everyone from the managing director to the dustman has a perfectly valid opinion on who should run their country – and how. No one could deny that in 1945 Britain was at a major crossroads with so many options that even a clever clairvoyant could only guess which way we'd go. . . .

Firstly, and most importantly; what was going to happen to the Empire that we'd ruled over (and milked) for so many years? Just like the French, who'd had to let go of Vietnam, or the Dutch, who were facing revolting Indonesians, Britain was hearing the faint, but ominous, beat of distant drums from India and Africa. Those natives were certainly getting restless. Indeed many countries throughout the world regarded us as a dangerous imperialist power on a par with Russia (which seems quite a hoot now!). Even the Yanks, who'd been the very first of our colonies to tell us where to get off, were now none too happy about the whole idea of a 'mighty' British Empire (probably, because they wanted one!). Understandably, a few politicians (like Churchill) seeing the writing on the wall, thought we should cuddle up to Europe, though admittedly, at this stage, for defensive rather than economic reasons.

Poor Britain was, therefore, to find herself in a fine mess as, not only was she getting it in the neck for being this wicked imperialist but, if she waved goodbye to any of her colonies, she'd be seen to be losing her grip.

The other great problem to face Britain, after the all-for-one-and-one-for-all war, was class. Could the huntin', shootin' and fishin' set still hang on to such a huge portion of the country's loot in a country showing signs of creeping towards the left, or would they end up short in the head department (metaphorically speaking) like some of their ancestors or French rellies?

Unfortunately, however, problems (and answers) are seldom as straightforward as this, and world events always put the spanner in the works of any plans a country might have for its future. If you want to see how all these and many other plots thickened, and how we got ourselves into the other fine mess we're in today, take a deep breath . . . and with the best of British luck read on.

Battling with Peace

Churchill, that fabulous fat man with the fabulous fat cigar, had shown the British what a brilliant leader he could be when his back was against the wall. When, therefore, he went into the General Election on 26th July 1945, he had every reason to expect that the shell-shocked nation he'd saved from the slavering jaws of the horrid Hun would welcome him, and his Conservative cronies, back with open arms. But you can always trust the fickle British to do the exact opposite of what is expected – bless 'em. They knew Churchill was fab at wars, but weren't at all convinced he knew how to cope in peacetime.

The war had had a strange effect on the British. For the first time in their history, the rich and privileged had stopped treating the working class like another species and had joined with them to fight the common foe (and those Krauts sure were common!). Countesses had worked next to shop girls making munitions, driving trucks, and working on the land and the bosses had rolled up their immaculate sleeves and joined the peasants on the shop

I say! Isn't work fun?

floor. When the war was over the lower orders (the middle class hadn't really been invented) were none too keen to return to the them-and-us, cap doffing, 'the guvnor's-always-right' system, which had flourished under the Tories before the war. So, much to the anger of Churchill and his none-too-merry men, they replaced the wartime coalition government (a mish-mash of the Conservative, Labour and Liberal parties) and voted in the Labour Party with the biggest majority in its history (before or since!). Foreigners were nothing less than gobsmacked at the result and one incredulous American political commentator reckoned the British population must have received a severe blow to its corporate head.

The practically unheard of motley crew of old lefties was led by a puny little pipe-puffing politician called Clement Attlee backed up by the brash but brilliant ex-miner Ernest Bevin as Foreign Secretary. The country they inherited, it must be said, wasn't that much of a going concern, but Britain knew that it had to dust the counters down, and open 'Great Britain Ltd' as quickly as possible.

Cutting the Cake
Before turning their attention to internal affairs, however, Attlee and a little posse of politicians went off to Potsdam (a dead posh house where all those horrid German leaders had once lived) to join Churchill, the head-American President Truman and head-Russian Stalin (him of the big, black moustache) in the squabble over how to slice up the seriously crumbly Kraut cake. The Western lot didn't like the idea of the puppet Poland (manipulated by Russia) taking a huge chunk of Germany and kicking out millions of its punch drunk inhabitants, while the soon-to-be-hated Stalin wouldn't entertain (surprise, surprise) the idea of free elections in the Eastern European countries.

Churchill, shrewd as ever, used the term 'Iron Curtain' which he accused the Ruskies of lowering, or rather slamming, down against the West. This was the beginning of what became known as the 'Cold War' which was to threaten world peace for years. On a

2

happier note in April, after 2,000 nights of blackouts, all the lights went back on throughout Britain and our parents and grandparents found yet another excuse to have a huge party (some thought it more fun with the lights out). In Croydon alone, which had been particularly heavily bombed (what could the Krauts possibly have had against Croydon?), 7,000 streets lights went on at once.

The UN is born

On 25th April, delegates from all over the world gathered in the San Francisco Opera House, not for a sing-song but to plan a new peace-keeping body to replace the League of Nations. The United Nations, as it was to be called, was formed on a cloud of optimism to make sure that a world war could never happen again. On 26th June delegates from 50 States signed an agreement to supply soldiers to an international force controlled by the new UN General Assembly. It basically meant that if any one of them started pushing their weight around, the other would cut him down to size. In other words it was 'peace with teeth'.

VJ Day

On 14th August, those pesky Japanese finally put up their hands and surrendered. Had the Yanks not dropped their ever-so-clever, but hideously effective A bombs (2000 times nastier than anything seen before), totally obliterating Nagasaki and Hiroshima and killing 7000 Japanese, the Japs might have fought on longer. Far from feeling guilty about our ally's dastardly deeds, we British had yet another huge party.

    The Ex-Premier of Japan, General Hideki Tojo, was so miffed at the prospect of being given the third degree by the conqueror's court that he shot himself in the heart. It really wasn't his year, however, as he 'missed' and had to stand trial like everyone else.

Nuremberg Trials

Meanwhile back in Germany, the allies opened the trials of all the now ex-Hitler's German mates at Nuremberg, where the Nazis had held all their flashest rallies (rubbing their noses in it or what?). Unfortunately (for them), guys like Goering, Hess and Ribhentrop, in their Germanic passion for thoroughness, had kept copious records of all their dirty deeds which, when retrieved, were enough to sign their death warrants.

Lesson One: If you're going to commit terrible crimes against humanity – for goodness sake don't keep a diary!

Meanwhile

January: The train takes the strain. The first boat-train for five years left for Calais.

June: Vampires in Britain! The RAF unveiled the Vampire Jet capable of a never-before-reached 500 m.p.h. A little late I'd have thought.

July: The BBC lightened up a bit too, with its Light Programme.

August: One of Germany's nastiest war criminals, Walter Schellenberg (the 'Butcher of Berlin'), was arrested by the Allies. He was almost more famous for having 'invented' Madame Kittie's, the brothel in Berlin famous for having every room wired with

Darlink! I sink I have vays of making you talk

recording equipment, in order that trained 'frauleins of the night' could elicit secrets from high-ranking foreign visitors.

October: George Orwell made the immortal comment in his brilliant, but scary *Animal Farm*: 'All animals are equal, but some are more equal than others.' (I bet the humble slug could have written that.)

Hit of the Year: 'We'll Gather Lilacs', a soppy song about . . . gathering lilacs.

1946

Britain Goes Short
Just as your forefathers (and mothers) were beginning to look forward to a life of plenty, the grumpy government told them that things could quite possibly get worse, despite a whacking great loan from the States (which was nearly spent by the end of 1947). The war had cost Britain a quarter of its national wealth – some £7 million – and we'd lost two-thirds of our export trade. Overseas investment? Forget it, we'd hocked just about everything but grandmother's false teeth to fight the war. And if that wasn't bad enough, there were other unforeseen problems connected with smashing the baddies, one of which was what to do with all those left, in this case 30 million peckish Germans. Britain found that having successfully ruined German agriculture, she then had to feed its people. You really can't win 'em all.

A world food shortage meant that rationing had to get tougher. This even stricter rationing was hard to take for a nation fed (or not fed) up with going without for so long. Bread, now much darker owing to a lowered wheat content, was rationed rather bizarrely according to how much energy you consumed at work. (I imagine civil servants got almost none.)

Churchill, now terrific in opposition, wagged his cigar, and claimed it jolly well served the British right for voting in the lousy Labour Party.

And Now the Jews

As with the Germans, there then emerged the problem of what to do with the Jews. A carefully considered Anglo-American report came out in May which hit the double jackpot by upsetting not only the world's Jews but the world's Arabs as well. It reckoned that the Holy Land (Palestine) should be regarded as the Jews' natural home but should not be regarded as purely Jewish because it lay at the crossroads of the Arab world. Unfortunately the Arabs didn't see it that way, saying that if it was anyone's natural home, it was theirs (well they would, wouldn't they?). It was a bit like someone coming up to your front door and demanding they live in half your house. They were, consequently, just a little miffed when in just one year, 100,000 of the Nazis' victims were plonked in what they reckoned to be *their* back yard. It was then added that the British mandate should continue till Arab-Jewish hostility disappeared. Nice one! I wonder what they'd have said if they'd had any premonition of what was going to happen. Let's face it, descendents of those Arabs and Jews have been fighting like Tom and Jerry almost ever since.

By August 1945 Britain, much to the annoyance of the Americans (who didn't want any more of them in their country), was actually keeping the Jews who exceeded the agreed quota *out* of Palestine by putting barbed wire across the harbour at Haifa, effectively imprisoning the poor refugees on ships that had become floating slums. Nobody seemed to have any idea what to do with them.

Love and Marriage

One of the more embarrassing effects of our prolonged war was exemplified by the fact that 40% of all girls under twenty had to have their wedding dresses let out for their wedding day (in those days having a nipper out of wedlock was almost unheard of). Let's face it, there was a limit to what our brave lads could do (that didn't cost much) during those home visits and one cannot deny that those flash American GIs often left our gullible girls with a lot more than chewing gum and nylons to remember them by.

Luckily, it was reckoned in those days to be as easy to get a marriage licence as a dog licence. This was all right as long as the youngsters were still friends after the war but unfortunately couples were often virtual strangers after those long separations (not to mention the black outs!) and found that getting rid of their partner was not as easy as getting rid of Rover the dog. In 1946, there were some 50,000 shotgun marriages waiting to be dissolved with simply not enough courts to deal with the crush, so they had to like it or lump it until their number came up.

Rover – do you take Harold to be your lawful master?

Nationalisation

Now that the Labour Party had got its feet safely under the table, it decided to hot up its nationalisation programme (just as the Tories these days are hellbent on denationalising everything). Nationalisation means that the State takes over large industries so that

    a. the profits can be shared amongst the population and
    b. they can run more efficiently.

That's the theory anyway. So, in that case, we ask ourselves, why aren't the railways brilliantly efficient and hugely profitable? Apparently railways were even more dreadful before nationalisation so they, with road haulage and ports, were the first to go, followed by coal mines. (At least our Tories don't want to denationalise the mines – they just close 'em.)

Shock Horror! Less Beer

In an attempt to hang on to the disappearing wheat stocks, beer production was halved. Far less serious, meat was rationed to one shilling's (5p) worth a week. Mind you, it was probably not as bad as you think. These days you couldn't buy a pig's ear for 5p. Then you could probably get a couple of pounds of sausages.

Meanwhile

February: Bananarama! A long lost visitor from foreign parts, the banana, turned up at our ports. Many children didn't even know how to eat them (unfortunately three year old Dorothy Shippey did – she ate one over the three, and died).

March: Black day for post-war squirrels. The government issued a recipe for squirrel pie. Take one large, fresh squirrel . . .

June: John Logie Baird, the inventor of the box, went into his. Not only did he invent the telly (what a responsibility), but also a weird electronic gizmo that detected objects in the dark. (A mechanical nose?)

August: A report came out claiming that the black market in chocolate, nylons and perfume was flourishing. Someone had to fill the gap after the flashy American soldiers had gone home.

October: At Nuremberg, twelve evil Nazi chiefs were sentenced to death and Rudolf Hess, who had claimed loss of memory, got life. C'mon Rudi, even the Brits wouldn't buy that one.

November: Hungarian journalist Ladislao Biro was on the ball. He invented the ballpoint pen which was a small sensation when it got to Britain even though it cost 55 shillings (£2.75). Was it called the Ladislao or something else? Answers on a postcard.

• IBM invented an electronic brain capable of doing in seconds what would take the average human brain hours (or, in my case, days). It was called the Electronic Numerical Integrator and Computer. To people's amazement, science fiction writers talked of a distant future when computers would be used in every field of science and business. Not that distant, we think.

December: Buffalo scientists (or should I say scientists in Buffalo) came up with what was thought to be a cock and bull story that smoking cigarettes might be connected with lung cancer. How right they turned out to be.

Britain Pulls Out

Talk about kicking a country when it was down. The 1946/47 winter was colder than a Siberian fridge and the post-war fuel shortage brought the already tottering British to their chilly knees. Any fuel that was available was piling up at the pits because transport had come to a snowy standstill. When the great thaw came, things got even worse especially if you were a sheep or a loaf! Two million poor little bleeters were washed away by the ensuing floods, and a month's bread was wiped out when 500,000 acres of wheat were all but destroyed.

Who gave you that loaf?

Way Out East

Over in hotter climes, the British were becoming really fed up with trying to keep people from killing each other. Jewish terrorists were now having a go at our soldiers who were only trying to keep those angry Arabs at bay by controlling the number of Jews flooding into Palestine.

If that wasn't bad enough, other troops were being run ragged trying to keep the peace in an India shortly due for independence. Lord Mountbatten had been given the dubious honour of becoming the Viceroy of India but could only watch helplessly as the Moslems and the Hindus curried – sorry – carried on slaughtering each other willy-nilly, as they couldn't seem to agree over who should have what territory. In May 1947, the British cabinet finally agreed to Mountbatten's idea of pulling them apart (called partitioning), a bit like you do with naughty kids. The Moslems would be put in the north west (where most of them had been anyway) to be called West Pakistan, and the Hindus would have the great big bit below to be called Hindustan (later India). Apart from this, there was a corner at the bottom right which was to be known as East Pakistan, also predominantly Moslem, and a bump on the top right hand corner to be called Kashmir (predominantly Moslem but with a Hindu ruler), the border of which was still being disputed.

So, did the colonials like this whole partition idea? Of course they didn't. For a first, the huge Indian army, with all its ships and planes and camels would have to be split up (an almost impossible task); for a second, nobody could decide whether or not the new countries should be in the Commonwealth and, for a third, many of the disgustingly rich maharajahs who, quite understandably, were perfectly happy being disgustingly rich (and had huge private armies to keep things that way), wanted to declare independence instead.

Oh dear Charles, what does one do with Jumbo?

On 15th August the British crated up their cocktail cabinets, emptied their elephant guns, paid off their thousands of servants, and cleared out to leave the Indians to fend for themselves. All except Lord Louis Mountbatten who was made Governor-General of the largest part – India (and made an earl to boot). This left the Moslems and Hindus to get on, uninterrupted, with tandoorying each other which they did with increased vigour. By the time the 8,500,000 Moslems and Hindus had a nice border between them, 400,000 had come to a sticky end and a further 100,000 had almost died on the journey, from either exposure or starvation. Obviously their gods moved in mysterious ways.

... and Palestine?

Within a few weeks of all this, Britain also decided to let the Jews and Arabs fight unhindered and cleared out of Palestine. On 30th November, the UN General Assembly inadvertently set up a lovely little scenario for an Arab-Jewish war by backing the British and American plans to partition Palestine formally so that the Jews could have a proper home of their own. Surprise, surprise, the Arabs were even less thrilled than they'd been before with the idea of lending half of what they thought was theirs anyway.

Elizabeth's Greek Take-Away

On a cheerier note, the Princess Elizabeth (our present Queen) announced that she was going to marry a young, unusually handsome Greek lieutenant called Philip Mountbatten (or, more probably, Mountbattenopoulous) who was the nephew of the aforementioned Indian Governor-General, Lord Louis Mountbatten. Great! Now we had Germans (our royal family) marrying Greeks in order to lord it over us British. Democracy?

At their highly expensive and glamorous wedding in November, the Archbishop of Canterbury said

> Notwithstanding the splendour and national significance of the service in this Abbey, it is in all essentials exactly the same as it would be for any cottager (?) who might be

married this afternoon in some small country church in a remote village in the dales. The same vows are taken, the same prayers are offered, the same blessing given.

That's as maybe, Bish, but I bet Liz and Phil didn't go back to fishpaste sandwiches and brown ale.

Meanwhile

January: The most popular programmes on the radio were 'Dick Barton Special Agent' (a really hammy detective series) and 'Woman's Hour' (a mumsy magazine programme).
• Al Capone, the best, or should I say worst, hoodlum in the world died.

March: Unbelievably, the Government banned all midweek sport so that the workers, bless 'em, wouldn't tire themselves out.

April: The Public Morality Council claimed artificial insemination was illegal as it was deemed to be adulterous. Obviously a case of better the husband you know than the test tube you don't.

September: The one-day-to-be-great Harold Wilson joined the cabinet aged 31, the youngest minister yet.

August: Princess Elizabeth had to go on her honeymoon without a trousseau, owing to the clothes' shortage. The poor dear must have been chilly wearing only a ring.

• British women were asked to economise by keeping their skirts short to save cloth! Predictably British men seemed relatively happy at the idea. This all proved a bit of a drag when Christian Dior's 'New Look' swept in from France. Although very flattering to women, especially after the austere utility wartime look, one of its main features was a hemline only inches from the floor.

1948

Health for All
The National Health Service was perhaps the fabbest thing that the new Labour Government (or any other, for that matter) had been responsible for. Almost unbelievably, everything from diarrhoea to dandruff or cancer to carbuncles was treated absolutely free. You could even get a wig on a prescription from

Well Mr. Jones - if you're absolutely sure.

your local doctor. It was largely achieved by Minister of Health Aneurin Bevan and was to make him one of the great figures of the history of British politics.

Everyone seemed over the moon with the new service, apart from the people actually carrying it out – the doctors – who were more concerned about losing money than anything else. They voted 766 to 11 against the NHS which is funny when you think that nowadays they are getting their stethoscopes in a twist at the prospect of it all changing back.

Nationalisation
Meantime, you must be dying to know how the new nationalisation programme was getting on. A bit early to tell but maybe the fact that the brilliant new Coal Board lost £5.44 million in the last quarter of 1947 gives you a clue.

Trouble Out East
1948 had started with the sad news from India of the assassination of Mahatma Gandhi, the funny little Hindu leader known for wearing only tiny round glasses and a tablecloth. The poor little chap-ati had only just finished fasting for Hindu-Moslem unity and was probably in a hurry for a curry down-town, when this guy jumped out of the crowds and shot him three times. When it was discovered that it was a Hindu who'd done the dirty deed, fresh riots broke out across India and Pakistan. The good news was that, just like all the continuing mess in Palestine, it just wasn't our problem any more. So there!

You Scratch My Back and I'll Scratch Yours
On 17th March Britain, France and the Benelux countries (Belgium, Holland and Luxembourg) signed a treaty promising that they would all jump to each other's defence if anyone big and horrid threatened any one of them. Nobody named names but few had any doubt that the threat was more than likely to come from that great bear – Russia. Hardly was the ink dry on the agreement, when the Russians slammed a blockade on all the

15

Western aid to Berlin, which it had had its beady eye on ever since the end of the war.

Birth of a Nation
On 14th May a new state, to be called Israel, was proclaimed by the Jews as their new home. All the British quotas were abandoned, making it a free for all for anyone (provided they were Jewish) to go and live in the Palestinian sunshine. The Arabs, predictably, went simply mad and Egyptian forces raided the gun cupboard and instantly massed on the southern border, looking extremely ugly.

Britain to the Rescue Again
On 30th June, back in Berlin, the RAF and the Western Allies broke the by now serious Russian blockade with only one month to go before the bewildered Berliners would have run out of grub. A mighty airlift to the western zone of the city smashed within a couple of months the Russian efforts to starve the Berliners into submission. The Cold War had reached freezing point.

Rubber Trouble
Nasty things were happening up Malaya way. Chinese Communist rebels had a new hobby – murdering British rubber planters. Britain bounced back on 30th July, sending a force of soldiers to sort the Commies out. At first the 'rubber bandits' ran away like scared bunnies, but it wasn't to be that easy. It seemed that the murders were only the beginning of a much bigger Communist plot to take over the country. The British had involved themselves in something a lot more serious than chasing a few terrorists away.

Babies Go Bonkers
The only area of production really booming was the baby business, probably due to the end of enforced wartime separations. Nippers were piling up at a rate never before imagined, and added to that, far fewer were lost due to the brill new National Health Service. This pushed the birth rate 21% higher than was actually needed to

keep the population stable. Even Princess Elizabeth got in on the act, and in December gave birth to two big ears with a baby boy (called Charles) in between.

I say Phil, where d'you think he got those features from?

Meanwhile

March: 'Orrible Oswald Mosley and his home-made, brown-shirted Fascists were silenced by a ban on all political marches in London for three months. Theirs was planned for 1st May.

April: The General Certificate of Education (GCE), that scourge of so many future generations, replaced the School Certificate.

June: Despite the Commons voting to suspend hanging, those bloodythirsty peers in the Lords chucked out the bill and the scaffold survived to service more criminals.

July: A brilliant little car called the Morris Minor was born.

August: Freddie Mills, who looked like everyone's idea of a cartoon boxer, managed to kerb his frantic, swinging style to win the World Light Middleweight Title. Poor Freddie was later murdered (to death) in a gangland killing.

November: The sugar-sweet child star Julie Andrews sang before the Queen. Let's face it, being royal does have its drawbacks.

1949

The Natives Get Restless

The Labour Government was beginning to lose its bottle over the nationalisation plan, realising that it was beginning to get right up the nose of the common man who was slightly weary of the economic state (especially the ever-reducing rations). Tate and Lyle, the huge British sugar refiners, decided to take on the Government who had been trying to nationalise their industry. They invented a daft little character called Mr Cube (original or what?) who appeared on 2,000,000 sugar packets, and all their delivery trucks, declaring in his sweet, cubular way how much he didn't want to be nationalised, thank you very much. The steel industry, also, saw the chink in the government's armour and took the Labour Government on with huge help from other private companies scared stiff that they might just be next.

Churchill, never one to miss the chance of jumping on a bandwagon, took the mickey out of the government, saying that every industry they'd got their horny hands on had gone from profit to loss in less time than you could even *say* nationalisation. Bevan waded into the slanging match, calling the Tories lower than vermin (rude to vermin I'd say), and a roly-poly battle-axe of a Labour MP – Bessie Braddock – screamed that she didn't care if the other side starved to death. Nice words from a party claiming to be striving for a more humane society.

On 18th September, the sh...illing hit the fan when Sir Stafford

Cripps, our particularly grumpy Chancellor of the Exchequer, announced that the poor, long-suffering quid was to be reduced in value by 30%. This meant that the battered British had now, on top of everything else, to face a substantial rise in the cost of living.

A survey was released proclaiming that Mr and Mrs Britain were spending more on booze (and who can blame them?) and less on food, than ten years earlier. Crime was on the increase (naturally!), but convictions for drunkenness were less than half. This could, of course, have meant that the cunning British had decided to get drunk at home (or the cops were sloshed too).

NATO Gets the OK

Updating the former agreement between European nations (to pitch in if anyone got into bother), Britain, America, Canada, France and the Benelux countries agreed on 8th March to a new peace alliance called the North Atlantic Treaty Organisation (NATO). Basically, if anyone took a swing at any one of the member countries, it would be construed as an attack on the whole lot. Many people were scared stiff that this might prod the sleeping Russian bear and make him cross. The far left, particularly in Britain, who still hung on to a loony admiration for Russia, saw the agreement as blatant bear-baiting. Many westerners slept happier in their beds that night, however, little knowing that, when push came to shove, NATO would prove a toothless wimp.

The Ireland Bill on 11th May, which finally recognised Eire as a republic, was passed almost unanimously by the British Parliament. Rather oddly, the Irish Republic didn't become foreign but something in-between. The people of Eire, for instance, were still allowed to vote in our elections, which even Attlee admitted was a bit cock-eyed for a new republic.

The Royals Revealed

The rot started here. For the first time in recorded history a member of the Royal Household spilt the beans (by appointment, of course). Marion Crawford (Crawfie) spoke to the *Ladies Home Journal* in the States. OK, it was pretty innocuous by today's standards. She said that the two princesses (she'd been their governess) were mad about horses and that the Duke of York (now king) had made a rare joke in which he claimed that his sister Mary had actually *been* a horse until she 'came out'. 'Coming out' was a cunning practice among the noble classes, in which girls of around eighteen were presented to the Queen and launched into society. It was really a sort of posh meat market where the 'debs' (short for debutantes) were paraded in front of eligible men much like they do, strangely enough, when selling thoroughbred horses. Just another way of keeping the bloodline pure I suppose.

China Chooses a Chairman
A cold wind blew in from the East on 1st October with the news that a chap called Mao Tse-tung had just become the boss of 40 million Chinese. He was the Chairman of the Communist-ruled People's Republic of China. The rest of the world showed very wobbly smiles as they grudgingly recognised the new regime, except Australia, Canada and America, who liked communism as much as snowmen do sunshine.

Dean Acheson, the American Secretary of State, said 'Communism is a very emotional subject in our country right now.'

Emotional! You're not kidding, Dean! I've never heard pure unadulterated hatred called that before. Britain, hypocritical as ever, didn't hesitate to recognise the new regime and didn't even put any conditions down. This just might have had something to do with the £3 thousand millions' worth of commercial interest they'd got running with the old regime. Velly funny how a litte cash can ease a greedy country's misgivings.

Meanwhile

January: The new micro-groove 7" discs came out in the States. This really hacked off established music-loving punters, as it meant buying completely new equipment in order to play them.

While the debate on hanging was still raging, the first woman for 12 years, Ruth Allen, was hung for murder.

February: The understandably sensitive Jewish community got itself worked up over the first showing of the movie *Oliver Twist* in Berlin. They weren't too happy about the way old Fagin was portrayed as a money-grabbing, Jewish crook (which he was, of course).

March: Bad news for British teeth. Rationing of chocolate and sweets ended. Also rationing on clothing finally ended. People generally got fatter and clothes generally got bigger.

April: Sir Alfred Munnings, famous for painting flat looking horses with small heads, called modern art 'silly daubs and violent blows at nothing'. Unfortunately for poor old Alfred, the statement caused exactly the wrong result. The Great British Public dashed to the Royal Academy to see what all the fuss was about.

May: If you didn't have a telly, you could watch your knickers getting in a twist at the first launderette in Bayswater, London.

June: Knickers again! American tennis player Gussie Moran showed hers (lace trimmed) at Wimbledon and upset the stuffy All-England Club.

July: The cost of health. The Government admitted that the NHS was costing 2/6d (12^{1}/$_{2}$p) a head per week, 1/4d more than they'd reckoned.

August: Starlings on the minute hand of Big Ben made it lose four and a half minutes. (A mystery to me. If they slowed it when it was going up one side, why didn't they speed it up when it was going down the other?)

September: Boy, are we British good at building white elephants. This time it was silver and called the Bristol Brabazon – the largest plane in the world. Unfortunately, it was so heavy and lumbering that it was put out to grass almost immediately.

Hit of the Year: 'Baby, It's Cold Outside'.

1950

The Fab Fifties
We are now half way through the century and it must be said that the British were still not happy bunnies. Much as we didn't want the Tory toffs back, we were none too thrilled at the performance of a Labour party that always promised so much and never delivered a bag of beans. This was proved by the results of the General Election in February. It turned out to be neck and neck to the finishing post, with Labour winning with the weeniest majority for fifty years. The British, however, were fed up to their back pockets with being used like laboratory rats, suffering the experiments – both social and economic – of, admittedly well-meaning, mad professors in the guise of politicians. They expected results from Labour.

Cold Comfort
Overseas, some chilly news crept under the rusty Iron Curtain. On

Do you do take-aways?

15th February 1950, Russia and China announced that they had jumped into the vast Commie bed together and were to unite against the world – which meant the West (that included us, folks!). It was a match made in heaven for them – and hell for us, as it meant that now old Joe Stalin could protect his endless frontier with Asia, whilst building up his military might in Europe. We Westies gulped nervously at the new Mao/Stalin love affair and wondered where it would all lead.

I Spy

All this East/West sparring and posturing required monitoring – and so began the spy era. Funny little grey men with wire-framed glasses, called Norman or Cyril, sat in their front rooms in Ruislip tapping out not-very-secret secrets on their crystal sets to their Commie controllers. Thousands of miles away, identical little fur-hatted grey men called Ivan and Boris, in Moscow suburbs like Ruislipovich, were sending similar stuff back to us. Occasionally, just to confuse future TV script writers, they'd pretend they were working for one side when they were really working for the other (double agents) or pretend they were working for one side while convincing the other that they were working for them too, while really working for another side entirely (triple agents), or occasionally they'd prete . . . oh, you get the picture!

Reds under the Bed

Communism had become the buzz word for everything that was horrid and not quite cricket (or baseball). Senator Joseph McCarthy in the States launched a crusade to wheedle all the filthy reds that were lurking not only under the bed, but in their insidious way throughout the federal government and, seemingly, throughout the entertainment industry as well.

First Blood

Just to kick things off nicely, over in Korea, the Communist northerners invaded the independent southerners and the Western allies put their hands to their holsters and prepared to interfere – or should I say – intervene.

The United Nations – who were all the nations that weren't Russia (who wouldn't come to meetings) or China (who weren't asked) – decided to chuck everything into defending the little Republic of Korea. Suddenly, like a cast-aside toy that suddenly becomes desirable when another kid shows interest, the whole world was getting worked up over the fate of a tin-pot country that weeks before they hadn't heard of (see the Falkland Islands). What had started out as a little foray by a few cheeky Communists was to turn into another full-blown, rip-roaring war which would eventually wipe out 5 million men, women and kids.

Troops Go In

On 29th August, the first of 4000 British troops landed in Korea to back up our dear old mates (and fightin' pardners) the Yanks. As they left Hong Kong, they were ordered by their Commander in Chief, Lieut. General Sir John Harding, to 'Shoot quickly, shoot straight, and shoot to kill,' which must have been about as useful as telling a trainee lion tamer to keep his eye on the wretched lions.

On 28th November, the troops of the United Nations paddled ashore off 260 ships, (scaring the wits out of the smallish North Koreans) and went on to occupy most of Korea in less than six weeks. Just as they were getting kinda comfy, they had to run for their lives as huge waves of Chinese troops started sweeping over them. Suddenly, the big boys were being threatened by the little boys. By 6th December over 200,000 Chinese had swarmed across the border catching not only the soldiers, but also the politicians at home, with their trousers well and truly down. Here we go again.

Fat Pharo

Just to make things even more complicated for Britain, the dreadful old Egyptian King Farouk pushed aside his many wives and, out of the blue, demanded that all the British troops, who were keeping the peace in the Middle East, scarper immediately. This demand was met with a chilly response by the British Parliament with the backing of the Americans. (You Limeys scratched our backs so we'll scratch yours.) Here we go again . . . again!

Out Goes Cripps

Life politics-wise was also becoming a touch tricky at home. Sir Stafford Cripps, the austere, vegetarian Chancellor, was finally 'sent off' due to ill health. The 'sub' was an ardent young man called Hugh Gaitskell, who was to become a familiar figure in British politics for many years. To be honest, the Labour Government was as good as clapped out. Along with Cripps, Bevin was shortly to retire, and Dalton, Morrison and Attlee were beginning to look likely candidates for the 'home for old lefties'. It was all a bit tricky for a party with such a tiny majority. In fact, the situation got so bad at one stage that some poor sick Labour MPs had to be dragged into the house on stretchers, just to boost the numbers at make-your-mind-up-time.

Cross Channel Telly

On 27th August, Auntie BBC beamed pictures across to our screens from France for the very first time. Richard Dimbleby, father of all serious TV presenters (and David and Jonathan) whizzed across from Calais on a cloud of micro-waves to be collected up and transmitted to our own front rooms.

Dimbleby only missed, by a few days, passing over Florence Chadwick, an American, who'd chosen a slightly slower route across the Channel. She broke the woman's cross-channel swimming record by an hour (see pointless things to do). Her poor appropriately named chum Shirley France wasn't so lucky; she was plucked from the Channel hysterical, and blue as a tit, eight miles

25

from the English coastline.

Scotland Gets Stoned Again

You might remember from my last book (available at all good bookshops) that the English nicked Scotland's very own Coronation stone called the Scone of Stone (or something like that) in 1296 and, despite many promises, had never quite given it back. It had since stayed tucked under our Coronation Chair in Westminster Abbey much to the annoyance of the stroppy Scottish Nationalists who saw it (and porridge) as a symbol of their independence. On 25th December a person (McSuperman?) or persons unknown broke into Westminster Abbey and relieved us of the 458 lb rock. Our brilliant police, with almost uncanny insight, put out an alert for a car looking – wait for it – decidedly back-heavy, driven by person or persons unknown with Scottish accents (how do you spot a Scottish accent?). The stone eventually turned up in another abbey in – no prizes for guessing – Scotland – Arbroath to be precise.

Meanwhile

January: Britain asked its rich chum America if it could spare us a pile of atomic bombs. We could have asked Father Christmas.

February: Sir Harry Lauder, everyone's caricature Scotsman, died aged 79. Among the deep and lyrical songs he penned was 'Stop Your Ticklin', Jock'.

26

March: The lengths some people will go to settle an argument. Thor Heyerdahl, the famous Norwegian explorer, reckoned that the Polynesians must have originally sailed from South America. His chum said no way, so Thor built a raft out of old balsa logs and, 101 days after setting sail, won the bet. *Kon-Tiki* (the name of the raft) became the subject of an all-time best selling book called *The Kon-Tiki Expedition*.

• Roger Bannister, a medical student, broke the world record for the mile with what seemed like an impossible time of 4 minutes 1.48 seconds.

• The British weren't half dirty, they were 48% dirty. In a survey it was revealed that only 52% of our households had bathrooms.

June: The National Coal Board thumbed its sooty nose at all its critics by announcing a profit in 1949 of £9.5 million.

August: The Royal stork stopped at Buck House again and dropped off Princess Anne.

November: The amazing George Bernard Shaw, one of Britain's greatest playwrights and author of *Arms And The Man* and *Man And Superman* (he reckoned he was better than Shakespeare) died aged 94. This stroppy, red-bearded Irishman, who lived on vegetables and wore daft clothes, was loved or hated by all who met him.

Hit of the Year: 'I've Got a Luverly Bunch of Coconuts'. (Roll on rock and roll!)

1951

Bevan Bows Out

Aneurin Bevan, that bad old boy of the Labour left, blew his Welsh top and quit the Government in a right paddy, on account of his colleagues' decision to make a mockery of his darling NHS by charging for false choppers and glasses. His resignation was also a slap in the face for new boy Gaitskell (the new Chancellor of the Exchequer) and became the high point in the destructive right v. left punch-up within the Labour Party that still goes on today.

Churchill Goes into Labour

Churchill's opposition to the tired Labour Government was really hitting them where it hurt most – in the lobbies (ouch!) – and on 26th October, he and his Tory mates beat the Socialists (i.e. the Labour Party) in the General Election, putting the smell of fine cigar smoke back in No. 10. Old Winny (as he was affectionately

labelled) was back, aged 77, fighting fit, and champing at the bit to undo all the harm that the lefties had done. There was no doubt that the old campaigner, never one to hide his light under a bushel, would have a far larger television audience than when he'd been

PM before. In 1951, telly sales had gone straight through the roof and the manufacturers were planning to make 250,000 in the following year.

Trouble in China
Velly, velly tlicky. 1951 opened with the approach of a full scale war with the yellow peril, China. To be honest, if you were to compare the conflict in Korea to a soccer match, at this point the score would probably have been 0-0, with the United Nations United threatening to break through with a goal at any minute. By March, General MacArthur was having a head-on collision with his boss, President Truman, owing to his belief that the Allies should take the battle to the enemy, and nuke China. This was dead popular with the anti-communist fanatics who saw it as a way of chop-sueying the Chinese once and for all. But Truman and the UN didn't go for this plan too much as they hoped to come to some political deal with the Chinese (and not risk having 3 million of 'em on their backs).

Big Mac Gets the Push
On 11th April, President Truman finally came to the end of his personal tether with the warmongering General MacArthur. Two other generals had whispered that the way MacArthur wanted to do things would lead to the wrong war, at the wrong place, at the wrong time, with the wrong enemy (China)! Truman obviously thought, this time, that four wongs didn't make a wight, and promptly fired him.

Watch Out! There's Mau Mau About
Just as we British were working out the possible consequences of all the Egyptian mess, trouble broke out in Kenya, one of our more prestigious (and profitable) colonies. The Mau Mau, a group of particularly unpleasant natives who nobody knew anything about, had decided they'd had enough of the thousands of white settlers (mostly British) who were doing very nicely, thank you, farming the fertile highlands, using African labour and, more to the point,

African land. What started as the odd burglary turned into arson, intimidation of peaceful tribespersons who wouldn't take the oath to drive out the whitie, and eventually widespread pangaring, using pangas (horrid sort of curved hatchets). One of their daftest, if somewhat spine-chilling, oaths went like this: 'When the reedbuck horn is blown, if I leave a European farm before killing the owner, may this oath kill me.' I don't suppose the poor reedbuck thought much of having his horns blown either.

By October 1952, the situation had got so out of hand that Britain was forced to dust down a load more troops and ship them out to Kenya. One of the colony's top men, Senior Chief Warahui, had been speared to death in broad daylight so the President of the Kenya African Union, Jomo (nicknamed Burning Spear) Kenyatta, and 500 further suspects, were rounded up and given the third degree. By January 1953, the whites (and the reedbucks) were in a state of total panic as whole areas of the Kikuyu tribes reserves had fallen under Mau Mau control.

Kenyatta (compared by some to Hitler) was eventually jailed for seven years for being head Mau Mau man. Poor Mr Spear (Burning to his friends) claimed rather feebly that the Mau Mau weren't really anti-white (of course not, Jomo!) but were just trying to get a better deal for African people.

Canal Caper
Just as life was getting a little quieter in Korea, due to a sort of

queasy unofficial ceasefire, trouble broke out in the East. Britain had a treaty with Egypt which was due to run out in 1956. This treaty had been of immense strategic importance to us during and after the war, as the Suez Canal allowed a nifty short cut between the Mediterranean and Indian oceans. In 1951, the Egyptians didn't want to play any more. They proclaimed King Farouk of Sudan (see Great Mistakes in King-Making) as their monarch, and started making life very tricky for our soldiers on the canal bases. The British then offered a jolly decent concession by suggesting a Middle East defence pact backed by France, America and the US, which included handing their base back. The Egyptians, however, had their blood up and replied with a gesture rather similar (but completely different) to Churchill's famous wartime victory sign.

So, out of the blue, British forces crept up the Canal Zone one night and surprised the Egyptian soldiers guarding it. When the sun came up, Britain held the key points. It was pretty clear, however, when all the wives and kiddies were suddenly shipped back to Britain a couple of weeks later, that the whole area was a powder keg that could go up at any minute. Finally, in November, the British agreed to withdraw from three towns, and the Egyptians agreed to stop their terrorism (but they didn't mean it). By January 1952, the situation was almost out of hand and British people were being murdered left, right and centre.

By July of that year, the legendary (and infamous) playboy King Farouk, who had by now suspended parliament, had hightailed it out of Alexandria, ousted by a military coup. Everyone had finally had enough of his over-the-top lifestyle and far-too-obvious links to corruption in high places. His nine month old son was left to rule the country with just a little help from General Neguib the army leader.

Britain the Brilliant
Before going under, the Labour Government had tried to divert the country's attention from the all-pervading gloom. No royal weddings this time (thank God). Instead, they went one better. They invented something called The Festival of Britain, a huge

extravaganza to show the rest of the world (and the menacing masses) just how clever we all were and just how well the country was doing. Herbert Morrison (a Labour Cabinet Minister) called it 'the people giving themselves a pat on the back'. Heaven knows what for. Probably for putting up with him and the rest of his geriatric cronies for so long. Mickey-taking apart, this festival was truly magnificent, bringing together some of the finest design and manufactured goods to be seen for many a long year. It occupied a 27 acre bomb-shattered site around Waterloo Station (which now looks rather similar again). Spanning a large percentage of this area was a vast dome called, just a little pretentiously, The Dome of Discovery. One of its most remarkable features was its almost invisible means of support (much like the British economy!).

Mint Spies
On 7th June a juicy scandal broke that was to set the scene for many to come. Two frightfully-frightfully British diplomats, Guy Burgess and Donald Maclean, suddenly disappeared much to the puzzlement of our brilliant police, who searched high and low to no avail. Eventually the two chums thoughtfully sent a postcard home, telling everyone that they'd gone on a long Mediterranean holiday. Even the police didn't go for that one (as the two absentees hadn't taken their swimming costumes) and so the search continued.

It took till 1955 for the penny (or should I say rouble) to drop. The naughty pair had been telling those horrid Russians all our best secrets for years and then, before they could be found out had, most unsportingly, hightailed it off to Moscow, to live happily.

Meanwhile

February: Good King George got a well-earned (notice, well-earned) pay rise, the first since putting on the big gold hat.

April: Taste hits the deck. Miss Sweden became the first winner of a contest to find the most beautiful (and most boring) bimbo in the world. Since then, every year, a troupe of multi-national bimbos has disrobed to never-to-be dampened swimsuits and white high-heeled shoes, in one of the most kitsch, politically incorrect shows ever to sully our telly screens – 'Miss World'. It's so bad it's good!

July: A survey pronounced that the average housewife in Britain worked 75 hours a week, let alone the overtime put in at the weekend. It was thinly disguised that she was simply a slave to the kitchen and the kids.
• World Middle Weight Boxing Champ Sugar Ray Robinson, arguably the finest fighter ever, was beaten by British boxer, Randolph Turpin, to the surprise of just about everyone (including Randy).
• The Admiralty rather sensibly banned the 'Snort' breathing tube on British Submarines as the one on the *HMS Affray* was found to be faulty. They weren't kidding; the *Affray* was found, full of water, 250 feet down under.

October: A single footprint was found halfway up a mountain in the Himalayas and reckoned to be that of the Yeti or Abominable Snowman. Either the thing had one leg or he sure had hopped a long distance. They never found another.

1952

King George Becomes Ex
The dreaded curse of the grouchy grouse struck again. It was reported that, after a pleasant day's shooting those rather dim dickies, on February 6th King George VI died in his sleep. Young Princess Elizabeth, the new Mrs Edinburopoulus, on safari in

Africa with Phil the Greek, woke up to find herself fatherless and a queen – or should I say *the* Queen. Her ex-dad was sadly mourned by nearly all the British people as he'd earned mega-brownie points by refusing to run for safety during the war with his wife (our Queen Mum), and sticking out the horrendous bombing with the rest of the brave but terrified Londoners.

Nuclear Peace

Churchill dropped his own bomb on 26th February by announcing that Britain now had a nice shiny atomic one. Our new toy was welcomed by America, whose spokesman proclaimed it would be a major contribution to world peace as a deterrent (which was a bit like Mr Nobel offering his famous peace prize after inventing dynamite). The tests were to be carried out from the top of a pylon so that, according to Downing Street, 'there would be no danger to people or animals' (providing you didn't mind them buzzing or glowing).

Shooting for Peace

In another weird attempt to promote peace in Korea, allied fighter-bombers obliterated the ancient city of Suan on 8th May with bombs and napalm. I suppose wiping out all the opposition is, after all, one way of assuring peace.

Back in Africa, just as the situation was beginning to go off the boil in Kenya, the first stirrings of racial unrest were seen down in the south. Black people and Indians began non-violent demonstrations against South Africa's apartheid laws (which had been designed to keep the blacks and the whites 'apart', or rather to keep the blacks under the 'protective' boot of the whites). By November, the situation took a dive when seventeen Africans were shot dead while throwing stones which, you must admit, doesn't sound altogether fair. An Irish nun and an insurance agent (sounds like the beginning of a dirty joke) were killed in the cross-fire.

All Change at Home

A tragic death occurred on the London streets on 5th July. The last, much loved, electric trams were taken out of service and scrapped, due to that favourite old government pastime of removing any trace of indigenous tourist attractions.

But that was not all that was a-changing. The economy was beginning to pick itself out of the gutter and with this awakening prosperity, social patterns were on the move too. On 11th July, a survey revealed that the British were:

a. Living longer (maybe not being shot at and bombed by Germans every five minutes had something to do with it)

b. Marrying earlier (10.00 a.m. instead of 12 p.m.)

c. Divorcing more often

The British were also drifting away from a lot of the traditional manufacturing industries (like tram-making, no doubt). Also, twice as many people were living alone compared to twenty years before, which doesn't take a genius to realise might have something to do with the divorce rate. Women were demanding the unheard of equal pay to men for the same work. Their cry was taken up by a Labour Party trying to tart up their shambolic image, which had been caused by the internal punch-ups, between the left and the right, the right and the centre and the centre and the left. Poor old Attlee, however, was far too close to his personal wits' end to concern himself with the women's issue.

Meanwhile

January: British headmasters criticised the new GCE examinations saying they were too hard for some kids. Isn't that the point of exams?

35

• The driver of a bus which killed 23 military cadets got a £20 fine and was banned from driving for three years. Life was obviously cheaper in those days.

April: In an effort presumably to wipe out mice, the cheese ration was reduced to an ounce a week.
• The Queen, in her infinite wisdom, decided to stick with Windsor for the family surname. Shame – we'd have liked some other town like Bootle or Scunthorpe for a change.
• The Queen, again in her infinite wisdom, gave Benjamin Britten permission to write about the relationship between Queen Elizabeth I and the Earl of Essex. See! Even our Queen's got one of Essex's girls somewhere in her ancestry.

June: The Government announced that they would introduce flashing orange lights to help zebras cross the road (or something like that). Actually, it was the first pedestrian crossing.

August: The first 'short, sharp shock' detention centre was opened for 'big, bad boys' in Oxfordshire.

September: John Cobb, the famous speedster, was killed when he hit 240 m.p.h. (and maybe the monster) in his faster-than-usual motor boat on Loch Ness.

October: More tea vicar? Tea rationing finally ended.

November: Talk about backing the wrong horse. The only left-wing Bevanite to get into the Shadow Cabinet was Nye Bevan himself.
• *The Mousetrap* by Agatha Christie, opened in London. It must have had something going for it – it's still running.

December: The Queen's Christmas Day speech in which our sovereign addressed us like naughty children, was broadcast for the first time.

• Anyone who thought that the A bomb was the ultimate weapon was in for a big surprise. American scientists exploded their new Hydrogen, or H bombs (hundreds of times more powerful), on a small island in the Pacific. Unfortunately, it destroyed the island completely. Whoops!

1953

That's Crowned It

This was the year that our Elizabeth was officially made queen and finally got to wear the sparkly hat on 2nd June. It had been a fairly uneventful five months leading up to the Coronation. Uneventful, but generally encouraging economically. The Tory Government under old Churchill were finally forging ahead and the British were beginning to enjoy the end of all that crippling austerity. Winston had surrounded himself with a brilliant young posse of super-posh, ex-public schoolboys. Macmillan, Butler and Eden were to become household names for many years. Harold Macmillan had been told, when put in charge of housing, that the job would make or mar his career. The former soon became the case as in 1953, 327,000 houses were knocked up for the public sector, far exceeding what Macmillan had been asked to achieve. Despite coming from a well-loaded family, Macmillan knew how to roll up his sleeves and get his hands dirty (metaphorically). He once said of Rab Butler – the colleague of whom he somewhat disapproved – 'He's one of those men who can't cook without meat! I, on the other hand, can cook with bread and water.' I bet he could . . . as long as someone else had to eat it.

Whites Only

The British and other white people in Africa, though pompous, exploitative and mean, weren't daft. They'd long recognised the dangers of keeping a whole continent under their manicured thumb and on 5th February decided to strengthen their position even further. A master plan for a new British state with a population of over 7 million, to be called the Federation of Rhodesia and Nyasaland, was published in London. 'Of course,' it claimed, 'the interests of the African people will remain paramount.' It didn't say, however, that that was as long as they were happy to work their butts off for the whites and help them get stinking rich.

Russian Roulette

The man who saved Russia and then punished it for years, old Joe Stalin, died of a brain haemorrhage on 5th March. Unfortunately (for them) Russian leadership was so often a case of better the devil you know than the devil you don't. Old Joe had been responsible for the most appalling treatment in his less than welcoming labour camps (to which he sent anyone who disagreed with him) but he had also been a key figure in the creation of the USSR, and had been reckoned to be one of the most brilliant military commanders of the war.

After bitter wrangling and in-fighting, his replacement, comrade Nikita Khrushchev, struggled to the top of the pile and was to prove to the West certainly worse than the devil *we* knew.

Coronation Fever
One of my strongest memories as a child was how everyone went totally bonkers over the crowning of Queen Elizabeth on 2nd June. Millions, throughout the world, saw the ceremony on huge black and white tellies (with tiny screens). It was the first Coronation ever to be televised. Kids got commemorative gifts at school; flags and bunting were draped from our humble houses and the procession route was full to bursting with a population who still knew their place.

Ain't No Mountain High Enough
It really was the month for going crazy over events. On the day before the Coronation, Everest, the highest mountain in the world, was finally climbed by a New Zealander called Edmund Hillary and a Nepalese sherpa (guide) called Tensing. The expedition had been led by Englishman Colonel John Hunt. Truly, there was more fuss made than when, later, men walked on the moon. These days, so many people go up and down that damn mountain that I'd be surprised if some entrepreneur doesn't open a tea shoppe on the top before long.

Winston Poorly
Later in the month, almost as if all the excitement had been too much, poor old Winny Churchill, now 79, had a severe stroke and could hardly speak (unlike later PMs who could hardly stop) and was ordered to take it easy. The seriousness of his condition was

kept secret by a press that in those days had something approaching integrity. Churchill didn't really take over the reins again properly and was replaced by Anthony Eden in 1956.

Korea Goes Quiet
On 27th July, the guns were put back in their boxes at 10 p.m. A month later everyone returned their prisoners, and everything went back to exactly as it had been before. Great, the only problem was that it had cost 2 million lives to get absolutely nowhere. That's war for you.

Baby King Deposed
Over in Egypt, poor little King Fuad was tucked up with his cuddly camel when the news was announced that he wasn't king any more. Still, what you never knew you had, you probably never miss. General Mohammed Neguib, the guy who had chased off his dad (see p.31), became President and Prime Minister and Colonel Gamal Abdul Nasser (watch this name) became his deputy.

Here Come the Kennedys
On 12th September in the USA, the brilliant senator with the film star looks, Jack (later John) Kennedy, married a pretty girl called Jacqueline Lee Bouvier in Newport, Rhode Island.

Young Jack was destined to become the most powerful and influential (and naughty) person in the world as President of America. The world stage was nearly set for one of the most fascinating and dangerous periods in history.

Meanwhile

January: An almost replica accident to the appalling *Herald of Free Enterprise* disaster occurred in the waters off Belfast. Someone didn't close the front doors after having loaded all the cars on to the Princess Victoria ferry, and the heavy seas burst in. Captain James Ferguson, in typical daft British fashion, saluted as he went down with the ship and 128 passengers and crew.

February: A young starlet called Marilyn Monroe shocked America by appearing on a calendar wearing nothing but a coy smile. Despite cries of 'Filthy!' and 'Disgusting!', she came to represent all that was glamorous in American womanhood.

• Red letter day for kids, and black day for teeth. Sweet rationing ended.

April: Two Cambridge scientists discovered deoxyribonucleic acid. If that doesn't mean much, it became better known as DNA and unlocked many of the mysteries of how living things reproduce themselves (no rude comments please!)

June: One of the most famous murderers, in the history of famous murderers, Reginald 'no dick' (as he was nicknamed) Christie, was sentenced to hang. The funny little man with the round, steel-rimmed glasses had gassed four women (one of them his own Mrs) and hidden them behind a false wall and under the floorboards of his home in Notting Hill, London. Apparently two meticulous police searches failed to notice that his garden fence was propped up by a human thigh bone.

October: The cheapest four cylinder car on the world market, the dear old 'sit-up-and-beg' Ford Popular, was sprung on a surprised British public. If a prize could be given for the most ugly and austere looking motor, the 'Pop' would have won wheels down. Take one look at what manufacturers were doing, car-wise, in the States, however, and you'll realise how they must have regarded their poor brothers across the pond.

November: The skull of the Piltdown man, thought to be the missing link between man and monkey (no football hooligan jokes please!) turned out to be a hoax.

• Smog, one of the curses of British urban living, was proved to be a killer to asthmatics or people with weak chests. Masks costing one shilling were offered on the NHS.

December: Young people flocked to their radios every Monday night to hear a programme that broke totally new ground. 'The Goon Show' featuring Harry (of dubious Highway fame) Secombe, Spike (of dubious sanity fame) Milligan and the late lamented Peter Sellers finally showed that you didn't have to be grown up to get the jokes.

Hit of the Year: 'Diamonds are a Girl's Best Friend' by Marilyn Monroe.

1954

Plenty for All

This was the year that saw the end of rationing for our long-suffering relatives. No sooner had it stopped than a report was published saying that the diet under rationing had been much healthier than their normal diet. Many adults were now smoking a great deal, but the habit was then regarded as rather good for weight control. On 12th February however, another report hit the headlines claiming that smoking was likely to make you much thinner than you might ever have bargained for, being now a definite cause of lung cancer. Oddly enough, yet *another* report claimed there was no proof of this, but lost a little credibility owing to having been issued from the Association of Tobacco Manufacturers.

More Mau Mau
You might be wondering how things were progressing up Kenya way. Events had taken a strange new turn as, on 4th April, British troops arrested 40,000 African suspects, on the premise, presumably, that if they managed to keep all the Africans in custody there wouldn't be any left to cause trouble. It was called the General China operation, after one of the Mau Mau's self-styled leaders. A bizarre little note which was supposed to have been written by one of the Mau Mau negotiators, who failed to show up to meet the security forces, was found in a cleft stick. It asked if the British would fly 'sky-shouting aircraft' over the forest areas equipped with loudspeakers to tell 'other terrorists' not to kill anyone that wanted to negotiate. We did fly aircraft over the forests – but they just fired rockets and dropped bombs. The bomb is mightier than the loudspeaker methinks.

Rock Hits the Brits
News came from America of their 'Rockingist Rhythm Group',

Bill Haley and the Comets. On 12th April, they recorded a number called 'We're Gonna Rock Around the Clock' which became a worldwide hit. Young Bill was an unlikely star, being a slightly podgy 29 year old with a daft kiss curl on his forehead. The sound, however, completely knocked British teenagers for six and at last it looked like there might be some alternative to all that dreary stuff (loved by their parents). Suddenly all those beehive-haired, big frocked songstresses like Eve Boswell and Alma Cogan looked and sounded decidedly past their sell by date. Not only that, but no longer did teenagers have to listen to naff songs like 'How Much is That Doggie in the Window?' or 'The Toothbrush Song'. The more fanatical followers of 'the devil's music', as some senior churchman called it, wore strange Edwardian clothes, weird haircuts and called themselves Teddy Boys. They didn't stop at music: their other great passion was cutting each other up (or anyone who got in the way) with old fashioned cut-throat razors.

We Love Billy

Another import from America came with the purpose of saving our souls. A clean cut, surprisingly handsome, hard-selling evangelist called Billy Graham hired anything from theatres to football stadiums to 'persuade' his wide-eyed converts to come forward and give themselves to the Lord. Thousands did but, unfortunately, the effects mostly wore off on the bus ride home.

Leave the Commies Alone

Back in America, MacCarthy's great Commie hunt was called off when the US Senate rapped him on the knuckles and told him that he'd been going over the top (a bit like Billy).

Suez Pull Out

After 75 years of occupation, British troops finally quit the Canal Zone following an agreement with Colonel Nasser who, as everyone had predicted, was now Head Egyptian. The British base was simply put into mothballs and maintained by civilians just in case of any more bother.

Meanwhile

April: British troops gave up trying to arrest all the Kenyans. The General China operation failed.

• At least as great a driver as Nigel Mansell (and relatively interesting), Stirling Moss won a race at the first ever motor racing event at the new Aintree course (now only used for horses).

May: The first electronic brain, or computer, by IBM, was moved into an office situation. Guaranteed to speed up calculating a thousand fold, the new machines looked positively elephantine compared to the stuff we use today.

• They all said it couldn't be done. Roger Bannister finally trotted a mile in under 4 minutes (3 mins 59.4). Who could have guessed that half a minute would still be chopped off that time?

June: Lester Piggot, who didn't always look like a dried prune, was the youngest rider to win the Derby at 18. He was to become the most famous jockey of all time.

• The old test for drunk driving was walking a straight line or reciting tongue twisters. Doctors suggested that there might be a more scientific way of working out whether one was out of one's box.

July: Bad year for bunnies. The rabbit population of Britain was in severe danger of total wipe-out owing to a sledgehammer-to-crack-a-walnut virus called myxomatosis introduced from Australia to keep the numbers down. Maybe they should have tried condoms.

Packet of 300 please.

September: The Federation of British Sun Clubs held its first annual meeting. All clothes had to be left in the lobby.
• Suckers for punishment, the Labour Party voted in favour of the re-armament of Germany. An audible chuckle was heard to come from Hitler's grave.

1955

Churchill Says Goodbye

After half a century in politics, Winston Churchill finally sat down and let the younger Sir Anthony Eden, a kind of latter-day Bertie Wooster, have a go as Prime Minister just before the General Election. It was a smart move to keep the job in the family (Eden was married to Churchill's niece). On winning the vote, Eden made his old mate Harold Macmillan, Foreign Secretary and Rab Butler, Chancellor of the Exchequer. Rumblings were also heard at the top of the Labour party when Attlee bowed out in favour of Hugh Gaitskell.

Sir Anthony Eden

Cyprus in Turmoil

Britain, still playing its part as fatherly protector of the world, had its work cut out keeping the Turkish and Greek Cypriots from making kebabs of each other – let alone the Greek Cypriot terrorists (EOKA) from attacking the British, who still ruled the island. Greek Cypriots had always resented this British rule and wanted the island to be part of Greece (obviously). The Turkish were not too delighted at this prospect (also obviously) and looked to Britain for protection. In other words, we were in another right mess.

Britain Invaded
According to some of the more red-necked, nationalistic Britons, we were undergoing our own mini-invasion. Hoards of black immigrants from the West Indies were storming our shores having been given the impression (probably from us) that this was the land of milk and honey (or rather money). When they got here, however, it was a different story. We might have wanted them to do all the nasty jobs but we certainly didn't want them living in respectable areas or (worse!) mixing with our sons and daughters. Consequently, the milk soon turned sour and the honey glued them firmly (and permanently) at the bottom of the social ladder.

Still Hanging On
The last woman to be hanged, ex-model Ruth Ellis, went to the gallows after shooting her racing driver boyfriend, David Blakely. It was the murder with everything, and the British public, who can always be relied upon to luxuriate in other people's misery, lapped it up. The case did, however, throw the barbarous act of the ultimate rope trick into public debate again. Whilst, in the past, it had been all right to hang weird-looking pervs like Christie, there was uproar about pretty ones like poor Ruth Ellis.

Gathering No Moss
Still, everything has a bright side. At least Stirling Moss had one less driver to beat. On 1st May, he became the first Briton to win the Mille Miglia, a tortuous road race through ordinary Italian roads and rather too often over ordinary Italian people. It was later banned for that reason (such spoilsports, the Italians). Motor

racing was obviously not the best spectator sport that year as a little later there was an appalling crash at Le Mans, when a Mercedes and two other cars left the track at 150 m.p.h. decapitating some eighty people. The Germans, still a touch sensitive about their reputation for killing innocent people, never raced again.

Warsaw Packed
Leaders from the Soviet Union, Poland, Czechoslovakia, Hungary, Rumania, Bulgaria, East Germany and Albania crowded into Warsaw to sign the Warsaw Pact, a treaty to balance NATO (the club formed by the West). All the signatories promised faithfully to be ever so good and not to solve any of their problems with violence, and to work towards eventually throwing all their nasty guns away. Unfortunately, no one looked behind the Russian delegates' backs to see if their fingers were crossed. Yugoslavia, ominously, didn't sign.

Jean Genie
If you ever wondered when the fashion started that was responsible for making everyone look exactly the same the world over, it was 1954. Like most crazes, the blue jean phenomenon came over the water from America and took our manufacturers completely by surprise.

Telly Sales
On 22nd September, the poor, long-suffering British were regaled with world-shattering messages like 'Murray Mints, Murray Mints – the too good to hurry mints' or 'The Esso sign means happy motoring'. Advertising had hit telly screens with a vengeance. Strangely enough, despite the huge fuss that had preceded commercial TV, the actual event was a bit of a damp squib.

Crying Out for Cash
The last famous singer of the old ballady school, American Johnny Ray, was reported as having earned half a million dollars in the last

year. Oddly enough, he is more famous for breaking down and sobbing during his act. Even oddlier enough, British women went crazy for this dorky-looking crooner who wore a hearing aid. Rumour has it he turned it off while singing.

Elvis Who?
Back in the States, a young truck driver called Elvis Presley was becoming, known rather embarrassingly, around Memphis as The Hillbilly Cat. Never mind Elvis, we've all gotta start somewhere. His shellshocked manager 'Colonel' Tom Parker told the press that the girls were literally tearing his clothes off, much to the annoyance of their parents.

Margaret Ducks Out
The Queen's rather wayward sister, Margaret, called off her wedding to Captain Peter Townsend on 31st October. She gave some lame excuse that, due to her duty to the Commonwealth, and the fact that the Church didn't go a bundle on divorcées, she felt she must do the noble thing and not go through with it. The fact that she would lose all the loot that she got from the Civil List, and her place in the queen queue, had absolutely nothing to do with it (and my name's Henry VIII).

My Bomb's Bigger than Your Bomb
The year ended with the chilling news that not only had the Ruskies got themselves a hydrogen bomb of their very own, but it was bigger and better than the Americans'. To be fair, they did tell us they only had it for national security (and to blast anyone who didn't believe them to kingdom come).

Meanwhile

January: Shock of shocks! Petrol went up to 4/6d (23p) a gallon.

July: Ullswater, in the Lake District, positively throbbed to the roar of Donald Campbell's (son of the late Sir Malcolm) hydroplane *Bluebird*, as he broke the world water speed record at 202.32 m.p.h.

August: A yuckily slick painting of the Queen was unveiled at the Royal Academy. It was by Italy's modern old master Pietro Annigoni and made him very famous – luckily only for fifteen minutes (see p.211 on Andy Warhol).
• A horribly embarrassed and embarrassing Irish TV host, Eamonn Andrews, compered the first horribly embarrassing 'This is Your Life' TV show on 3rd August. It doesn't seem possible that we're still putting up with it. It's interesting to note that the other great telly host, Terry Wogan (who we're also still putting up with) was born on the same date 17 years earlier.
• It's also interesting to note that yet another syrupy chat show host, Jimmy Young, was Top of the Pops that October with the appalling 'Man from Laramie'.

November: No more soccer by candlelight. The first floodlit international football match was played at Wembley.

September: Role model for a million spotty teenagers, James Dean, kicked off his legend by killing himself (and his brand new Porsche) in a crash just outside Los Angeles.
• *Health Warning:* Legendary status is not guaranteed by this course of action.

December: Not only had those Ruskies developed their pesky hydrogen bomb, but now they claimed to have a rocket which could deposit it 4000 miles away.

1956

Cyprus Hots Up

It was the same old British piggy, but in a different middle. Stuck bang in between the age-old hatred of the Turks for the Greeks (and vice-versa), it was beginning to look like a no-win situation. More and more British troops pitched up on the island of Cyprus to patrol the streets of the main cities of Limassol and Nicosia. The British Governor, Field Marshal Sir John Harding, secretly met the Greek Cypriot leader, the formidable farmer's son Archbishop Makarios (who looked like a demonic negative of Father Christmas), but there was absolutely no way that he was going to allow the Greeks (who outnumbered the Turks four to one) the independence they were clamouring for.

Bring the Cows In, Dad

It was reassuring to know that Britain was on the ball as far as nuclear attack was concerned. It was announced that we were to get a really fab early warning system. Members of the Royal Observer Corps were to be spread around the country at 15 mile intervals, linked by an underground telephone. When it came right down to it, however, one can only suppose that they were to look out of their bedroom windows and, presumably, ring up their colleagues and Central Office if they saw anything suspicious coming. They would then rush out in the streets and tell everyone to go indoors and shut all the windows, as radiation could apparently be rather unpleasant (it could cause one to feel a little dicky for up to three months they claimed). Farmers would be asked to go out and get all their animals in and, no doubt, cut all their crops quickly. Meantime, one can also only suppose that the approaching rocket would either park up and wait for us all to be ready or go round the block a couple of times. 'Dad's Army' lived again.

More Cyprus

Cyprus was becoming a nightmare chess game. Whichever way the British authorities moved seemed to get them into check. Finally, Sir John Harding, who was near the end of his tether, made a move that really stirred things up. He removed the Bishop (Makarios) and deported him to the sunny Seychelles (it's a hard life). EOKA the Greek terrorists, then went totally crazy, whipping up riots and bombing anything that stood still long enough. Hugh Gaitskell, the opposition leader, leapt in and ridiculed the move as 'an act of pure folly'.

On 25th March, reports came through that poor old Sir John had literally been sleeping on top of his own personal time bomb. One of his servants, an EOKA supporter, had put one under his bed (you just couldn't get the staff in those days). Fortunately (for Sir John) his unfaithful servant had set the time wrong and the device was later exploded harmlessly in his back garden.

Dans alarm clock

Khrushchev Comes to Visit

Nikita Khrushchev, having rocked the world by renouncing old Joe Stalin as a brutal, despotic and criminal murderer (weren't they qualifications for the job?), came to Britain to have a friendly pow-wow with our Government. Everything went well until the wonderful George Brown, a Labour Shadow Minister famed for getting pi . . . e-eyed and saying the wrong thing, got into a furious argument with the Commie boss at a rather boisterous dinner party. Unbelievably, Nikita responded by saying that if he was British he'd vote Tory, which was like George saying that if he was Russian he'd try to reinstate the Csar.

The Case of the Disappearing Crabb

While Khrushchev was visiting with us, a scandal broke that embarrassed the pants off the British Government. A naval frogman, Commander 'Buster' Crabb, was caught 'doing underwater tests' underneath the Russian ships that had brought their leader. The Russian newspapers accused Britain of 'shameful underwater espionage' and accused us of undermining international cooperation.

Poor old 'Buster' was never seen again and although the press suggested he'd drowned, most people thought he'd been nicked by the rotten Ruskies. A year later, speculation ended when Buster was found (unfortunately *sans* head) near where he'd disappeared. The question then was – how did he lose it? And was it now on Khrushchev's mantelpiece?

Naughty Nasser

On 13th June, Colonel Nasser waved goodbye, with an insincere smile, to the British troops who'd been occupying the Canal Zone. Thirteen days later, he dropped a bombshell by nationalising the Anglo-French controlled Suez Canal Company, saying, rather rudely, that if they didn't like it they could jolly well 'choke to death on their fury'. And fury there was, particularly from the

Colonel Nasser

French who'd built the canal. Nasser then said he would spend all the cash that he was going to charge foreigners for using the Canal on building the Aswan Dam, which doubly miffed the Brits and the Yanks who'd reckoned they could make a killing by financing and building the damn dam. It almost makes you think that international affairs are really only about money.

Eden, who nearly blew a gasket, said that we couldn't allow a creep like Nasser to 'have his thumb on our windpipe'. In truth, the crafty old Colonel had us by a much more delicate part of our anatomy.

Oh dear, oh dear – the next thing the poor long-suffering British heard was that their forces and the French forces had jumped into the gun boats and were heading for Suez. On 9th October the Israeli army, always ready to have a pop at the Arabs, stormed across the border and headed towards the Canal from the other direction. Nothing to do with helping us, however: they were just retaliating against Egyptian attacks across their border. The plot thickened!

On 31st October, all hell let loose when Anglo-French aircraft dropped their guts on to the Egyptians before they could even put their camels away. They'd given Egypt and Israel twelve hours to get all their soldiers out of the Canal Zone but although the Israelis did as they were told, the Egyptians (surprise, surprise) ignored the warning. For the first time in recent history, Britain and France were chums. The UN, America and even Russia were refusing to have anything to do with this reckless action. After a rather ragged little war, the Anglo-French troops captured the Canal Zone on 6th November: but that was, by no means, to be the end of it.

On 12th November, there was a ceasefire, brought about by the UN who set the terms (and threatened to send in 6,000 troops if they didn't agree).

The Canal was by now clogged by loads of sunken ships; Britain was shunned by world opinion; relations with the States were at their worst ever; sterling was near collapse; Sir Anthony Eden was suffering from exhaustion; Britain was accused of setting up the Israeli invasion; and the Government was in total disgrace. Not bad going, eh?

Dear old Eden's famous quote of the year went: 'We are not at war with Egypt – we are in armed conflict.'

Hungary for Freedom
On 26th October Hungary rose as one to show two fingers to their Russian oppressors. The brave Hungarian people fought the

occupying Soviet troops with their bare hands, and thousands were killed for their trouble. When the huge bronze statue of Stalin was chopped off at the knees in Budapest, it looked as if the people had got away with their bid for freedom. No way! On 5th November, the fireworks really went off and the dream became a nightmare when a thousand surly Soviet tanks rolled in and over Hungary. All that could be heard from Budapest radio was 'HELP, HELP, HELP' as the merciless Russian bear literally squeezed the life out of the opposition. But the United Nations, when push came to shove, was too chicken to pitch in, and by midday the brave revolution was ground into the mud.

In Britain, the little Communist Party was left with so much egg on its already red face that a huge proportion of the almost quaint bunch of idealists quit the party, totally gobsmacked by their Russian idol's gross actions. It was never actually to be the same again.

Meanwhile

January: The Astronomer Royal, known to have his head in the clouds, said that the whole idea of space travel was 'bilge'. Only ten years later he would have been able to watch the moon landing on television.

• For the first time (surprisingly) in Britain's history, the import and export of heroin was banned.

February: A piece of wood shaped very roughly like a mule went on British TV. Needless to say 'Muffin the Mule', the mute puppet, was a huge success with us deprived kids.

May: Self-service shops were seen for the first time in Britain. Critics feared overspending, pilfering and the death of the small shopkeeper. It was a watershed in retailing history. These days we are hard put even to find a shop assistant – alive or dead.

June: Every red-blooded man's toes curled with envy when the gawky playwright with the Buddy Holly glasses – Arthur Miller – married their favourite fantasy, Marilyn Monroe.

August: The man who made fame and fortune splattering paint against his canvases, Jackson Pollock, splattered himself against a tree when his car ran off the road. I wonder if he was a James Dean fan?

September: The film *Rock Around the Clock* proved to be too much for the hordes of Teddy Boys who flocked to see it. Near riots rocked around Britain's cinemas as the lads in the drainpipe trousers and drape jackets jived in the aisles and ripped up the seats. What would they have done, we ask, if they *hadn't* liked it?

October: Frozen pea-man Clarence Birdseye finally went to the great freezer in the sky.

1957

All Change on Top
Who says it's fun to be prime minister? Even after a long holiday in Jamaica, Sir Anthony Eden came back brown but knackered. He resigned on 9th January, both as Prime Minister and, two days later, from parliament. 62 year old Harold Macmillan (who by now looked like a kind but worried walrus) got the top job, putting poor Rab Butler's nose out of joint. (He'd been favourite with the bookies.)

Fool's Gold
Poor old Britain really was having a hard time abroad. The British ruling classes (God bless 'em), though realising they would have to give up their lucrative dominions one day, weren't prepared to rush into it. They thought independence should wait until the 'natives' had proved they could handle it – a policy which history has proved to be not that daft.

On 6th March the British Gold Coast decided to drop the 'British' bit . . . and then the 'Gold Coast' bit – becoming the all-black state of Ghana. The brand new President Kwame Nkrumah told the cheering crowds that at last they were free from the chains of imperialism (which meant us, folks!). He also told them he wanted to get back to the dim distant past when black Africa had all the power and cash.

No sooner had they all stopped jumping up and down in Africa, than a new cry of joy went up in Malaya as they ended their 170 years of British rule. They, however, were not so dismissive of their old masters, thanking us for recently saving them from the slavering jaws of communism, but presumably *not* thanking us for exploiting them rotten for years.

Britain Misses the Boat

On 25th March, France, West Germany, Italy, Belgium, Holland and Luxemburg signed the Treaty of Rome, so forming the European Common Market. It was formed to banish tariffs and promote the free movement of people, goods and money. Britain, who still thought it was a great major power, had decided not to join the flash new club, preferring to stick with the dear old Commonwealth. Many people (including the Prime Minister) were not at all sure we had done the right thing and wondered if we should talk some more . . . The French, always ready to get one over on the British, could hardly conceal their Gallic glee, saying like cocky enfants that we should have thought of it earlier and that we couldn't join in their game . . . What's French for 'Yah Boo Sucks'?

You Lucky People

There's nothing like a good old, top-of-the-pile, true blue, millionaire Tory Prime Minister to dish out patronising statements. On 20th July Mac (as he became known) told his loyal subjects 'Let's be frank about it. Most of our people have never had it so good.' Maybe Mac (and even Frank) was doing OK, but a lot of us Brits, especially the newish immigrants, felt like ramming those words down his aristocratic throat. To be fair, however, the standard of living for the newly invented lower middle-class was one hell of a lot better than when the Tories had gained power.

Dogs Rule OK

3rd November was a red letter day (literally) in the canine world. A Russian dog called Laika had been booted into space by his Communist masters and was now doing mega-walkies round the world without leaving his tin kennel. The good news was that

Laika became the most famous dog in all history. The bad news was that the spacecraft, six times heavier than the first satellite (called Sputnik 1), was not designed to come home, so poor Laika eventually ran out of oxygen (and dog biscuits). They should have called him Pluto as, for all we know, the poor mutt's still in orbit, like a little planet, in what became a flying coffin. Ah well, it's a dog's life!

Lordesses
On 30th October the Government proposed the creation of life peerages and baronesses (women lords). The former meant that, for the first time, the privileged classes (toffs) would no longer have a stranglehold on the House of Lords. Common folk could, if they did really well in their working lives, sleep all day on those lovely red leather benches like the others. Little did the Government know that one day it would let in the likes of cocky, pulp novelists like Lor . . . (I can't even say it) Jeffrey Archer.

Rock On
Far more important, Bill Haley and his Comets finally hit a rapturous London. There were even lofty, murmurs of approval from our more than stuffy Royal Family. Mind you, it was Princess Margaret who did the murmuring, and she always said and did the wrong thing.

British teenagers were now wallowing in the waves of American rock and roll talent that were gushing over them. Elvis was in full flow; Fats Domino, Frankie Lymon, Paul Anka, Jerry Lee Lewis, The Everly Brothers, Buddy Holly and Little Richard to name but a lot, heralded what became known as the golden age of rock and roll. In retaliation (and trying to cash in) British singers like Tommy Steele, Lonnie Donegan, Marty Wilde (Kim's Dad), Adam Faith and Cliff Richard squawked valiantly to make themselves heard, but their sound, to us 'experts', was positively weedy compared to all the fab imported stuff.

Meanwhile

January: No more free telly. GPO detector vans became a common sight in Britain's streets designed to catch licence dodgers.
• Everyone's favourite prince, Charles, went to school for the first time.

April: Tom Finney became famous for having the biggest shorts in soccer (and as Footballer of the Year).
• The 'Sky at Night' presented by the man who always looked like he dressed while escaping from a fire, and spoke faster than anyone could think – Patrick Moore – was broadcast for the first time.
• Only Yanks could invent something called the Drunkometer, designed to measure the alcohol on the breath. Was this an omen?

July: MPs voted themselves £750 a year increase on their expenses. Great idea, I vote we should all try it.

August: Despite plenty of work at home, 2000 British people a week were heading off for somewhere better (like Australia or Canada) to live. Their boats probably passed all the foreigners on their way here to find somewhere better to live.

• Chelsea Football Club caused a sensation by playing 17 year old Jimmy Greaves. Unlike most footballers, Jimmy refused to go away and has now joined the ranks of all those other boring TV sports 'experts'.

September: The Wolfenden Report came out of the closet saying that homosexual acts between consenting adult men should no longer be against the law. Lesbians carried on gay-ly.

October: Christian Dior, the man most responsible for making women look like women after the war, died in Italy.

1958

Talk's Cheap

1958 heralded the age of economical, speedy communications over far greater distances. At last, you could call your Auntie Ethel in Scotland without having to go through some surly operator. Also a new phenomenon called a motorway was built to by-pass Preston (no comment!). This eventually came to mean that, instead of sitting alone in a traffic jam, you had cars either side of you. The first bit of the, later-to-be-awful, M1 was opened in December. Huge new traffic signs had to be designed that could be read at 70 m.p.h.

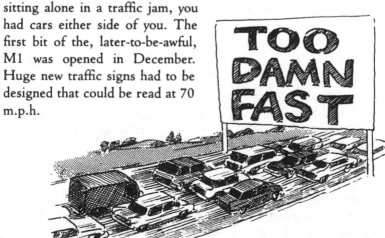

The Dreaded Meter Maids

While giving with one hand, the Government, typically, took with the other. Suddenly our urban roads sported gaily painted yellow lines which meant, for the first time ever, that one couldn't park where and when one wanted (provided there was a space). The downtrodden driver was allowed, however, to stop in *some* places but would, also for the first time, encounter horrid little meters which demanded payment for the privilege of doing just that. And if you didn't pay? Lurking on street corners, dressed in yellow and black battle gear, like psychotic wasps, were the instantly recognisable (and instantly despised) traffic wardens, whose only pleasure in life seemed to be stinging the motorist. The British, of course, accepted these new infringements on their liberty without a whimper.

Ban the Bomb

One group who didn't mind telling the government exactly where to shove its politics, formed the Campaign for Nuclear Disarmament or CND. Led by the one-day-to-be-PM Michael Foot; the brilliant, if somewhat potty philosopher, Bertrand Russell; the author J. B. Priestley; and the late, great journalist James Cameron, they were to become a force that would one day embarrass the hell out of the Government and *nearly* influence its nuclear policy.

'Ban the Bomb' became the battle cry of just about every socialist, student, or anti-establishment rebel in the country. Unfortunately, their famous scruffy marches looked so much like queues for soup kitchens that, predictably, their message tended to be ignored by the Great British (Oh dear, we'd better not make a fuss) Middle Class who thought that anyone who didn't wear a collar and tie was either a drug addict or on the payroll of the KGB.

Blacks Break Out

It just had to happen. On 9th September our coloured brothers, fed up with being taunted by white racists, suddenly blew their cool and fought back. The Notting Hill race riots dragged to the surfac the sort of tension that had been bubbling away in the States for years. For the first time, petrol bombs were lighting up British streets and from this point blacks, hacked off with being taken for granted, were seen to be on the case as far as racial discrimination was concerned. It was also, interestingly, the first time the press was censured for whipping up an already tense situation in order to make their story a bit sparkier.

Would you mind picking a fight with those chaps?

Nasser Rattles His Sabre

On 30th July, the Middle East erupted yet again. A gaggle of young Iraqi soldiers (heavily whispered-to by Nasser) overthrew their boss King Faisal. This put the wind up Iraq's neighbours Jordan and Lebanon, who immediately rang up America (on reverse charges) and asked for help. The Yanks, never ones to miss the chance of flexing their mighty muscles (especially where oil's concerned), got 1700 marines out of bed and rushed them to Beirut the following day where, instead of being fired at, they were greeted by a gaggle of bikini-clad Beiruti beach bimbos who offered them ice-cream and all sorts of other things.

Not to miss the party, and following our destiny as the world's co-prefect, 2000 British troops landed in Amman, Jordan to help King Hussein. The plot to invade Jordan by Nasser's United Arab Republic troops (really Syrians) had been cut off at the pass.

Nasser and his new best mate, the Soviet Union, were well miffed and ordered the UN to tell the British and Americans to leave the pitch for an early bath.

In England, Aneurin Bevan made a right prat of himself when he declared that Britain really shouldn't do anything to upset the Ruskies, while Khrushchev sent a postcard to Nasser saying that Soviet 'volunteers' could be available if required. Let battle commence.

Pick-a-Pope

The world's Catholics heaved a sigh of relief when, after twelve false starts, the Vatican managed to decide on a new head man and yellowy white smoke was seen issuing from the chimney (their way of telling the world that a decision has been made). Pope John XXIII, as he became affectionately known, was a surprise choice as, owing to his leftish views, he'd got right up the noses of the ultra-conservative Papal Court up Venice way.

De Gaulle est le Boss

Over in France, General de Gaulle, who looked more French than frog's legs, became the first President of the French Republic by an overwhelming majority. As far as we were concerned, this was 'pas bon' as it was well known that the ridiculously tall Frenchman thought we British were creeps.

Thalidomide Horror

The year ended with the horrendous discovery that the 'wonder' drug thalidomide, used to treat pregnant mothers for morning sickness, may have seriously deformed thousands of newborn babies.

Meanwhile

January: The net was closed. The first radar speed checks were used on London streets.

• Jerry Lee Lewis, the dynamic rock piano thumper, shocked a still puritanical world when he announced that he'd married his cousin. Tricky, but not as much as the fact she was only thirteen. (Great balls of fire!)

• Civil servant Irene Ferguson cracked how to be the first woman to be paid the same as a man. She turned herself into one!

February: Probably the most talked-about air crash in history. The fabulous Manchester United football team was all but wiped out when their plane crashed on the runway at Munich Airport.

March: Always guaranteed to put his foot in his mitre, the late Bishop of Woolwich claimed that women who went out to work were the enemies of family life. Blimey Bish, it's a good job you've gone to the other place; you'd be hard put to find a mum that *doesn't* work these days.

May: Christopher Cockrell shocked the car, boat and aviation world by making a cross between all three. His 'Hovercraft' was the first vehicle to float on a cushion of air.

July: Nasser gets nasty. In Baghdad, King Faisal, the Crown Prince, and Iraq's prime minister were murdered in one of Nasser's more unpleasant plots.

August: High Fidelity, or Hi Fi, was the new buzz word in the record world. Would you believe it, you had to use two loudspeakers placed at either end of the front room, as well as the equivalent of your radiogram, somewhere in between.

October: Surprise, surprise! The USSR agreed to loan Egypt $100 million dollars to build the Aswan dam. Funny how things turn out.

• Just about the daftest looking machine ever built, the Bubble Car, went on display at the Motor Show in London. One variety of the car, designed to foil urban traffic congestion, required the driver to sit in front of his passenger and climb out of the roof.

65

The other type had the driver sitting next to his passenger and exiting ... through the front. Either way, both driver and passenger looked pretty damn stupid. The first were built by BMW who now own what remains of Britain's car industry. Now what does that tell you?

1959

Carry on Cuba

2nd January saw an event which at first looked as if it would have very little to do with Britain. The glamorous rebel leader Fidel Castro (him of the big beard and trendy fatigues) proclaimed to the world that he'd taken over Cuba after two years struggling against the infamous and desperately cruel dictator Batista. So far so good. Nobody likes dirty dictators and Britain was one of the first to suck up to – sorry, 'recognise' – the new regime.

Despite refusing to side with America against Russia in the exciting new game called Cold War, Castro laughed off any suggestion that he was a communist (what a porkie!) and even became the toast of Washington when he buzzed over there to convince them. Can anyone guess where this is going? Wait and see.

Cyprus Deal

More seriously, a deal was finally worked out for Cyprus. The new republic would have a Greek-Cypriot President and a Turkish-Cypriot Vice-President (that's diplomacy for you). Britain ducked out after 80 years of rule (most of them miserable) but was allowed to keep one or two military bases on the island. EOKA (the terrorist organisation) jumped up and down when they heard the details of the agreement and claimed their boss, Archbishop Makarios, would never either agree to the deal, or to be president. They couldn't have been more wrong. He did – and was . . . on 12th December.

You want the tooth fairy? What about the truth fairy?

Supermac Makes Moscow
Looking like a pint of Guinness in a too-tall white fur hat and a long black overcoat, Harold Macmillan landed in Moscow on one of his famous goodwill trips. After a brief meeting, Khrushchev claimed he had toothache and couldn't carry on with the discussions. Nice one Nikita – don't they have dentists up Russia way? British officials were not amused.

Good Cod — It's War
On May 6th Britain had a go at Iceland because they were using bully boy methods to enforce their new 12 mile fishing limit. This dispute had come to be known, rather obviously, as the Cod War, but had become a bit serious when Iceland's patrolling gunboats actually started firing live ammo at our trawlers (still using the old four mile limit). This simply wasn't cricket (or fishing), though I don't suppose the individual cods gave a monkey's *who* caught them – they'd end up as fish fingers either way.

Got Any Spares?
Hammer films came to life on 25th June when doctors at Hammer-smith Hospital announced that they were setting up a spare parts department. It worked like this. If you were unfortunate enough to be snuffed out by a road accident (for

example), a chap would come along in a refrigerated van and whip out your liver and lights before you were cold on the road. These personal bits would then be stored back at the ranch until needed by someone whose own were knackered. Meantime, you'd be buried somewhat lighter. That was the theory anyway.

Mini Madness
One of the vehicles that could well turn you into spare parts if you crashed it, was the new Mini Minor, manufactured by the BMC (British Motor Company) to fit nicely under a speeding juggernaut. This four-seater motor, designed by Alec Issigonis, looked rather daft when it first came out, but the shape soon caught on and, to this day, has been a common sight on British roads. Its most remarkable feature is that it is actually bigger inside than out. Perhaps it was Issigonis who later designed Doctor Who's 'Tardis'. Dead clever these Italians.

Mac 'n' Ike
Carrying on his crusade to be mates with all and sundry, Harold Macmillan appeared with President Eisenhower (Ike) of America on the 'Downing Street Show' on telly, casually discussing world events in a manner that seemed about as natural as warm ice cream. It was, strangely enough, a huge hit, and the two old campaigners, flushed with success, proposed to do the same thing, a little more formally (if that was possible), with De Gaulle and Khrushchev.

Telly Takes Over
Distressing reports from the cinema industry claimed that telly was beating them hands down in popularity. This wasn't helped by Auntie BBC buying 20 American feature films. It was around this time that cinemas began mysteriously turning into a brand new scourge – the dreaded bingo hall.

Mac Does it Again
8th October saw a new General Election, and Supermac, 'never

having had it so good', pulling one of the hugest majorities ever seen. Gaitskell, the loser, put his failure down to squabbling within his party. He did agree with Macmillan, however, that the class war was dead. Dead? They obviously didn't read *The Tatler* or *The Lady*.

Europe Does the Splits
Just as the European Common Market Club was settling down with a self-satisfied feeling of superiority, Britain, Austria, Denmark, Norway, Portugal, Sweden and Switzerland formed a club of their own, effectively showing two digits to the others. EFTA (European Free Trade Association) as it was called, made no secret of trying to upstage the rival gang. Talk about a damned cheek – they even asked the others to disband and come over to their clubhouse. Who was to get the last laugh! Read on.

Meanwhile

January: Sit-ins on London Underground's Northern Line prompted the powers-that-be to warn against strikes. 35 years later the line's still a disgrace.
• Being overweight was reckoned for the first time to be more of a problem in Britain than malnutrition. Simple! Why didn't all the thin people eat the fatties? Next!
• Henry Cooper, a much loved British hero, with a face like his own punch bag, became British and Empire Heavyweight Champion on 12th January, aged 24. 'Our 'Enery is still, thankfully, alive and kicking (or punching).

February: A brat is born. A black day for all those tennis fans who like a quiet life. John McEnroe entered the world.

April: The Queen Mother and Princess (I dig rock and roll) Margaret had an audience with the Pope. I've heard of being desperate to get your daughter married off, but this was ridiculous.

May: Talking of marriage. The state of Alabama banned a kids' book in which a black rabbit married a white rabbit. They were probably far too young to get married anyway.
• Talking of rabbits, two American monkeys became the first living creatures to return to earth in one piece (or should I say two pieces) when they splashed down in the Atlantic. They'd just been cruising around 360 miles above the Earth.

August: A survey reported that the average British household spent 18s 1d a week on food. These days that would hardly pay for the plastic bags to carry the stuff home in.

September: One of the funniest events in world politics occurred when Khrushchev lost his rag (red) because the Americans (for security reasons) wouldn't let him visit Disneyland. Sad really – he could have got a job as a Dopey (of *Snow White* fame) look-alike.

November: Talk about jobs for the boys. Fidel Castro astounded the Cubans (and the rest of the world) by making his old revolutionary chum, and pin-up, Che Guevara, Head of the National Bank. It was a bit like making Ronnie Biggs (see page 86) Chancellor of the Exchequer.

1960

Mac's Wind

On February 3rd, good old Supermac came out with another famous one-liner. He pronounced in a speech to the South African Parliament, referring to black unrest, that the 'wind of change' was blowing through the continent, whether we (notice the we) 'liked it or not'. Oh boy, did that go down like a lead balloon with the whities. He then went on to say that, if they weren't careful, all the African countries would shack up with the Communists who, in the short term, had so much more to offer. Let's face it, it doesn't take the best offer in the world to attract people who have little more than they stand up in.

It was no pie in the sky prediction either. Those saucy Soviets were definitely huffing and puffing at the African hut doors and they knew they wouldn't have to blow that hard. Hardly had the words left Mac's mouth when the appalling Sharpeville massacre gruesomely underlined what he'd been saying. 56 Africans were mercilessly slaughtered and 162 injured, at a rally in Sharpeville in the Transvaal. The police had waded into blacks demonstrating against having to carry pass cards. This was very much the thin end of a wedge that was to widen for years to come.

The Cold War Bites Harder

The Russians were now really throwing their weight around and everyone in Britain and the rest of the West was getting pretty nervous about what they might do next. Over in Germany, floods of people (mostly farmers) were crossing over from East Berlin following the Communist enforced collectivisation of small farms. Then, the summit conference, planned the previous year by Mac and Ike with De Gaulle and Khrushchev, fell through owing to the shooting down of an American plane (flown by Gary Powers) which the Commies outrageously claimed had been spying on

71

them. Actually, to be totally truthful, it had (tee hee!).

Kennedy Gets In
The whole of the western world was delirious at the news, on 9th
November, that the handsome John (or was it Jack?) Kennedy had
beaten the sleazy Richard Nixon to the presidency of the United
States. It effectively made this boyish-looking, youngest-ever,
president, the most powerful man in the world. It would not be
exaggerating to say that young people, throughout the free world,
believed that he was the one person who might prevent us all from
being blown to kingdom come by the follies of our elders and
worsers.

Maggie Marries
The 60s also opened with the world-shattering news that Princess
Margaret, after all that earlier fuss, was going to marry a common
person after all. The lucky man was Anthony Armstrong-Jones
who, although only a mere photographer (passports and wedding
photos to the nobility), was actually rather posh. The rest of the
Royal Family didn't make as much fuss as the last time because he
wasn't divorced and they were no doubt beginning to wonder if
they'd ever get poor Maggie off their hands.

Ship Ahoy
One of the great events to take our minds off all that Russian
breath on our necks, came to a finale on 21st July. Francis
Chichester (later to be Sir'd), a 58 year old Briton, suffering from

lung cancer (and, as some people thought, total insanity!), successfully sailed the Atlantic alone, in the new world record of 40 days. His little boat, which looked not much bigger than a bath-tub, became almost as famous as its driver-sorry-captain when it went on display in London.

Pornographic Penguins

An even better worry-diverter was the hilarious trial of Penguin Books who were charged with the publication of an 'obscene' book, *Lady Chatterley's Lover*, by D. H. Lawrence. There's nothing more likely to make a book a bestseller overnight than to suggest that it's dead rude. Sales of this otherwise rather weedy book rocketed and schoolboys in every playground in Britain could be seen huddled in corners hoping the book would spring open at the dirty bits.

Mr Mervyn Griffith-Jones, prosecuting, came out with a classic remark. He asked the jury if it was a book that they would wish their wives or servants to read. Barristers were then, as now, not always completely in touch with the common man. Joking apart, if you were fortunate enough to have a wife or a servant, they'd probably have already read it. Case dismissed!

The Choice to Fight

Even more good news was announced on 31st December, unless you were one of the poor unfortunate lads to receive the last National Service call-up cards. No longer would youngsters of eighteen be press-ganged into playing soldiers for two years with the vague possibility that if they did well they could get killed for Queen and country.

New Old-Fashioned Music

Traditional jazz, with its almost quaint plinky-plonky charm, had been like an underground music amongst trendy art students. These Beatniks as they were labelled were the very first to wear high pointed boots, long hair, heavy make-up and black Gothic style clothes (and that was the boys!). Suddenly trad. jazz leapt across to the hit parade and bands led by Acker Bilk, Chris Barber and Ken Colyer couldn't believe their luck (or their bank balances). But it wasn't to last. Rhythm and blues, sweeping through all the clubs and bands, led by guys like Georgie Fame, Long John Baldry and Alexis Korner soon made Acker Bilk and his mates look like tired old muso-saurs.

Meanwhile

January: The sale of pep pills, like Purple Hearts, much loved by the modern teenager, were given the thumbs down by our caring Government.

February: Top of the hit parade was a song called 'Teen Angel' sung by American Mark Dinning. This little ditty was all about a guy singing to his recently-ex-girlfriend who has been smashed to bits in a car crash. Charming!
• The star hovered again over Buck House heralding the birth of Prince Andrew (later known as 'Randy Andy' for reasons unknown).

April: Ace racing driver Stirling Moss lost his licence for a year. He'd been driving his ordinary motor, on the ordinary roads, forgetting he wasn't on the race track. Thirteen days later he won the Monaco Grand Prix . . . remembering that he was.

May: Those naughty Teddy Boys were creating such a stir that the government passed a bill to clip their wings, or D-A's (popular abbreviation for their 'ducks-arse' hairstyle).

July: To give you some idea of what British record buyers were into in 1960, Rolf Harris (that ghastly professional Australian) had a major hit with his heart-rending version of 'Tie Me Kangaroo Down Sport'. At that stage grown-ups, as one might guess, still represented the lions' (or kangaroos') share of the record-buying public.

August: Two Russian dogs managed to get home to earth alive after their outing in space. This encouraged their masters to have a go.

1961

South Africa Quits
You might have thought that when South Africa told us that, like most other Commonwealth countries, it wanted to become a republic, the British Government would have jumped up and down with relief. Macmillan, on the contrary, stated in his most sincere, paternalistic voice, that he was sorry, maintaining that being mother of the Commonwealth was the only way we could influence the lot of the poor down-trodden black Africans.

Horrid, cynical people might claim that Mac's motivations were not quite that big-hearted. South Africa was one of our major trading partners and worth shed-loads of loot especially as the two countries enjoyed preferential treatment as Commonwealth members. The solution was simple. South Africa would go it alone politically, but tradewise would cooperate with Britain in all possible ways. In other words, we're all right, Jack, tough luck on the natives.

Cuba Libre!

Meanwhile something very ominous was going on up Cuba way. That definitely 'non-Communist' Fidel Castro and his brave boys were fighting off an invasion by the exiled lot that used to control the country. The Cuban Revolutionary Council, as they called themselves, had apparently set up an airstrip at the Bay of Pigs. Big deal you may say! Yet another tin-pot revolution. Why should that be any concern of ours? It was when we realised that all Castro's planes, tanks and armaments were being supplied free from communist Russia, and that much of the weaponry used by the old regime was American, that the piquancy of the situation became clearer and more scary.

Khrushchev had a furious argument with President Kennedy demanding that the Yanks should, like them, help Castro. New boy Kennedy told him, in no uncertain terms, that if Russia poked its snubby East European nose into Cuba, or anywhere else for that matter, it would get severely bloodied. For a while they pushed and pulled at each other like two snotty kids in a playground, while the rest of the world wondered if we were teetering on the edge of the long-awaited World War 3.

Postscript: The invasion failed, and on 1st May Castro proclaimed Cuba as a socialist nation and, surprise, surprise, banished elections.

Walled In and Out

Yet another huge event that indirectly made our knees wobble happened on 31st August. What had seemed like a nice little brick wall, separating East and West Berlin, suddenly grew and became covered in barbed wire. All the 50,000 East Berliners who worked in the Western bit were turned back, and anyone who tried to cross over was promptly shot. The only ones who did escape were the few East German guards who saw that it was their last chance to get out. There was absolutely nothing the other Berliners could do about it. By October, British and American tanks literally faced Russian ones across the border.

Children's Hour Axed

Britain's children were also getting a rough deal. Auntie BBC had decided to take 'Children's Hour' off the wireless and away from her nieces and nephews. To be honest, it wasn't the greatest loss to us sixties' kids as it was hopelessly out of date, catering for nice children of a bygone age: the telly was much better!

Rock Rolls On

Although British artists like Cliff Richard and Adam Faith were making a few quid they were still small potatoes compared to the hip-swinging Elvis, bug-faced Roy Orbison or the super-smooth Everly Brothers, who were dominating the charts. The greatest news in music this year was that Little Richard, the totally-round-the-bend High Priest of Rock and Roll, came back into the business after four years as a proper preacher. Praise the Lord!

Meanwhile

January: The 1,000,000th Morris Minor trundled off the production line. In slight contrast, the Jaguar E Type, maybe the prettiest car ever, had a very easy birth. It cost an unbelievable £2196.

• There was an investigation as to why the poor Queen's personal train was held up for an hour. Perhaps she needed a break from all that coal shovelling?

April: The Soviet Union put the first human, Major Yuri Gagarin, sneakily into space. The Americans congratulated them with forced smiles, well aware that they'd lost the man-in-space race. They quickly bunged up the first person they could find with an astronaut's suit, a month later.

June: The first push-button pedestrian crossings were seen in London.

July: With not a little embarrassment the British Government, cap in hand, asked if we could join their Common Market. The special terms, asked for by Macmillan, really miffed the French (can you believe?) who threatened to spin out the talks for as long as possible or use their veto to keep us out.
• A report was published, saying that Britain's population had rocketed by 2.5 million in the last ten years. It now stood at 52,675,094.

August: The GPO announced that the tower they were planning in central London was going to be much taller than at first planned. This white elephant, the Post Office Tower, now has a mere handful of people working in it.

September: The first chain store to deal with the Baby Boom – Mothercare – opened in Kingston, London.

15,000 people demonstrated in London against the possession of the nuclear bomb. Dear old Bertrand Russell was jailed for 'inciting a breach of the peace'.

October: The Queen was obviously not that wild about having a 'commoner' brother-in-law, so she made Anthony Armstrong-Jones, Princess Margaret's new hubby, the Earl of Snowdon. Wasn't there a story about a princess who kissed a frogotrapher and got a prince?

December: Adolf Eichmann, a jolly nasty German, who had helped in the extermination of thousands of Jews, was finally sentenced to his own extermination after a lengthy show trial.

1962

Mac's Spring Clear Out

The most exciting event for years in British politics occurred when Harold Mac-the-knife-Millan cut a third of the cabinet in one slash. It followed an appalling by-election result, in which a Liberal overturned a Tory in Orpington. The party was pretty shaky anyway, and we British were becoming disillusioned with continual Tory promises of good times. It's nice to know some things never change!

Jeremy Thorpe, the up-and-coming Liberal MP, came up with the best joke about the Cabinet sackings when he said of Mac, 'Greater love has no man than this, that he lays down his friends for his life.' Ironical really – the same was to happen to Jeremy years later.

Blacks Stays Back
Now Britain had most of its unglamorous jobs filled (prime minister, etc.), the British Government were unkeen to have all those eager immigrants turning up from the Commonwealth, cluttering up our Labour Exchanges (now Job Centres). They

therefore searched for a way to get themselves out of the promises they'd made. Enoch Powell, at the Ministry of Health, didn't mind if the immigrants were skilled doctors or nurses as he was running a bit short, but he was getting a bit worried about the 'outrageous' habit the underprivileged ethnic minorities had of living together in little inner city communities and carrying on their customs. In July, therefore, the Government brought in the Commonwealth Immigration Act which stated, in so many words, that to get into these fair isles an applicant should either:
a. Have a job to come to.
b. Be able to do something that was needed in this country (see spying).
c. Have enough cash to be able to support themselves. (In which case, why would they want to come here?)
The opposition parties called it a nasty little piece of racist

legislation as it was fairly obvious that the Act was directed at 'coloured' immigrants.

Satire at Last
At home the British had a new craze: taking the mickey out of itself. A new telly series called 'That Was The Week That Was', hosted by a sharp, young, clever David-called-Frost, broke new ground by lampooning everything pompous and anachronistic about our Establishment. (It's interesting to note that he is now *Sir* David Frost and part of the very Establishment that he used to laugh at.) It was around this time, too, that a new magazine called *Private Eye* hit the newsagents. The *Eye* (as it was known) also debunked the system and anything that stood still long enough.

Vietnam Looms
The beginnings of the Vietnam War were set in motion when that 'hope for world peace' Jack (or was it John?) Kennedy sent 5000 troops into Siam to check the expanding Communist military offensive. Nobody in America quite realised what he was getting America into and, anyway, the wonder-boy President could do no wrong.

World on the Brink
Everyone in Britain held their breath on 28th October when John (or was it Jack?) Kennedy put his hand to his holster and challenged Khrushchev once more to a draw. A high, spy plane flying over Cuba (again) had spotted lines of missiles pointing straight at the United States. America had never been threatened before and they sure didn't like it. Before you could say 'Coca-Cola', they'd put loads of ships round Cuba and stopped anything going in or out. Kennedy then demanded that Khrushchev took his missiles and shoved them anywhere he liked – as long as they weren't in Cuba. For one whole day the world swayed on the edge of nuclear war with nobody knowing which way Khrushchev would jump. In the end, he saw that 'peacemaker' Kennedy wasn't going to chicken out and backed down himself. Castro was most cross

when he realised he was just a pathetic pawn in a much larger power struggle, and really smarted when he had to watch American observers supervising the dismantling of his lovely, shiny new toys.

Jobs Vacant

If you wanted a job that offered loads of cash, plenty of foreign travel, extreme danger but loads of excitement, then the big word down the local Labour Exchange was 'espionage'. Seriously, the early sixties was open season for spies. Every country was spying on every other country and every spy was spying on every other spy.

On 22nd October, an Admiralty clerk, William Vassall, was jailed. It turned out that the filthy Russians had found out that poor William didn't like girls much (know what I mean?) and invited him to a rather gay little party where they took lots of rather explicit photos (use your imagination) while he wasn't looking. They then blackmailed him into selling secrets about the navy and, no doubt, what colour underwear certain politicans wore.

On 22nd November, the Russians got their own back for his arrest and captured British businessman Greville Wynne, who'd gone to Hungary to demonstrate caravans (and my name's Marco Polo). The Soviets then began to prepare a major show trial.

Meanwhile

February: A little known group called The Beatles were turned down by the huge Decca recording company, who thought they'd didn't stand a dog's chance of making it into the charts.

• *The Sunday Times* brought out the first colour supplement. Critics, like those of The Beatles, turned it down saying the idea would never catch on. These days, even your local parish newsletter has a colour supplement.

• By now, both Russia and America had fine collections of each other's spies, so it was time for swapsies. Russia traded Gary Powers (of spy-plane fame) with KGB Colonel Rudolph Abel (America's most valuable prisoner). It wasn't really a fair swap as

Powers was only doing ten years as opposed to Abel's fifty.

June: Anyone want to bet on where Britain's first legal casino was situated? Brighton wins the money.
• The first edition of 'Police Five' was broadcast. Shaw Taylor, its presenter, became known in the underworld as 'Whispering Grass' proving that even crooks have a sense of humour (even if Mr Taylor didn't).

August: Yet another country rejected its mother. Jamaica gained independence after 307 years of British rule.
• Tragic news for male movie fans. Marilyn Monroe, arguably the most glamorous lady in the world, died in mysterious circumstances. Since then, the official verdict of suicide has been thrown into serious doubt and 'connections' with at least two of the Kennedys have come to light.

December: London's air was known to be filthy and, as if to prove it, a three day pea-souper fog caused the death of at least 60 people.

1963

Another Day — Another Harold

18th January was a black day for the Labour Party – literally. Hugh Gaitskell, the controversial leader of the party, died of a mystery virus infection. Harold Wilson, who looked like a slightly secretive pipe-puffing hamster, got the job after a savage fight with the brilliant, if unconventional, George Brown, who'd been Gaitskill's deputy (and who presumed he'd one day be sheriff). Brown decided to stay on as number two, but all their mates had a sly bet on how long they'd last before a major tiff.

De Gaulle Puts 'Le Boot' In

At an enthralled Paris news conference, President Charles de Gaulle delighted the agog frogs when he finally came out of the woodwork and trashed Britain's hopes of joining the Common Market. He told them that as far as he was concerned England would always act like a little two-bit island nation and, therefore, had no business trying to get into the big boys' 'gang'. Also he quite rightly recognised that we were not about to chuck away what

was left of our Commonwealth (even though most of the Commonwealth countries were trying to chuck us). The final insult came when he looked condescendingly down his huge Gallic hooter and suggested that maybe Britain could be offered some paltry junior associate status. Macmillan, highly miffed, accused de Gaulle of trying to dominate Europe. Who said the Battle of Agincourt was forgotten?

Super Scandal Begins

There had been rumours flying around London for some time that the immensely boring-looking Minister for War, John Profumo, was carrying on with a pretty young model (not that boring eh?). Like all MPs caught with their pinstripes down, Profumo tried threat, bluster and writ at first, and must have thought he'd got away with it after his boss Macmillan called the matter closed. When, however, the 'model' Christine Keeler, who admitted doing a little more than just disrobing, was also connected (in the biblical sense) with Russian diplomat, Eugene Ivanov, the whole delicious concoction started fizzing again.

On 5th June, Profumo finally admitted that he'd been telling privileged porkies and promptly resigned from the Government and Parliament. The silly chump had been shopped by a rather suave West End osteopath Dr Stephen Ward, who was later charged for living off the earnings of up-market prostitutes like Keeler and her drop-dead-gorgeous chum, Mandy Rice-Davies, the epitome of the new term 'dolly bird'.

It was fab reading; the more that came out, the more the British public realized that just about all areas of lowlife and highlife (including royalty) were somehow intertwined. During his trial, the dirty doc, Stephen Ward, described a world where aristocracy mixed with drug addicts and sexual perverts (so what's new?). At one point, you could count the influential people who *weren't* involved on the fingers of one foot. The gutter press, who usually didn't require more than a whisper to create a scandal, could hardly believe their ears or luck. But Ward was very much the scapegoat and the whole sleazy business took a sad turn when, while waiting to be sentenced, he topped himself.

Macmillan, who'd tried his level best to sweep the whole thing under his plush Downing Street carpet, could hardly be seen for all the egg on his face. The poor chap was blown away by the affair and resigned as Prime Minister. The end of a perfect scandal.

New Home for Alec

Our favourite Prime Minister was replaced by Sir Alec Douglas-

Home, putting poor Rab Butler's nose out of joint even further. He'd been waiting in the wings (like Cinderella) for the star part for two years but had been kept from going to the ball by a secretive little in-group later labelled 'Mac's Magic Circle'. Ian Mcleod and Enoch Powell obviously thought Douglas-Home was a right prat and refused to work with him, accusing the poor toff of being lightweight, which was not surprising as he looked a bit like a skeleton dressed in MP's or rather PM's clothing.

The First Great Train Robbery
On 24th March, Dr Beeching, the man brought in by the Government to run their train set better, did something that not only changed the face of Britain, but literally ruined thousands of people's lives. He closed 2128 stations, mostly on branch lines. It effectively stranded the very people who needed their railways most.

This was the beginning of the end of the great battle between road and rail and heralded the car becoming the god it is today. If you want to blame anyone for all those hideous smelly multistorey car parks or those horrid, traffic-free shopping centres, full of the sort of people you only see in horrid, traffic-free shopping centres, then it's all down to Doctor Beeching.

The Second Great Train Robbery
On 4th August, another crime occurred that is still talked about today. A group of fifteen hooded hoods held up a train in a manner better suited to a bad cowboy film. They jumped the train knowing it contained over £1,000,000 in used (thereby untraceable) banknotes and got clean away. Most British people, it must be said, had a slight admiration for the audacity of their crime. Even so, over the following years, the police had caught up with most of them. Only one, Ronald Biggs, managed to escape and hole up in Brazil. Despite numerous attempts to extradite him, Ronnie continues to thumb his nose at the British authorities while cavorting with tanned Brazilian bimbos on Acapulco beaches. Who says crime doesn't pay?

Beatlemania

The last great robbery of 1963 involved the stealing of the hearts of practically every teenage girl in Britain. The Beatles, that group that Decca said would never make it, suddenly did, and were hotter than Bill Haley or Elvis put together. Many of us boys were to become sick of the sight of John, Paul, George and Ringo; firstly, because our girlfriends fancied them more than us, and secondly, because we were fed up to the back teeth of always hearing about how fab Liverpool and the dreary Mersey Sound were.

Not bad Kevin - but what about the accent?

Bye-Bye John or Jack

The year ended with news that made everything else, including Beatlemania, pale into insignificance. On 22nd November, John Kennedy's brief career as President was cut short by the assassin's bullet. Everyone, the world over, froze at the news, and the prospect of a world without him. The controversy over who shot him still rages on. The man who was instantly arrested, Lee Harvey Oswald, was himself plugged by a gangster with Mafia connections called Jack Ruby, who then in turn died three years later of a mysterious 'bloodclot'. There's always been a strong rumour that the dreadful 'Commies' might have had a hand in it (at least it couldn't have been Marilyn Monroe).

The Bomb Gets Banned

At last the Brits, the US and the USSR hung up their egos and signed the Moscow Treaty, banning the testing of nuclear weapons in the atmosphere, outer space, under water or in back gardens. De Gaulle wouldn't join in – probably because everyone expected him to.

Meanwhile

February: The worst learner driver in Britain, Margaret Hunter, was fined for 'erratic' driving after her instructor jumped out, claiming it was pure suicide to stay in the passenger seat.

April: British 'caravan' salesman Greville Wynne (see page 82) was sentenced to three years in a Russian prison followed by five in a labour camp for spying. Guess they didn't want any caravans.

June: Our 'Enery (Cooper) stopped all our hearts when he floored Cassius Clay – probably the best World Heavyweight Champion in the history of boxing. Trouble was, Cooper always had dodgy eyes and was pulled out in Round Five with a bad cut.

July: Viscount Stansgate became the first peer to renounce his title so that he could be common like us (well, a bit like us). Anthony Wedgewood Benn, bless him, has been a thorn in the side of the rich and privileged ever since.

November: Whether the BBC were 'leant on' or not, we'll probably never know, but 'That Was The Week That Was', which had reached cult status, was suddenly axed.

December: Poor Christine Keeler (who only wanted a fair day's pay for a fair night's work) was jailed for nine months for conspiracy and perjury.

1964

Labour In

This was the year that the Labour party, despite its hobby of inflicting wounds on itself, beat the floundering Tories after fifteen years of rule. Harold Wilson, the new PM, won instant popularity because, for once, Britain had a leader who hadn't been born with a silver

spoon in his mouth (but didn't he let us know it?). 'When I was a lad we were so poor . . . ' and so on, and so on.

The Socialists had an ambitious set of plans and a new determination to carry them out.

Vietnam Explodes

President Lyndon Johnson, who had eased into the dead Kennedy's boots, managed to get Congress to form a posse to hunt and contain those darn Communists in North Vietnam. His action followed an attack on US destroyer Maddox in the Gulf of Tokin, and the retaliation was fast, furious and extremely unpleasant. This was the official beginning of the Vietnam War, which was to influence and frighten the British for years (even though we managed to keep our noses out of it).

All Change

Nothing remarkable had happened since the war fashion-wise. Men and boys looked basically the same as they always had, and women were mostly influenced by what was happening in Paris. Trousers for ladies (popular during the war) had disappeared; hemlines had gone up and down (but always a decent distance below the knee); bras had changed from soft and rounded to wired and pointy; knickers had shrunk from voluminous to fairly brief; shoes had lost the clumpy look of before and during the war and were now stiletto-heeled and narrow. If anything, after the American-inspired big petticoats and bobby socks of the newly invented fifties' teenagers, grown-up women's clothes had become even more conventional, with hardly a dividing line between the post-teenagers and the older mob.

Nothing prepared the British female (or male for that matter) for the revolution that was to occur on 13th Jan 1964 when a young art student named Mary Quant suddenly launched a stinging attack on the whole French led *haute-couture* scene, saying it was *très* boring and out of date. From her small shop Bazaar in Chelsea, she started a look that was to take over the world including Paris (though the French would never admit it). At last girls could buy clothes that their mums would look silly in. Shorter than short skirts, bold patterns that hurt your eyeballs, pink lipstick, false eyelashes, clipped elfin-like haircuts and paler than skin colour tights (necessary if your bottom was practically showing). The swinging sixties were born.

Sex, drugs and rock and roll were becoming available to all. If your mum and dad didn't like it . . . all the better. It was a period when anyone over, say, 25, was past it. At last British kids had found their own identity and even the Yanks, for the first time, started peering rather inquisitively over the water.

But it wasn't just in fashion that our youngsters began flexing their muscles. The Beatles had for some time been the toast of America, but now rhythm and blues, that had been filling all the British clubs and pubs, was becoming the honey on top. Bands like The Rolling Stones, The Animals, The Zombies, Rod Stewart and Alexis Korner were playing a kind of raw aggressive music that was not only knocking the kids sidewise but shocking Establishment America. Even when, the following year, the Labour Department of the US Government rescinded all visas for visiting British groups, it failed to halt their growing popularity.

Mods and Rockers
This new youth freedom had some sensational side-effects. A new cult group called Mods, who wore clothes inspired by Quant and her growing bunch of imitators, would speed in magnificent convoys to seaside towns all over the south coast. There, they would have magnificent punch-ups with their sworn enemies The Rockers, a group of sadly dated, motorbike-riding, leather-jacketed, greasy-haired, American-inspired tearaways (who lived with their mums).

It's interesting to note that racial prejudice between black and white youth was practically non-existent in those days. In fact, the racism displayed by their parents was yet another thing to rebel against.

Meanwhile

January: One of the first of the hilarious truly British sitcoms,

'Steptoe and Son', was declared Britain's most popular telly show. The first episode of the last series had claimed 9,653,000 viewers.
• Machines hit Underground stations. Automatic ticket machines that nearly ripped your fingers out of their sockets were first seen.
• Can you believe it, the average weekly wage in 1964 was £16 14s 11d.
• A gloomy month for Britain – *The Sun* newspaper rose in the east.

February: The Government announced the building of the Channel Tunnel. I think they must have had one Frenchman and one Englishman doing the digging from either end ever since.

March: Yet another baby for our parents to support. The Queen had a fourth sprog, called Edward.

April: The twelve members of the Great Train Robbery gang got 307 years in prison (but not each).
• A chap who was to be a thorn in the side of the British was made Prime Minister of Rhodesia. Ian Smith, a butcher's son, looked more like a strict Presbyterian minister than a politician.

May: Music fans, bored with the stodgy old BBC, had a new, deliciously illegal girlfriend called Radio Caroline. She was a 'pirate' ship parked somewhere off the east coast, blasting out non-stop-pop to the fury of the Beeb and most parents.

July: Never have so many people owed so much to so few. To one, in fact. Dear old Winston Churchill left the House of Commons for the last time aged 89.

August: A telly that didn't take ten men to lift was introduced to England. Having said that, it still weighed 26 lbs.

October: One of London's oldest institutions, The Windmill Theatre, was closed. It was famous for having naked women on stage. Typical of this country's loony obscenity laws, they could wear, or not wear, whatever they liked as long as they didn't move.

November: England got out its begging bowl and borrowed £1080,000,000 on the never-never from eleven nations.

December: Here's a well deserved Christmas present. Lord Beeching (Lorded for services to railway murder) was himself chopped by the Government. I bet he didn't have to travel home by train.

1965

Bye-Bye Winnie
On 25th January everyone who'd survived the war shed a tiny tear at the news that dear old Winston Churchill, the fat guy with the acid wit and the broad girth, had gone to the great parliament in the sky. He had been, no doubt, the greatest statesman that anyone could remember and few dared even a cynical whisper of criticism at his passing.

But life had to go on. The years of Tory rule were now dragged out and examined more closely – particularly Harold Macmillan's rash statement 'We've never had it so good'. It had finally dawned on the working class that the only people who'd 'had it so good', in the past ten or so years, were the lucky so-and-so's that had had 'it' in the first place. If, by chance, the common folk had shown any rise in their standard of living, it was due to their new ability to buy things on the never-never.

It now seemed, in retrospect, that the haughty Tory Government had spent more time losing sleep over whether Britain was still one of the world's big boys, than keeping their eyes on the ball at home. Okay, towards the end of their reign they'd waved their manicured hands around and sworn blind they'd do something about the state of our hospitals, schools and social services – but it had all been a bit too late, the horse had not only bolted but had taken the stable door with him.

Not only that, but due to several almighty cock-ups abroad, like the Suez fiasco; the refusal of those other Common Market countries (mostly France) to let Britain join their game; a seeming inability to be able to brandish our very own nuclear weapon (sorry 'deterrent'); and all the African countries giving us the old two fingers, Britain could be said to have not only lost its money and its empire but its role in the whole damn business.

Resignation

Alec Douglas-Home, realising he'd made a dog's breakfast of practically everything he'd got his skeletal hands on (and also that he didn't need the PM's salary), happily resigned, making way for a man who couldn't have been more different. Edward Heath, the new Opposition Leader, seemed a rather jolly Dickensian sort with a big, red, round face, a pointy nose, and shoulders that shook uncontrollably when he laughed. He hadn't been to public school (tut, tut) and came from unfashionable Broadstairs where he led the local church choir and was not married (not that those two things are connected).

Britain in Labour

The Tories had had 13 years to muck up the country and now Britain had a bright new (well! brightish, newish) Labour Government. Most people thought everything was now going to be all right (welcome to cloud-cuckoo land!). Wilson had been elected on a programme of 'purposive planning' (which could have meant just about anything), and his 'national economic plan' included the state control of steel, water and building land. Sidekick George Brown, now the new, posh-sounding Secretary of State for Economic Affairs, told his eager followers 'Brothers, we are on our way.' But which way?

Certainly not onward and upward. Having got rid of the skin-head Alec Douglas-Home and the Tory toffs, the poor, long-suffering Brits soon found that his replacement, the seemingly down-to-earth Harold Wilson, also suffered delusions of grandeur; believing that Britain was still a major world power and that he, therefore, must be a major world leader. In fact, it could be said that although some things were never to be the same after 1964, they never really seemed any different either.

It was all a bit pathetic really: we seemed to be world famous for things that, at the end of the day, people could actually live without: fashion, pop music and a booming tourist trade (based on the fallacy that London was actually 'Swingin''').

On 15th June, those pillars of society, The Beatles were informed that they were to be presented to HRH and given MBEs. (Actually that's nothing, she even knighted Jimmy Savile later.) I don't think the Queen actually liked the Beatles (or Jim for that matter). In fact, I doubt if her Majesty had even heard of them: but The Beatles were earning more foreign loot than the rest of industry put together and, besides the Government decides who gets the honours anyway.

Hilariously, some old buffers gave their MBEs back claiming, as Canadian politician Hector Dupuis put it, that the award placed him on the same level as 'vulgar nincompoops'. The Fab Four probably agreed with him.

God Loses to Telly

At this stage of Britain's history 94% of Britons belonged to a church and two thirds of that lot were Church of England. Only 2% dared risk being struck by a thunderbolt from above by saying they didn't believe a word of it, while the rest floated somewhere between heaven and hell, hedging their bets.

The statistic that made everyone sit up, however, was the fact that only 10% of those that claimed to be God-fearing actually went to church on Sundays. The rest stayed in and watched the new devil's tool – telly – probably making do with the, almost kitsch, 'God slot'.

On the TV in those days there were very few programmes that the devil might have enjoyed. 'Ready Steady Go', however, was certainly one (according to our parents), and by 1965 (its third series) it had reached cult status. It brought into our front rooms every pop group or star that had ever upset mum and dad. A lot of the music came from kids who were hoping to crack stardom and did, for only five minutes, but most of the later-to-be-huge British bands like The Rolling Stones, The Animal and The Who also got their early exposure on this icon of the sixties.

Trouble in Gib.

Britain had owned the strategically important Gibraltar since 1713 (and still does), which had really got up the nose of the arch-fascist Spanish boss, Franco, who thought that Spain should have *their* rock back as it was attached to *their* country. He, therefore, decided to put up a comprehensive blockade which effectively made life impossible for border-crossing workers and visiting tourists – not to mention all those baboons who, for some obscure reason, lived on the rock and thought they were British. The argument was not resolved until 1967 when a referendum decided over whelmingly to stay British.

Trouble in Rhodesia

Oh dear, oh dear, Britain only had one colony left in Africa, Rhodesia, and now even they hated us. Ian Smith, their new super-grumpy Prime Minister, issued a Unilateral Declaration of Independence on 16th November. Smith was to turn out to be only a lightly disguised dictator, imposing censorship on all media, rationing and any money going out of the country. The old Governor, Sir Humphrey Gibbs, furious at having been sacked by Smith, turned round and sacked him back; but Smith wouldn't take his turn. He was running the show and everyone knew it.

Our Harold Wilson called it a 'rebel regime' and refused to trade with them, but it was all a bit tricky, as many people in high places still had close relatives (and, more to the point, loads of dosh) in Rhodesia. Representatives of the 4,000,000 blacks (there were only 20,000 whites) beseeched Wilson to go in with guns blazing (à la Thatcher) but Wilson thought he could break Smith and his rotten regime by being reasonable and setting a good example (silly fool).

Smith then put the cat amongst the corgis when he claimed that our Queen, God save her, on the night before the breakaway, had asked him 'not to sell the white man down the river'. What she probably meant was – don't sell the white man down *my* river.

Saved from Sex

Britain had its own housewife superstar. Mary Whitehouse decided, without so much as a by your leave, to be the guardian of Britain's morals, by setting up the National Viewers and Listeners Association. She and her followers sat by their tellies and radios every night, searching for the rude bits – before kicking up a huge stink. It must be said, however, that many people would have had more sympathy for her views if they had been presented in a more open-minded manner.

Skirting the Issue

In November, Customs and Excise got themselves into a right pickle over skirts. It appeared that women's skirts were liable to a

10% duty if over a certain length. Anything less was regarded as children's wear and was therefore exempt. Some bright spark came up with the idea of including a bust measurement when measuring garments in order to differentiate between children's and women's skirts. This was all very well, but supermodels like Jean Shrimpton were noted for the shortness of their skirts and flatness of their chests. Back to the drawing board!

Meanwhile, mini skirts (at that time they were still only an inch or so above the knee) were condemned by our moral watchdogs (like old Mary) as reflecting the fall of standards and rise of the 'permissive society' (and so say all of us).

Meanwhile

January: It's nice to know that kicking an old bit of leather around a field can push you up the social ladder. Sir Stanley Matthews, him of the short hairy legs and big shorts, became the first knight of football.

February: Beatle Ringo Starr married a Liverpool hairdresser, Maureen Cox. Unfortunately she never managed to do anything about his stupid hairdo.

March: Goldie, London's zoo's favourite golden eagle (brilliant name eh?) broke out of jail and stopped the traffic for three days around Regents Park. At first they were worried about him starving to death until they noticed some of the park's ducks had gone missing too.

June: Major Edward White, a US astronaut, went for the first space walkies. He liked it so much that, like Goldie, he had to be coaxed back in by mission control.

June: The Japanese announced that they were going to have a go at motor racing, as a way of introducing themselves to the British car market. How silly! As if we British (who practically invented the car) would ever buy Japanese.

August: Elizabeth Lane was made the first female High Court Judge.

October: The Queen wrote ever such a nice letter to Ian Smith (Prime Minister of Rhodesia) saying that she hoped he was well and that they would be able to find a solution to the crisis in her country.

November: Britain stopped swinging. Murderers would no longer swing for their sins, as hanging was finally abolished.

December: Roy (call me Woy) Jenkins became Home Secretary, and Barbara (call me anything you like) Castle became Ministress of Transport.

1966

Wilson Gets Worried

Harold Wilson (of whom Aneurin Bevan said 'All facts, no bloody ideas.') turned out to be just about the most cocky Prime Minister we'd ever had. His inflated opinion of himself was further pumped up by being told by the country, at the May General Election, that he could hang on to the keys of Downing Street for another term. Despite his huge popularity with the common man (who misguidedly thought he was one of them), his government was allowing the economy to get into such a tangle that even those old Tories began to look good.

On 16th May, the situation came to a head when the National Union of Seamen downed ships and went on strike, effectively paralysing anything trying to float in or out of the London docks. This caused the £ to tremble and then slip off its precarious perch and forced Harold to announce a nice new 'state of emergency'.

Wilson had blown his cool and blamed Commie agitators for the unruly mess his party was in. It's funny now to think anyone could have been frightened of this quaint little Yorkshireman – but they were – and the seamen did, eventually, go grumbling back to their boats. But Labour's cred. was blown. This was just the beginning of the bloody battle between the unions and the Government that was to rage for years. So what did our Harold do about it?

First, he announced a wages freeze which made it illegal for bosses to pay their slaves any more money (which must have pleased them lots). He then, in an effort to stop anyone with any money shoving it abroad, forbade any more than £50 being taken abroad. This was a disaster for travel agents (and abroad), but totally brill for English resorts like Bognor or Scunthorpe (where it was very difficult to spend *more* than £50!).

He then slapped a massive increase on purchase tax (father of VAT) which meant that, just as more and more people had less and less money to spend, all the good things in life were going up as well. It's funny, but if a government starts to tax luxuries like fags and booze it tends to become a little less popular.

Nevertheless, these steps sort of worked and Wilson went on holiday to the Scilly Isles (with £50? You must be joking!) feeling relatively safe. By November, however, Britain was in a minus £162 million position and poor Harold was forced to look at the prospect of devaluing the pound. Everyone blamed everyone else, as always, but despite a desperate cabinet reshuffle, the Labour Party, once again, found themselves skating on the thinnest of ice.

Abroad?

Britain's position abroad continued to totter from one crisis to another but that was nothing compared to our old chums, the

Americans, who were happily digging the hugest pit for themselves in Vietnam. Although the Government claimed that they were right behind them, it became fairly obvious to all that if we British were actually ever required to take our jackets off and get our own noses bloody, things might well change.

Meanwhile three labour MPs traipsed over to Rhodesia to see if they could do any better with Mr Smith and his whities. All they got for their trouble was a severe heckling from an all white crowd who called them 'stupid nits, liars and communists'. Blimey, they were used to worse than this at home. But it was when the mob closed in and dowsed them in itching powder that the meeting was promptly scratched.

A Match Made in Heaven?

Over in Italy, the Pope and our Archbishop of Canterbury were caught kissing. Don't worry, it was the first time in 400 years that the Anglicans and the Catholics had been in each other's houses, and the ceremonial kiss was to cele-brate the building of a bridge between the two churches. God proved to be fairly unimpressed by the event, though, as the bridge never seemed to carry much weight.

Murder Most Foul

On 6th May, two of the most horrendous murderers in the history of horrendous murderers were brought to book. Terence Brady, aged 27, and Myra Hindley, aged 23, were found guilty of torturing and killing at least three children, one with an axe. After a trial that made even the most unfeeling person's eyes water, they received three and two concurrent life sentences respectively and both are still languishing in their cells today.

What a Gas!
Talk about the luck of the British. Just as we were grovelling in the depths of an economic crisis something turned up to help. Phillips Petroleum, who were poking around the bottom of the sea off the East coast, noticed some bubbles from the sexily named Block 48/30 zone. With a little encouragement, the bubbles grew into a stream of 17 million cubic feet of gas a day (that's quite a lot of bubbles!), which was the equivalent of 3.5% of Britain's daily use. They reckoned that eventually they would be pulling enough gas out to supply all Britain's needs.

England on Top
England had taught footer to just about every country in the world – just so they could all beat us at it. Well, they didn't in 1966 – so there! Under the fab captaincy of, the now sadly deceased, Bobby Moore, England beat Germany in the final of the World Cup. Actually the celebration was nearly as big as when we beat the Krauts (with a little help from the Yankee squad) twenty odd years earlier.

London Tops the World
Despite the poxy economic situation, this really was the year that London became the centre of all things fab and fashionable. Mary Quant was now almost Establishment, but a bright new sensation, in the form of Barbara Hulanicki's clothes shop, Biba, blew away any doubt that if you wanted to be IN then London, and particularly the Kings Road, 'Kenny' High Street and Carnaby Street were the only places to be seen.

   The clothes were often silly, always loud, mostly badly made, but unlike anything that had been seen before. Never, since Regency days, had men dared to be peacockish; and although pink, flared hipster trousers, huge 'kipper' ties and platform-soled, glittery boots were not exactly macho, girls seemed to lap them up. All this dovetailed in the late sixties into the new hippie movement. Now most ex-hippies will tell you that hippiedom represented a philosophy dedicated to loving one's fellow man and casting away

OOH! He's so butch.

all aggression. Baloney! It was almost purely a fashion and drug club. American kids, of course, had a damn good reason for all this soppy peace and love mumbo-jumbo, as they were trying to find any excuse to forget about the crazy Vietnam war.

Even those Beatles, who really should have known better, abandoned their sharp little suits, grew out their silly hair cuts (into sillier ones), and trolled off to Wales to sit awe (or dumb)-struck in front of a 'guru' called Maharishi Mahesh Yogi who had a long white beard and a voice like Minnie Mouse.

The only musician who came out of the whole period with any real brownie points was gravelly Bob Dylan though – if we were to be totally honest – many of us didn't understand a single word of what he was droning on about.

Meanwhile

February: Britain's beer drinkers gulped in amazement when Watneys put the price of a pint up to 1s 8d. I bet they'd have choked if they could have foreseen that in 20 odd years they'd be paying a couple of quid.

March: The stolen World Cup that our football team had striven so hard to win was found by a dog named Pickle who dug it up in someone's front garden.

April: At least we only lost a priceless trophy. The American air force went one better, losing one of their very best H bombs when it fell off the back of a B52 bomber. Luckily they found it on the sea bed two months later – still ticking!

May: Graham Hill (Damon's daddy) won the Indianapolis Grand Prix in his Lotus Ford. He was also Formula 1 World Champion.

June: The BBC, in their infinite wisdom, showed a TV sitcom called 'Till Death Us Do Part' for the first time. Its hero, Alf Garnett, was fiercely nationalistic and totally racist. The Beeb thought they were being ever so modern by showing Alf up as the bigoted fool that he undoubtedly was. Some of us, however, realised they'd shot themselves well and truly in the foot, as it became fairly clear that loads of viewers quite liked old Alf, and that he was merely echoing what they'd been thinking all along.

October: Double agent George Blake (on the Ruskies side) escaped from Wormwood Scrubs using a home-made rope. There was little doubt that he'd had a little help from his old Commie chums.

December: Harold Wilson met his new enemy Ian Smith on a boat called HMS Tiger in the middle of the Mediterranean to try to sort out the Rhodesian mess. Presumably they didn't want to be overheard. Not that it made any difference – the talks were a flop.

1967

Cold Comfort

The wages freeze had now been going for over a year so little Harold Wilson, who was definitely no longer flavour of the month (or year), decided to call it something else. The aptly labelled 'period of severe restraint' seemed to correspond with an upturn in world trade and, for a while, everything seemed to look a little better. So much so that in July the 'wage freeze' or 'period of severe restraint' ended. Well, sort of ended – the Government reserved the right to delay increases for yet another year. Heads they win – tails you lose!

The poor old £ was still limping along like a three-legged tortoise and Wilson tried to blame the horrendous Six Day War between Israel and its Arab neighbours for its nosedive on the world money markets. This was highly dubious as the £ had begun on its slippery path downward at least six weeks before the Jews and the Arabs had even begun to get their guns, tanks or camels out.

Down We Go

The economy was plummeting in direct proportion to the Labour Government's popularity and, to cut a long, sad story short, hapless Harold was forced to chop the value of the £ by a massive 14.3% in November. It was the worst financial foul-up for over 20 years.

Then, in a desperate attempt to cheer everyone up (and hang on to his job), Wilson came into everyone's living room one night (on the telly) and told them in his honest, no nonsense, Yorkshire way: 'It does not mean, of course, that the £ here in Britain in your pocket or purse or in your bank has been devalued.' Not only was it dodgy grammar but daft logic. Maybe Harold should have mentioned that if anyone wanted to take their money *out* of their pocket, purse or bank to actually *buy* anything that remotely originated abroad (like the odd banana), it would cost them about 14.3% more.

Travel Trouble
Donald Campbell had this thing about fast motorboats just like his late, lamented dad. At his attempt to break the world water speed record on Lake Coniston, the 'boat' (really a floating plane with no wings) called *Bluebird* suddenly reared out of the water and flipped over backwards. All that was ever found of Donald was his helmet, his mask, his shoes and, strange as it might seem, his teddy bear. Obviously, if there was such a thing as a Loch Coniston monster, it didn't eat record-breaking cuddly toys.

Over in the States, three astronauts missed their trip around the planet when the blasted rocket caught fire before blasting off. Their deaths severely curtailed the Apollo mission to get men on the moon. Only a couple of months later, a Soviet astronaut was zapped when the brakes didn't work as he came back into orbit. The Ruskies claimed he should have used his ejector seat but anyone whose ever been in a Russian car would realise that they might well have forgotten to put one in. Astronauting obviously has its ups and downs.

Oil Abroad
Sadly 1967 turned out to be a very good year for very bad disasters. On 19th March, a ginormous oil tanker called the *Torrey Canyon* carelessly ran aground just off Land's End and instantly started spewing its load. It was described as 'The greatest peacetime threat to Britain' (after Harold Wilson). The only solution was to use incendiary bombs and napalm to break up and set fire to the oil in a vain attempt to avoid mucking up some of England's most beautiful beaches (before the English did).

America the Brave
Over in Vietnam, the Yanks were using their personal napalm slightly differently. On 16th February, 25,000 men attacked the

Viet Cong stronghold known as War Zone C. Their bombers dropped fireworks anywhere and everywhere, which disgusted the rest of the world. Strange logic to think it's okay to kill thousands of innocent people if you're defending their freedom.

Throughout the world, youngsters were losing patience with the war-mongering Americans, especially in America itself where, unfortunately, the peace and the hippie movements were becoming inseparable. Unfortunately, because about the only effect they had, was that new soldierlings spent most of the war wearing headbands and being stoned out of their boxes (before going into them).

Royal Meeting

All the Royals wore extremely thin smiles on 7th June at the unveiling of a small slate plaque (mean or what?) to commemorate our Queen's grandmother, Queen Mary. The reason for the tension was the appearance among the guests of that bad old Duke of Windsor (the one that preferred American chicks to ruling us) and the American lady herself. It was rumoured that the Queen Mum actually blamed the death of her husband on these two. Poor old King George IV (her hubby) had, apparently, never quite got over the shock of having to drop everything and rush out to hire a King kit.

Could you tell me of which country you will be becoming king, sir?

Concord or Concorde?

Was it really possible? Britain and France finally managed to do something together without it ending in tears. A staggeringly pretty supersonic airliner was unveiled on 12th December, designed to get you to the other side of the Atlantic exactly one hour before you set off. Did I say the project ended peacefully? Silly me! It must be recorded that as the plane rolled out for the first time, a huge scrap broke out over whether Concord or Concorde should or should not carry the French 'e'. After months of terse deliberations at the highest diplomatic level, they came up with a staggeringly inspired solution. The French one should carry the 'e' and the British one shouldn't. Mon Dieu!

Meanwhile

January: Plans to build the most boring city in the world were launched. Milton Keynes was to (and now does) ruin – whoops – occupy 22,000 acres of (once) beautiful Buckinghamshire.
- Jeremy hits the top. Old Etonian Jeremy Thorpe became the leader of the Liberal party on 18th January. Everybody seemed to like this handsome, slightly extrovert, rather top-drawer chap and few could have guessed the sticky end he was to come to.
- There used to be a paper for all those boys who did as their parents told them, helped old ladies across the street and brushed their hair in the morning. It was called the *Boy's Own Paper* and was about as exciting as a day out in . . . er . . . Milton Keynes. Thankfully it closed down owing to the severe decline of 'good' boys.

February: There also used to be a very silly teenybopper group in America called The Monkees (definitely an insult to apes). Heathrow airport became a war zone when their British fans went sub-human on their arrival.
- Talking of monkeys, the man in charge of them at London Zoo, Desmond Morris, wrote the first of his many quasi-scientific books called *The Naked Ape* and informed us, among other things, that

orang-utans are the sexiest primates alive. Was Mr Morris pulling our legs?

March: A strange (and rather silly) underground hippie magazine struggled up to street level in London. Run by a group of loony Australians, *OZ* used any writer or artist (including myself) prepared to take the mickey out of British society.

April: One would have been forgiven for wondering if the invention of the Ombudsman was some kind of April Fool's joke. It was, in fact, the name given to a chap whose new job was to help people stung by government departments. He'd have got home a lot earlier if he'd only dealt with those that weren't.

May: Those naughty Rolling Stones got stoned once too often and ended up in court. Mick and Keith both received prison sentences but in the end they got off. Rumour has it they offered the judge a joint . . .

• Never one to mince his words, Enoch Powell called Britain 'The sick man of Europe'. Isn't it about time we started feeling a little better?

• Elvis Presley married his childhood sweetheart. The cake had six tiers, and the female fans shed thousands.

August: Who says we live in a free country? The Marine Broadcasting Act fired a broadside and sunk 90% of the brilliant and popular new pirate radio ships by making them illegal.

October: Brian Jones of the Rolling Stones, not to be outdone, finally got himself jailed for drug offences.

December: South African surgeon, Christian Barnard, actually managed to find a new heart to install in a 53 year old grocer. Denise Darvall, a 25 year old bank clerk, found dying after a road accident, had contributed hers.

1968

Castle Strikes Out

Unofficial strikes by the unions were continuing to pull the Labour Government to its knees. Just as one crippling strike was killed off like weeds on a lawn, another couple would rear up. Barbara Castle (the Employment Secretary), in an effort to bring the unions to heel, introduced a bill called pretentiously 'In Place of Strife'. Senior government ministers, like Jim Callaghan, gulped at its cheek, being fully aware that if it wasn't for all that union loot ('donated' by its members), the Labour Party wouldn't have a pot to p... put water in. Not only that, but there was a General Election looming and the last thing the Government needed was to enter it with the Trade Union Congress tearing at their throats.

Basically, 'In Place of Strife' demanded that the TUC agree to compulsory legislation to deal with any industrial relations problems and recommended that unofficial strikes should be punished by cash fines, which was a bit like asking condemned murderers to help tie their nooses.

After a long drawn out (and terribly tedious) tug of war, both in the Commons and at the TUC, both Wilson and Castle realised they were massaging a dead duck and gave in the following year. The trade union leaders, hardly able to hide their honest, working-class grins, promised (with all their fingers crossed) that they would try to behave better in future.

I'm Backing Britain (Maybe!)

Talk about pathetic. Five typists from a two-bit heating firm deep in the Surbiton suburbs suddenly couldn't stand all the appalling news about their country's economy. They declared, with chins held high, 'We're Backing Britain' and, much to the delight of their bewildered boss, promised to work an extra half hour a day for nothing. The Government and the press (always game for a silly story) rushed round to sunny Suburbiton to slap the women on the back (and use up more hours of their working day). A huge press campaign followed, in those silly small papers, but the kiss of death came when Brucie Forsyth (yes, we've put up with him that long) made a record called – you've got it – 'I'm Backing Britain'. It became obvious that the crass campaign had just become a vehicle for flagging circulations, flagging governments . . . and flagging show-biz careers.

Keep 'Em Out

Immigration was the other big buzz word of 1968. Thousands of Asians were pouring in from East Africa and Kenya carrying completely kosher British passports. The Government rushed out a quota system, in an effort to stem the flow, with Home Secretary 'honest' Jim Callaghan telling us that he had a responsibility to all those at home (hey folks, that meant us!).

On 21st April, old misery-guts, Enoch Powell, made a speech that was to make him famous (and seal his fate) for the rest of his career. He proclaimed, 'As I look ahead I am filled with foreboding. Like the Romans, I see the River Tiber (I think he meant The Thames) foaming with much blood.' He went on to say that we were mad, literally mad, to let 50,000 immigrants in every year. We were, he ranted 'heaping our own funeral pyre'. I wonder if he realised he was heaping his own.

111

Edward (I'll be PM at all costs) Heath immediately fired him from the Tory Shadow Cabinet labelling him an 'inflammatory racist'. Many other politicians buttoned their lips, realising that Enoch was merely saying what they and lots of Britons thought (remember 'Till Death Us Do Part'?). Politicians might be stupid, but they ain't daft!

Up, Up and Away

Just about the only thing booming in this country was the fashion industry. Mini skirts were reaching new heights and seemed to be turning into wide belts. Dry cleaners got so concerned that they started charging by the inch. Girls were all trying to look like half-girl, half-stick-insect Twiggy, the unbelievably pretty ex-shop assistant who had shot to modelling superstardom. Unfortunately, most had about as much luck as I would imitating Arnold Schwarzenegger.

Up America

Every time the Americans thought that the Vietnam War just couldn't get much worse . . . it did. President Lyndon Johnson was obviously feeling a little chilly around the feet area and announced to a shocked nation that, thank you, but no thank you, he wouldn't be running for President again. The dead John Kennedy's little brother Bobby, now a senator himself, obviously saw the ad in the Jobs Vacant section and decided to have a go himself. He did follow his brother, but not quite in the way he might have hoped. On 6th June, poor Bobby was fatally shot in the lobby of the Ambassador Hotel in Los Angeles. A young Palestinian Arab admitted the crime, claiming he did it for his country (which you may think sounds a bit like shooting the leader of India because you had a bad time in Spain. Oh well!).

The end of the year saw Richard Nixon (later known as Tricky Dicky) as the new President. Remarkably, Nixon looked like Pinocchio's psychotic uncle, and was later to share some other Pinocchio characteristics.

Meanwhile, the uncrowned king of America's blacks, the Reverend Dr Martin Luther King, was shot dead by a white man in Memphis. They sure know how to treat their leaders over there. This seemed to sum up the state of race relations in America, and riots suddenly exploded in major cities throughout the country.

Meanwhile

March: Road deaths fell by 23% as a direct result of the introduction of alcohol breath tests. No survey was done about how many people were getting rat-faced at home.

April: There's hard up and hard up but it really comes to something when an American oil millionaire can buy one of your capital city's major landmarks. Tycoon Robert McCullough bought our London Bridge for a mere £1,000,000 so he could put it in his backyard in Texas. I wonder how much he offered for the Royal Family?

• The fantabulous Jim Clark, twice World Champion Racing Driver, definitely saw the wood for the trees. Poor Jim spun off the road at 125 m.p.h. into a wood and was killed instantly.

• Chaos hit the streets when the first few decimal coins hit the purses and pockets of the British. Many people, including me, looked into their palms in total confusion when given change including the new 5p and 10p.

May: Ronan Point, a huge grotty tower block in East London, decided to save the demolition men a job by simply falling down like a pack of cards. Somebody on the eighteenth floor had unfortunately left the gas on. A major investigation began into shoddy building methods.

• What started as a little demonstration against American action in Vietnam, broke out into a major riot between French students and police in Paris. (NB French police are the sort that bludgeon you to death for bad breath.)

June: Black, black day for comedy lovers. Tony Hancock, just about the funniest man that ever lived (please debate!), killed himself in an Australian Hotel. C'mon Tony, even Australia's not that bad (also debate!). Apparently his totally despairing view of life on screen was little different off.

Tony Hancock

August: Those rotten Ruskies were at it again. This time it was Czechoslovakia that got the full treatment for trying to give socialism a 'human face'. Alexander Dubček, the Czech leader, was gobsmacked as the tanks rolled into Prague. He thought they were a bunch of rotters for stabbing him and his country in the back after years of cooperation.

September: Two members of the cast of the hit musical *Hair* appeared stark naked two days after the relaxation of theatre censorship was announced.

Hit of the Year: 'Those Were The Days', by the ever-so-prissy Mary Hopkin. Significant title or what?

1969

It's All Irish

It's always difficult to put one's finger on when the Irish started hating each other. Anyone who has stood outside a pub at closing time on a Friday night will gather that they're a pretty warlike race. As you probably know, this disharmony between the Catholics and Protestants started hundreds of years ago, but you'll have to read my last books to find out why (and that's called marketing, folks!). On 23rd January, violence reared its ugly head during a Catholic march in Londonderry demanding 'one man one vote' in the province. The Catholics trapped their arch-enemy, that priest with the voice and nature of a demented Rottweiler, the 'Reverend Dr' Ian Paisley but he, as always, managed to bark his way out of it. Several of his followers, however, were slightly injured.

Bottled Babies

For the first time ever, British scientists managed to fertilise human eggs outside the body (free range?). The method had first been tried out successfully with rabbits – the only hitch they encountered was keeping the darn critters apart! One of the greatest problems scientists foresaw was the possibility of deformities in the foetus caused by this technique. (Who wants a nipper with long ears and a fluffy white tail?)

A Kray Day

Two of the nastiest villains that ever walked the streets of East London (and there's been a few) were sentenced to 30 years prison each. Ronald and Reginald Kray (who both looked a bit like

Jonathan Woss) had a nasty habit of murdering friend and foe willy-nilly in pursuit of their gangland activities. The terrible twosome are, thankfully, still in separate jails, though one is now said to be totally round the bend.

The Oil Fairies

You may remember a couple of years earlier when the gas fairy visited this country and waved her wand over our coast line (see page 102)? Well, she'd obviously told her mates that Britain was still in the sh . . . ambles (despite all that buckshee gas). On 30th June, high grade crude oil was discovered under the bottom of our bit of the North Sea. The oil companies weren't sure at the time whether it was commercially a goer, but I can tell you now, with the privilege of hindsight, that the find was to save our extremely vulnerable bacon.

The Men in the Moon

Anyone who was around in 1969 gets a slight shiver down the spine when they remember looking up at the man in the moon and realising that, almost unbelievably, there were earthlings walking on his face. Watched by trillions of awe-struck telly viewers throughout the world, American astronaut Neil Armstrong out-astronauted all the rest by stepping out of his little spaceship and taking 'one small step for man, and one giant leap for mankind.'

Predictably, the poor old moon was about as interesting as an empty car park in Slough but it didn't matter, it was just great to be somewhere that McDonald's hadn't got to first. Neil and his two mates brought back a few lumps of moon rock for the folks back home. These were instantly pounced on by brainy boffins who rushed them to the most sophisticated laboratories in the world, where they discovered, after months of painstaking study, using the most sophisticated of scientific equipment, that they would have been marginally more interesting if the moon had really been made of green cheese.

Ulster Explodes
On 15th August, British troops were actually *cheered* as they put barbed wire all the way round the Catholic Bogside district of Londonderry. The troops had been *asked* in by the Ulster Government to try and put the tin lid on the furious fighting between the Catholics and Protestants. It didn't take long for the situation to erupt into violence though and five were killed and hundreds injured.

Royal Skint?
The Duke of Edinburgh, on an American TV programme, claimed that unless he and his Mrs got a pay rise, they'd have to give up Buck House and live somewhere cheaper (like one of their other fab homes). He then said they'd already sold off a small yacht (the *Queen Elizabeth?*) and that, unless something turned up pretty smartish, he'd have to give up polo. Now either Phil was telling Royal porkies or since then both of them have been doing paper rounds, as they sure seem to have made up for it since. Crikey! If you can't make ends meet when you're married to one of the richest women in the world, then what chance have we got?

Meanwhile

January: All bad things must come to an end. 'Mrs Dale's Diary', the Beeb's longest running radio soap, which made 'The Archers' seem like *Terminator II*, ended

March: Oh what a lovely war! Britain invaded the postage stamp island of Anguilla in the Caribbean, to put down a revolution by the fearsome Republican Defence Force led by that infamous revolutionary Ronald (a revolutionary called Ronald?) Webster. The whole population of 6000 turned out to welcome the troops and the event turned into a bit of a party, televised by the BBC. There was no resistance, and 40 British bobbies were left to keep the peace. Watch out Russia, it could be your turn next!

April: Sikh bus conductors in Wolverhampton finally won their battle to carry on wearing their banned turbans at work.

July: Rolling Stones don't float (epsecially when stoned). Brian Jones drowned in his own swimming pool in Hatfield.
• Yet another Kennedy – Edward – hit the headlines. He failed to report an accident in which a girl, travelling in the passenger seat of his car, drowned when it plummeted over the side of a bridge in New England. It put the kibosh on any dreams he had of getting shot (like his brothers) as President. Nobody knows what really happened – except Teddy.
• Our Gracious Queen gave Charlie his very first crown to play with when she made him the Prince of Wales. If only the poor lad had known that he'd probably have to wait till his mum's dying breath to get his hands on hers.

I knew those ears would come in useful

118

September: ITV broadcast in colour for the first time, though it didn't seem to make 'Coronation Street' any less dreary.

• The super-trendy boutique Biba grew into a huge department store, only to prove that little ideas don't always grow into big ones successfully. It closed after a few years because the tourists, who flocked to see this hyper-trendy new phenomenon, mostly forgot to buy anything. Most of what wasn't bought was then nicked by the staff (allegedly).

October: The Divorce Reform Bill was passed, making the irretrievable breakdown of a marriage sole grounds for divorce. Can anyone think of a better reason? How about snoring?

• Just as mini skirts were reaching the point of no return, some bright spark invented the nearly-touching-the-ground maxi skirt. Cynics thought it had something to do with the imminent winter, the floundering textile industry and a preponderance of chubby legs.

November: A London woman, Mary Hanson, tried the new fertility drug gonadotrophine (from the Latin 'gonad'?). Good news, she became pregnant. Bad news, she had five!

December: While some people were desperate to have nippers, some were desperate to avoid them. A sterilisation clinic was opened in Birmingham, offering the 'cruellest cut of all' (vasectomy for men) for £16 (a mere snip).

1970

Hurrah for Heath

Everyone was, finally, well fed up with Wilson and his not-so-merry men. Despite Harold's protestations that we were coming out of the economic mess (does this sound familiar?), nobody believed him. Even so, most of us were amazed when, at the General Election in May, Labour lost to the Conservatives, especially as the opinion polls had been telling us that it was going to be a walkover. The complacent (and lazy) Labour voters had obviously stayed at home thinking their little individual votes wouldn't be necessary.

After four years in opposition, Edward Heath, the jolly man with the plummy voice and the shaky shoulders, was clearly over the moon at being the Prime Minister, and vowed to undo all the Labour cock-ups (my words not his!). He told us he'd take us into Europe – which we liked – and he also told us he wouldn't make rash promises (like Wilson) just to catch the headlines – which we also liked. He then told us he'd tackle the unions – which we sort of liked, but dreaded the ensuing battle because, as far as industrial relations were concerned, the unions had had their foot on the Government's windpipe for as long as we could remember. In his new government, he gave the job of Minister of State to a grocer's daughter called Margaret, little knowing that she would eventually cause his downfall.

Votes for Youngsters

The year had opened with the news that the age of majority was to be changed from 21 to 18, which meant that teenagers could vote for the first time (if they could find anyone to vote for). Most young people thought this meant we might be in for a decade where the wrinklies would have to start taking account of what *they* thought, so bringing a period of fresh optimism. No way! The seventies were to be a period of pessimism, and worse, apathy. If Britain had ever been 'swingin'', it certainly wasn't any more, but (to be honest) nor was the rest of the world.

Hero rock stars like Jimi Hendrix and Janis Joplin were dropping like flies from drug overdoses; a new man on the world political stage, Colonel Gaddafi, introduced his new national sport, terrorism, to the world pitch; that funny (but insignificant) magazine *OZ* (see p.109) was prosecuted for depravity; and, worst news of all, The Bee Gees announced they were getting back together again. Perhaps the greatest indication that the sixties were over, however, was that The Beatles had fallen out of love and were now trying to divorce each other.

The Women's Movement

The early 70s saw the virgin birth of what came to be known as the 'women's movement'. Women had finally reached the end of their tether with regard to their subordinate role to men. Australian, Germaine Greer, led the cavalry with her analysis of how your 'women's-place-is-in-the-home' average man stereotyped the role of the opposite sex, in her book *The Female Eunuch*. Some believed, however, that the more extreme bra-burning, man-hating, over-the-top faction did the movement more harm than good.

Jumbo Journeys

On 23rd January, everyone looked up into the sky with amazement as a huge shadow passed over London. Was it a bird? Was it Superman? Was it pollution? No, it was a big fat plane from the States nicknamed Jumbo. The trouble with any kind of jumbo is that it won't fit into your average quarters, and this vast Boeing 747, carrying 352 passengers, had airport authorities tearing their hair out as they struggled with inadequate baggage and passenger handling facilities. They were also worried that the turbulence it caused would disrupt all the other littler planes as they went about their everyday business. As we now know, nothing of the kind occurred and before long, there were troupes of Jumbos – trunk to tail – in and out of London Heathrow.

Filthy Foreign Flu

But if the jumbo wasn't going to flatten us, a new strain of Hong Kong flu was. In one week alone 2850 people died. There's nothing like an epidemic to cause us to turn to the Lord, even though he often moves in mysterious ways. A new version of his old bestseller started selling like hot cakes. *The New English Bible* caused a great deal of fuss because, for the first time, it used language that people could almost understand (and, oh Lordie, the High Church didn't like it).

It wasn't all plain sailing for God, however, as on 22nd June, the Methodists announced that they were going to allow mere women to become priests. The Church of England giggled into its beard, safe in the knowledge that such a dreadful thing could never happen to them. Could it?

Terrorism Triumphs

In September, three airliners (one of them a young Jumbo) were hijacked by members of the 'Popular Front for the Liberation of Palestinian' (the PLO). The world watched nervously as the planes sat in the sweltering heat of an airstrip in Jordan, while officials tried to talk the terrorists out of it.

Meanwhile, on the same day, the crew of an El Al jet jumped two would-be hijackers, killing one of them. The surviving member, a rather pretty girl (for a terrorist) called Leila Khaled, was handed over to British police when the plane landed in London. The PLO, (who'd by now evacuated the first three planes and blown them up) then had the damn cheek to ask for the release of

Leila as swapsies for the passengers that they were still holding in the other hijacking. There was one hell of a fuss when the British wimped out and gave them their girl back.

De Gaulle De-Dead

Stroppy old General de Gaulle always had to have the last word – even when dead. He'd insisted (when not dead) that none of his government colleagues should be allowed to attend his funeral. Instead he invited everyone else, and his graveside was besieged by tens of thousands of weeping French. Our dear old Harold Macmillan was there with all the world's leaders, though one suspected that he might be one of many glad to see the cantankerous old f...rog safely underground.

Flying Circus

Just about the best thing to happen in Britain in 1970 (which wasn't difficult) was the start of a new TV comedy called 'Monty Python's Flying Circus' which was the nearest thing to the old radio 'Goon Show' from years ago. Some of the sketches, including the one with the dead parrot, have gone down in comedy history.

Meanwhile

January: The Football Association, who always knew best, suspended George Best, Britain's most famous soccer player, for disreputable behaviour.

March: Most people were slightly surprised (and his mum and dad relieved) when David Bowie married a girl. Nobody had been quite sure (including Bowie) on whose side this somewhat androgenous pop star batted.

April: It was announced that the Morris Minor, the longest ever car in production (in time – not length!), and now a minor dinosaur (or minosaur), was to cease production the following year.

July: A 50 year old woman was given the first heart pacemaker powered by nuclear energy. It was a great success (and nobody seemed to mind that she glowed in the dark).

August: George Brown, who'd always resembled an inebriated owl, was made a peer, so that he could join all the other doddery oldsters in the House of Lords.

November: Pope Paul IV banned all Cardinals over 80 from voting in Papal elections. Five days later, he was attacked by a man carrying a dagger in Manila. I reckon the guy must have escaped from a Catholic old people's home.

December: MPs rejected a move to keep British Summer Time through the winter. Heaven knows why – there's no difference anyway.

More of the Same

Heath's brave attempts to give the British economy a kick up the backside were sadly to no avail, and the Government, with their coat-tails firmly between their legs, skulked back to a lot of the economic policies they'd ridiculed Labour for. Not only that but, as might have been expected, the Tories' new policy of confrontation with the unions made the Labour/union relationship look like a teddy-bears' picnic. In the first quarter of 1971, the days lost by strikes were four times that of the same quarter the year before. Even our dear old postpersons went on strike on 20th January causing total mayhem. Heath, determined to be the hard man, refused to budge and even allowed private entrepreneurs and wide boys to set up alternative services (Postman Prat Ltd), which gave the British an eerie premonition of the major flogging-off of utilities that became such a feature of the eighties.

Holy Rollers

Another shock came on 4th February when Rolls Royce, that very British symbol of engineering excellence, went bottom up. The Tories, in a complete about-turn, decided to nationalise the aero-engine and aerospace activities and let the poor car bit fend for itself. The Rolls Royce company had been brought to its immaculate knees by a disastrous contract with the US company, Lockheed, who'd screwed them (in more ways than one) down to an almost ridiculous price and time restriction.

Happy Heath

The only thing that did cheer Heath up was when the EEC (with de Gaulle safely out of the way) decided that the terms were now right for Britain to join. To be truthful, everyone was now bored to death with the endless yapping so, although the faithless French whinged that things would never be la même if we joined, most of the other members thought we'd stayed out in the cold long enough.

Death in Ulster

Things were hotting up over in Northern Ireland and on 9th February the first British soldier was killed during rioting. Up to this time, the Protestants and Catholics had seemed perfectly happy just slaughtering each other. On 11th August, occurred the most controversial development so far when 300 IRA suspects were arrested and banged up in prison without any trial. This practice was called 'internment' and the IRA went crazy (or should I say crazier), embarking on an orgy of killing within hours of the announcement. The British Government then banned all marches and demonstrations, but it was like trying to hold back a pack of rabid dogs. Four days later, 5000 Catholic houses and 2000 Protestant houses were burned to the ground. Ireland was now at war with itself, with the poor British soldiers getting it in the neck from both sides.

Up to this time, the Great British Public had looked over to Ireland with only a little more than a vague casual interest. If they want to wipe themselves out, let them, we thought. It really wasn't anything at all to do with us. It all became very different when we heard that the IRA had decided to bring their bombs over the water.

New Money for Old

On 14th February, everyone was thrown into complete and utter turmoil when complete decimalisation became official. Our dear old pennies, threepences, shillings and half-crowns were finally kicked into history.

Cold War

Meanwhile, back at the Cold War with Russia, a KGB defector had spilled the beans on all his mates working in Britain. We reacted by kicking out 90 of their diplomats and officials which really cheesed off their bosses back home. The USSR responded by sending only five of our chaps home and so we got off relatively lightly.

Hot Pants

On a lighter note, the British (particularly men) were getting bored with maxi skirts, and so were girls with good legs. The solution was 'hot pants', which were tiny shorts that should have been locked up for their brevity.

Hi Twigs!

Foreign Parts

On 24th November, six years after that nasty Ian Smith had proclaimed Rhodesia's independence and told us to go forth and multiply, an agreement was signed with Alec Douglas-Home (now our Foreign Secretary) to legalise their independence and to open up all the links that had been lost with Britain (well, surprise,

surprise!). The Labour Party didn't waste any time pointing out that nothing had changed for the blacks, and that they were further from being in charge of *their* country than they'd ever been. Silly Billies! Didn't they realise that international affairs have nothing to do with ethics or morality – at least not when there's hard cash involved.

Meanwhile

February: Still on the war path, Enoch Powell went one further and suggested that we should start sending immigrants 'home' as he foresaw an 'explosion' of not-quite-white people. On 24th February, the Immigration Bill was passed ending the right of Commonwealthers to settle here.

March: The *Daily Sketch*, which was a more awful paper than the *Daily Mail*, or the *Daily Express*, closed after 62 years. It was sadly (not) missed.
• A very weird guy called Charles Manson who, with his 'family' of hippies, chopped up the gorgeous film actress Sharon Tate and a few of her glam chums, featured in the most bizarre murder trial that the States had ever seen (and that sure is bizarre). Charlie, who was barking mad, was eventually sentenced to life on death row.

June: Just to prove that the British public have always enjoyed their fair share of junk on TV, 'Opportunity Knocks', a 'talent' show, was top of the ratings. Hughie Green, its slimy presenter, displayed about the same amount of talent as the contestants.

August: Edward Heath led his crew of jolly sailor boys to win the Admiral's Cup on his own boat *Morning Cloud*. Many people accused him, however, of sailing while Ireland burned.

October: When the diminutive Emperor Hirohito of Japan drove through London on a state visit, he was a little surprised when the commoners, who could normally be guaranteed to cheer or wave flags at anything in a state coach, remained silent. The Queen told him 'We cannot pretend the past did not exist. We cannot pretend that relations between our two peoples have always been peaceful and friendly.' This was really a polite way of saying 'Look you little creep, don't go thinking we've forgotten what you did to our boys in the war. The only reason you're here is because we want your loot.' Or words to that effect.

November: Princess Anne was not just a pretty horse – sorry – face! She was also good at riding. The British Sportswriters Association made her Sportswoman of the Year.

The BBC was flooded with complaints after a boy used a four letter word on 'Woman's Hour'.

December: I bet the Queen was secretly delighted with her husband's claim that the Windsors were going broke. Anyway, her allowance was doubled to near on £1,000,000. I bet that kept her in horsy headscarfs for a bit longer.

1972

EEC at Last
The only possible chink of light at the end of our economic tunnel of doom seemed to be the European Economic Community which we finally joined, much to the disgust of the French, in January. We were now part of a population that was even bigger than that of the United States.

But, for a veteran yachtsman, poor old Heath never seemed to enjoy any plain sailing. As he was entering the Egmont Palace to sign for Britain, a woman jumped out of the throng and chucked a bag full of black printing ink all over him. Strangely enough, it had nothing to do with the EEC but turned out to be a rather misplaced protest over Government plans to redevelop London's Covent Garden. It was obviously to no avail, as the dear old fruit and veg market was soon to turn into the yuppie fairground it is to this day.

Ireland Hots Up

At least it was only ink that flowed over Ted. Eight days later, British paratroopers opened fire on what was soon to be known as 'Bloody Sunday', killing 13 civil-rights-marchers-turned-rioters and injuring a further 17. The IRA then announced, charmingly, that they planned to kill as many British soldiers as possible. The 'troubles' in Northern Ireland had so far only been sauntering along in the slow lane – now it was all-out war.

Heath, realising the nightmare ahead, announced that Northern Ireland would henceforth be run from England. (Oh boy, did the IRA like that!)

Heath S(t)inks!

During 1971, the Heath Government had done everything they could think of to bludgeon some life into the economy and get unemployment down. All to no avail. By January 1972, nearly

1,000,000 were on the dole (these days that sounds pretty good) and the value of the £ abroad was sinking faster than a Page 3 girl's suntan. Industrial relations couldn't have been worse (they thought) and Heath's blood pressure went through the roof when 280,000 ungrateful miners rejected his £31 million pay offer. Their president, Joe Gormley, called on all the other unions to add muscle to the first total pit shutdown since 1926. Gormley was assisted by a guy who was to become famous for his terrier-like tactics. Arthur Scargill, a funny little rodent of a man who seemed to be wearing someone else's hair, was one of the first to lead 'flying pickets' – groups of men who travelled round the country effectively shutting off any pit they felt like.

Just to make Heath squirm even more, the Wilberforce Commission, set up to look into the deadlock, awarded them a 20% pay increase, which they grabbed with open arms.

Prices Soar
To make things worse, all the world's commodities like copper, cotton and cocoa (not just for the drinking of) started going through the roof price-wise owing to the success of those countries like Germany and Japan who'd (thank God) lost the war, but were (no thanks to God) whipping us in the peace. By November, things were so dreary that the Government was forced to do a complete U-turn and, instead of trying to inflate the economy, set about squeezing it down with a 90 day price and pay standstill to try to stop wages going crazy. The TUC giggled behind their horny hands, flushed with the knowledge that they had finally got the Government by the short and curlies

Strangely enough, the electorate were becoming well hacked off with the union's bully-boy techniques and starting to let it be known that they might well back Heath if he took off his kid gloves and had a proper no-holds-barred fight.

It was time to shuffle Heath's bratpack again, so all the Cabinet changed seats when the music finally stopped. All that is, except poor Reggie Maudling, the Home Secretary, who was left without one. He'd been found, not exactly with his fingers in someone else's till, but at least 'involved' with the newly infamous John Poulson. Poulson was the rich, successful and extremely dodgy architect at the centre of a huge scandal in which it was proved that he had been bribing bent officials with fat backhanders to gain lucrative Government contracts. Funny, ministers are usually such good judges of character!

Scandal in Washington

In the USA, five men were arrested for trespass in the offices of the Democratic National Committee (the opposition party). No big deal. When, however, it turned out the men were trying to bug the Democrats, the whole business became a lot more sinister. Bug-eyed Senator Hubert Humphrey, the Democratic candidate, demanded an explanation from President Nixon. Nixon denied all knowledge but his Pinocchio-esque nose grew another inch. (This was the beginning of the Watergate Scandal (see p.138).) Later in the year, he obliterated the challenge from Democrat George McGovern with an overwhelming vote of confidence from the American people (if only they'd known what was about to break). I suppose by then he'd found out all there was to know about their election strategy from his spies.

Trouble in Uganda

The party was over in newly independent Uganda. Suddenly General Idi Amin who had seemed 'such a decent chap' to the British Home Office, was turning out to be a dictator just like his hero, Mr A Hitler. He claimed that the Asians (who were carrying British passports) were sabotaging his economy and said he was kicking them out in three months. Some of these Asians thought the whole thing rather brilliant as it meant they could bypass the quota system controlling their entry to Britain . . . until Amin's soldiers nicked all their money at the airport.

Meanwhile

February: Psst! Wanna buy some lions? Billy Smart's Circus, the biggest and best in Europe, closed due to rising costs.

• Bernadette Devlin, the Ulster MP, flew at poor Reggie Maudling, in the House of Commons, pulling his hair and scratching and punching his face, like a demented witch. All he'd said was that he was launching an enquiry into the 'Bloody Sunday' massacre. I wonder what she'd have done if he'd said he wasn't? He was probably relieved to resign later in the year.

April: Cambridge scientists claimed that putting salt on your food led to heart disease. So what? Just about every sort of food you could sprinkle it on was apparently bad for you anyway.

June: Thousands of people turned up to say a last bye-bye to the Duke of Windsor, the uncrowned Edward VIII who was buried on 5th June.

July: Brilliant news! Women were to have a bigger role in TV current affairs programmes. Not so good news, the women in question included Esther Rantzen.

August: The Bishop of Kingston claimed that London was on the brink of collapse because of a sickness that was affecting the whole world. He was referring to the lack of community brought about by hideous tower blocks and the pressures from urban and industrial life. 18 years on we're still waiting.

September: Auntie BBC still had some taste. The powers-that-be asked the slippery smooth Jimmy Young to stop singing on his morning radio programme. He had to content himself in future to crooning and crawling to senior politicians. Bring back the singing I say.

November: American firmly believed, in their inimitable way, that they'd done so much damage to North Vietnam that the enemy would be forced to agree to a ceasefire. The Commies replied by shooting down the first American B52 bomber.

December: I've heard of aircraft food being revolting but this was ridiculous. A plane carrying 45 passengers crashed in the Andean mountains. The sixteen that were left, a rugby team called the Old Christians, having eaten all the peanuts, survived their long wait for rescue by eating the others. That's old Christians for you.

Oh no, not the scrum-half again.

Hit of the Year: 'Amazing Grace'!

1973

Inflation Inflates

Basic Economics: Lesson 1

If you happen to be a country and you want to trade with other countries, it's rather important that you try to sell them as much as they sell you. Otherwise you have what is known as a balance of payments deficit. Britain in 1973 was really good at buying loads of gear from abroad, but really lousy at shifting any of our stuff over there, which resulted in a deficit of over a £1,000,000,000,000 (and a very embarrassed government).

Basic Economics: Lesson 2

If you happen to be a country that is manufacturing less and less (for whatever reason), it's rather important that you don't pay the workforce – who is making less and less – more and more. Between 1963 and 1973, despite a weedy increase in production, average weekly earnings soared by 249%. All this, with added problems like stroppy unions threatening strikes, go-slows and work-to-rules at the drop of a cloth cap, indicated a country in big, big trouble. This was Britain at the beginning of 1973.

The only glimmer of hope lay in Europe. On 5th January, we finally became (theoretically) working members of the EEC, much to the disgust of the Labour Party, the trade unions and, true to form, Enoch Powell. It could never be said that dear old Enoch's racism was based solely on colour; he just seemed to loath the idea of *any* foreigner setting foot on our shores. EEC entry must have been a real blow to him as, no sooner had his party managed to curb the flow of Commonwealth immigrants into the country, than the floodgates were opened to a whole load of Europeans. He really shouldn't have worried, however, as no European with half a brain would have wanted to come here anyway.

Three Day Week
By the end of the year, the economic situation was said to be the worst since the war (again) and Edward Heath was no longer the jolly red sailor we knew, and sometimes loved. The Government was at total loggerheads with the unions and industry was flattened by the industrial action of the miners, power and railway workers. 'Who rules the country?' everyone cried, and the Conservatives sussed that, if they couldn't squash the unions, they would soon be forced into a General Election. Talk about stalemate! It was just like two kids' gangs facing up to each other in the playground. Edward Heath's lot refused to give in to the workers, and the workers refused to be pushed around by them. On the 13th November, he called another State of Emergency which put the wind up the whole country. No one was allowed to heat their home by electricity; no advertising signs could be lit up; drivers couldn't go more than 50 m.p.h. (apart from in aeroplanes); heating was restricted in factories; and horror of horrors, telly had to finish at 10.30 p.m. – and still neither side would budge! Worst of all, businesses – be they big or small – were only allowed to work for three days a week. This, obviously, became totally ridiculous and so it became commonplace to black out windows (like wartime) and work illegally (er – so I'm told!!). It was a cold and miserable Christmas with only turkeys managing to keep warm for just a few hours.

In January, Heath, in typical nautical manner, tried another tack and told the nation that things weren't as bad as the Government had at first expected and that the country might well go back to a four, or even five, day week. This scared the pants off the miners' leaders who then, in desperation (and seeing the writing on the wall) threatened an all-out strike.

Keeping the Punters Quiet

What do our betters do to divert the attention of their worsers when at the point of rebellion? Right first time. They either start a war or give us a royal wedding. This time it was the latter. The day after the announcement of the State of Emergency, Princess Anne got herself hitched, and everyone forgot the lousy situation, went soppy and waved Union Jacks. The subject of her affection was a right Hooray Henry called Captain Mark Phillips who, like Anne, was a world class rider (and twit). The day after the wedding the happy couple scarpered off to the sunny Caribbean to escape the misery that all us commonfolk had to endure.

Distillers Lose Spirit

The huge group of companies under the Distillers umbrella suffered a blow when a leading supermarket chain decided to boycott their products, owing to their tardiness in settling the compensation claims for the poor little mites disfigured by their mums' use of the drug thalidomide during pregnancy. Their biggest loss was in the booze market, as Distillers produced many leading brands of whisky, gin, vodka and brandy.

IRA Targets London

Well, we might have guessed that the IRA wouldn't like the idea of Northern Ireland being run by the British Government, and they showed their wrath by blasting the Old Bailey in central London. They managed to kill one person and injure 250. From then on, nowhere was safe. Still, we all felt better when we found out that they weren't using their own pocket money to make bombs. No; that nice Mr Moamar Gaddafi of Libya was footing most of the bill, saying that he 'must support any little country which has taken up arms to defend its rights and freedom.' Ah yes, freedom to go into a shopping centre in another country and blow up innocent kids and their mummies. Nice one Moamar!

Dickie's So Tricky!

Just so that you know that Heath wasn't the only leader in a deep mire, Richard Nixon was revealed to be far more deeply involved in the Watergate bugging scandal than was ever imagined, and had gone to great lengths to hide his tracks (even though his nose was now two feet long). The world's press were after him like a pack of hyenas, and it seemed to all that watched him squirming on telly (before 10.30!) that even he couldn't survive this one.

Then unbelievably, some tapes were discovered which were said to put the finishing touches to proof of Nixon's involvement but, at the last minute, his loyal secretary said that she was ever so sorry, but she appeared to have accidentally erased 18 minutes of the most important tape. And this, dear readers, was the secretary to the President of the United States of America. Read on.

Meanwhile

January: Jim didn't fix it this time! Smarmy Jimmy (good works for maximum self-publicity) Savile made a bundle promoting the silly 'Klunk-Klik' TV commercials to enforce the new seat-belt laws. It was then noticed that his own flashy new motor caravan wasn't fitted with them. Ow's about that then, guys and gals?

March: Teeny-bopper band The Osmonds arrived on our shores for the first time. The squeaky-clean Mormonlings came from Salt Lake City in the US. Five sixths of the singing troop were pretty awful, but the sixth, 9 year old Jimmy ('I'm your Long-Haired Lover from Liverpool'), was just about the worst thing to land on Britain since the horrible Hun's flying bombs.

April: Pablo Picasso died. Whether or not one thought that he was the world's greatest twentieth century artist or an overrated self-publicist, nobody could deny he made the most loot.

May: Wanna buy a bit of Rolls Royce? When nobody came up with a decent offer for the whole company, they decided to sell off the £38,400,000's worth of shares to anyone who wanted them.

July: David Bowie announced at a London concert that he would never perform live again. It turned out to be like a fish saying it was going to give up water.

October: President Nixon, who'd been withholding some significant tapes, gave in to a court order to give them up.

December: St Michael, the patron saint of underwear (and millionaires), sure had his protective eye on Marks and Sparks boss Joseph Sieff, who was gunned down by an assassin in his own home. Mr Sieff, a top Jewish figure, had always been a major target for Arab terrorist groups. The bullet, fired at close range, failed to kill him.

1974

Welcome Back Wilson

Edward Heath was smarter than he looked. He managed to turn the 'Who runs Britain?' question to his own advantage when he asked the British people whether they wanted the Government or the miners to call the shots. Unfortunately, poor old Ted, battered and bruised from probably the worst year of his life, was committed to putting his head on the block at the General Election in March, even though the country was still in a State of Emergency and collapsing under a three day week. On top of those little confidence boosters, the miners, never known to miss a trick, threatened to strike for the whole duration of the campaign. If all this wasn't bad enough, on the final Monday of the campaign, trade figures were published that made anything that had gone on before in our country's history look like a cocktail party.

With the timing of a fine strip-tease dancer, Enoch Powell (the famous Tory rebel), removed the final garment covering Heath's humiliation, and said he was going to vote – can you believe it – Labour.

Labour Knows Best

The Labour Party's strategy was, of course, to try to show us all that they could get us out of the fine mess the Conservatives had put us in (the same Conservatives who'd once tried to get us out of the fine mess that Labour had put us in).

The voters, however, were so punch-drunk by the messy affair that most of them really didn't give a monkey's either way, and this showed in the results. The Tories and the Socialists all lost hodloads of votes, mostly to the lacklustre Liberals and Scottish Nationalists. Neither Heath nor Wilson had a majority and despite Heath's fruitless attempt to snuggle up to Jeremy Thorpe (the leader of the Liberals) in order to form some sort of pact, Wilson became the first Prime Minister since 1929 to lead a government without a majority in the House of Commons.

Wilson's first action was to make Heath's head-on fight with the miners count for nothing by chickening out and giving in to all their demands. The unions had won – grubby hands down.

Another Election

Talk about boring. No sooner was that election over than the politicians started creeping round their electorate again. There had to be yet another election as soon as possible because even cocky Harold Wilson found it impossible to run a country with a minority government. This time Labour got a small majority (if you call just three seats small), but it was enough for clever little Harold to do what he wanted. Unlike Heath, who had gatecrashed other parties like a cut-price tart, trying to get them into bed with his Conservatives, Wilson had decided to go it alone.

Anne Nearly Gets the Bullet

It was a good job that Princess Anne's and Captain Mark Phillip's relationship was already cooling down, for if they'd been cuddling in the back of the Royal limo on 20th March, one of them would almost certainly have been hit by the assassin's bullet that went straight between them. A car slewed round in front of theirs, only yards from their front garden at Buck House, and a guy jumped in and dragged our Anne out in order, as we all found out later, to

It's OK Anne, I think he only wants our autographs

ransom her for £1,000,000 (a lot more than he'd have got for poor old Mark). As might be expected, everyone around got hurt apart from the royal couple and, when eventually arrested, the chap (called Ian Ball) claimed he was doing it to bring attention to the lack of mental health facilities. I suppose it *did* make us all realise that there are still a lot of nutters on the loose!

Counties on the Move

Just to show how powerful they were over those who couldn't answer back, the Government (who always knew best) decided to muck around with names and borders of towns and counties going back to the *Domesday Book*. Only 10 of the 45 English counties and one of the 13 Welsh counties remained unscathed and some, like Rutland, Cumberland, Huntingdonshire and Westmorland, went altogether.

Nixon Hands Over

Over in America, the Watergate scandal was hotting up nicely. Tricky Dicky Nixon had handed over the infamous tapes to avoid impeachment from the Congressional Committee (see page 138). On one of the tapes, he could be heard telling his counsel, John Dean, that he reckoned he could get hold of the odd $1,000,000 required to stifle any blackmail attempts from a conspirator called Howard Hunt. No wonder he'd tried to 'lose' the tapes. On 8th August, he could hang on no longer and chucked in the Presidency. He had now become famous for being the first American President ever to resign.

Nixon was replaced by the one President that everyone forgets when listing presidents – Gerald Ford. He'd got to the top, not particularly for his own merits, but simply because all the others seemed so bent.

Meanwhile

January: Brilliant schemes (and wide boys) were emerging to beat the restrictions of the three day week. One enterprising hairdresser in Dagenham thought up a great wheeze. As food shops were exempt from the three day week, he offered baked beans for 75 p a tin with a 'free' shampoo and set thrown in.

February: Dr Spock, the world famous millionaire American doctor whose book on child-rearing had been a bible for millions of young parents, was suddenly blamed for the rise in hooliganism in later life. When challenged, he simply turned round and said sorry he'd got it all wrong. Fair enough Doc!
• Too healthy for his own good, a fitness freak called Basil Brown drank eight pints of carrot juice a day and died, bright yellow, of an excess of vitamin A. His condition was indistinguishable from alcohol poisoning. Moral: if you're going to die from drink, you might as well enjoy yourself on the way.

March: Abba, the dreadful Swedish band, who looked as if they'd just raided a pantomime dressing-up box, won the excruciatingly embarrassing Eurovision Song Contest.

April: Chinese Take-Aways had taken over from good old fish and chips in the affections of the British. All velly deplessing.

May: The term Ms (pronounced Miz) was introduced at the passport office to placate all those women who found it embarrassing to be either Mrs or Miss.

July: The perfect actress and bishop scandal. Jess 'the bishop' Yates presented the most yucky religion-cum-showbiz programme called 'Stars on Sunday' on the weekly God slot. This tubby, balding, slippery-smooth example to us all, turned out to be having an affair with a blond 'actress' who'd recently appeared topless in the *Daily Mirror*. No wonder poor daughter Paula turned out the way she has.

August: Would you believe it? A Tory MP called Jeffrey Archer had to stand down because of severe financial problems. To be fair, the rise in the fame and fortunes of the now Lord Archer should be a lesson to us all. Quite what the lesson is, I'll leave up to you.

September: Discrimination against women was finally outlawed in a new White Paper by Woy Jenkins. Anyone who refused a woman anything from a job to a pint of bitter because of her sex became liable to prosecution. (Nice try, Woy, but many would argue that things aren't much better now.)

October: The IRA had different ways of dealing with women. They blew up, in their cowardly manner, two pubs in Guildford known to be frequented by members of the WRACS (Woman's Royal Army Corps).

November: Nobody realised that when the dashing Lord 'Lucky' Lucan disappeared, having allegedly murdered the family nanny and nearly his wife, that he would still be missing to this day. If you had a £ for the number of alleged sightings, you would be nearly as rich as the errant Earl. C'mon Lucky, where are you? I won't tell.

December: Everyone was slightly amused when Margaret Thatcher told us that she was entering the ring to fight for Edward Heath's job. Equal opportunities fine, but a woman (and a bossy one at that) as head of the Tory party? No chance!

1975

Thatcher Hatches

It had to happen. On 11th February, Margaret Thatcher, a 49 year old mother of twins, finally became the first woman to become leader of a political party, despite frantic efforts from her chauvinist colleagues to block her passage. Willie Whitelaw, who looked like a sycophantic toad, and was soon to act like one, nearly blubbed, as he, and most public opinion, had thought he had the job in the bag.

Maggie's timing was brilliant as always. Wilson was scrabbling around for hide-saving ideas and longed to get back to the homely, pipe-smoking, confidence-inspiring leader of a few years ago. He showed what a wily old fox he was, however, when, on 18th March, nearly half his cabinet, totally fed up with the Common Market, rebelled. Nothing like it had been seen for over 40 years. Wilson neatly side-stepped his personal dilemma by stating that he was not that bothered either way and certainly wouldn't resign over the final decision. Cabinet members were left free to campaign according to what they truly believed (for nearly the first time before or since) as opposed to having to toe the party line. Any fool could see that this was just a sign of a desperate government that couldn't even make up its own mind, let alone persuade anyone else.

Drooping Pound

On 16th March, the £ took a nose-dive to only 75% of its value four years earlier. At the same time, prices were rising by 22%, and unemployment hit the 1,000,000 mark for the first time ever. You don't have to have a first-class degree in economics to realise that the Labour Government had lost it, and even they knew it.

In June, there was a referendum to find out, once and for all, whether we British were still into being European. The vote was a surprisingly overwhelming 'Yes please', which put the tin lid, once and for all, on any arguments. We were *in* the EEC now and we could like it or lump it.

Uneasy Education
This was the time when the Labour Government, in its infinite wisdom, was trashing the grammar schools (much loved by middle-class Britain) and replacing them with comprehensive schools (much loved by er . . . ?). Many of the finer grammar schools, like Manchester, refused to play ball when their funding was whipped away, and went totally independent, relying on a payment-according-to-means fee structure. The joke was that this method was really more socialist in practice than the smart new comprehensive system which still failed to give the poor kid from the working class background the same chance of a good education as those better off.

Of course, all this played into the hands of the posher public schools whose administrators were bowled over by the rush of applications from 'nice' mummies and daddies, who didn't want their little treasures going to school with (let alone talking to) those awful little oiks from the poorer areas.

Fashion

It certainly wasn't a bright idea to go into gent's hairdressing in the mid 70s. The only young men that didn't wear their hair long were soldiers, prisoners or the follicly-challenged (bald to you!). The hippie movement, now (thankfully) on the way out, had left funny little reminders that had crept into everyday fashion. Trousers still flared below the knee; shoes made you at least an inch taller, and big moustaches (on men) were politically correct. T-shirts, which had once been called vests and worn under the shirt to keep you warm, had now become a major fashion garment. Kids exhibited controversial, or really rude, one-liners on their chests and advertisers saw them as an excellent way to promote their products and, for some totally obscure reason, punters of all ages seemed to love to be seen advertising God-knows-what for no money. Beats me!

The mid 70s were a kind of fashion no-man's-land for women. Bits of ageing Biba gear were worn with hot pants or maxi skirts. Clumpy platform shoes were coupled with floaty flower power frocks and hair couldn't decide whether to be long and wispy or short and permy.

And Music?

Musically it was similar. Strong diving forces like rock and roll, rhythm and blues and soul were still alive, but fighting against a very unpleasant, 'easy listening' virus. People like Barry Manilow, The Carpenters, Englebert Humperdinck (his singing matched his name), or Paul McCartney's rather weedy Wings were increasingly popular. Hit of the year was 'Sailing' which was about the blandest song Rod Stewart (by then nearing his sell-by date) ever sung.

Hip kids of the time were listening to some brilliant bands from the States like Steely Dan, Bruce Springsteen and Velvet Underground. In Britain, we had The Average White Band, David Bowie, the now great Eric Clapton, and a much more jazzy Van ('the man') Morrison; but the really good sounds seldom made the singles chart.

Meanwhile

January: Having spent a cool £40 million buying buckets and spades to dig the Channel Tunnel, the whole thing was put on ice yet again by the Government. A lot of non-Francophiles heaved a hugh sigh of relief.

March: What a comedown. The once highly regarded Shadows led by Hank (dorky-looking) Marvin actually entered the Eurovision Song Contest and came in second behind a Dutch group who sang a song called 'Ding-a-Dong' (which is what all those songs seem to be called).

April: Another comedown. Aston Martin-Lagonda, perhaps the finest British car firm ever, was sold to the International Semi-Conductor Company of America. Good job they didn't call the car that. (Hey! Wanna lift in my International Semi-Conductor!?)
• On 1st April, the wholly disgusting Vietnam War officially ended when North Vietnamese tanks rolled into Saigon, the capital. The Americans had already pulled out of a 15 year war which had achieved nothing but the deaths of thousands of young men, women and children and the end of America's belief that it could do and go anywhere, whenever it damn well wanted.

June: A brilliant new TV series called 'Fawlty Towers' was launched on British TV. Starring John Cleese (ex-Monty Python) and Prunella Scales, it proved conclusively that British comedy was the very best in the world (unless you're foreign).

July: Fact meets fiction. Police discovered that Carlos Martinez, otherwise known as the 'Jackal' the most famous international assassin ever, had been living in London, when his heavily weapon-stocked lair was found. He is still on the run.

August: A Japanese ex-army mechanic offered Britain a dream. The Honda Dream became the first of a flood of Jap. motorbikes that completely destroyed Britain's stick-in-the-mud industry. Served 'em right I say.

October: Trust the British to catch something horrible from the Dutch. Over 6.5 million elm trees died from the cleverly named Dutch Elm Disease.

November: He should have stuck to cars. Graham Hill (Damon's dad) became an ex-racing driver when he ploughed his plane into a field near Elstree and died.

1976

Room at the Top
On 5th April, James Callaghan became the new Labour Prime Minister following the shock resignation of worn-out Harold Wilson. As when Heath replaced Douglas-Home, if you'd looked for anyone more different, you'd have found it difficult. For a start, everyone seemed to like Callaghan. For a second, unlike Wilson, who'd been dead clever at school and later Oxford, Jim

Callaghan (who was no spring chicken at 64) had come from a dead ordinary elementary, and then secondary school, education. For a third, he was a non-smoker, non-drinker, regular church-goer and about as straightforward as you could get (for a politician!).

Callaghan came from the right of centre, but was well clued up as to the growing power of the left. His great intention was to unite the party and he was therefore hellbent on swatting the leftie minority groups, who were multiplying like flies while trying to hoist their views on to party policy. In a way, he came into the job with one hand firmly tied behind his back, as Wilson had made himself and the Labour Party extremely unpopular and his government had been losing loads of by-elections to the Liberals.

Jobs for the Boys

Wilson had gone out under a hail of bricks owing to his resignation honours list, which had been drawn up in conjunction with his very personal secretary Lady Falkender and published in May. Amongst the group of extremely dubious 'friends' he'd showered with knighthoods and lordships was one Joe Kagan. Kagan was an extremely dodgy, self-made millionaire northerner who, amongst other things, manufactured the hideous raincoat (called a Gannex), that looked as if it was made out of reconstituted chewed-up cardboard, and was much favoured by Wilson. The lengths some people will go to for a free mac! A few years later, Kagan was 'de-lorded' when charged with cheating and defrauding the Inland Revenue.

And Another

MP John Stonehouse had arranged a 'disappearance' by leaving his clothes on a Miami beach before heading off to Australia under a forged passport. He then turned out to be a forger, a cheat, a fraudster, a liar (as well as a politician). This brilliant man, who'd been tipped to be the future leader of the Labour Party, was found guilty on 6th August of a whole series of naughtinesses and sentenced to seven years hard 'labour'. I would have thought that his ingenuity was just what the Labour Government needed. Stonehouse for PM I say.

Thorpe Backs Out

Probably one of the greatest and most fascinating scandals began in May when Jeremy Thorpe, the ultra-posh leader of the Liberal party, suddenly resigned after allegations of sexual relations with a model. Not any old model, either, as this one was called Norman. If you think I'm going to descend into all the sordid details of this business, I'm afraid you're absolutely . . . right, but you'll have to be patient and wait until 1978 for the next bit.

Snowdon Slides Out

Just as the Royal Family are never seen visiting the toilet, they never discuss personal problems either. It was, therefore, quite a shock when it was announced that Princess Margaret and her hubby, Lord Snowdon, were splitting. At the press conference, Lord Snowdon, who'd looked miserable for years, seemed positively ecstatic. The only problem the Royals had was who would now take the family snaps (and whether it would cost 'em).

Phew, Wot a Scorcher!

What do we British moan about more than anything else? You've got it – the English summer. Why is the weather so unpredictable?

Why can't we have barbecues without the fear of wet sausages? Why do we sometimes have to wear overcoats on the beach? And so on, and so on. The summer of 1976 was the driest, hottest and longest this century. So were the British people, at long last, happy? . . . Don't be silly!

You just can't remove the British pastime of complaining at the drop of an umbrella. Before long, sunburnt people were happily moaning about everything from the state of their lawns, the queues for ice cream, the water rationing, the forest fires, the hole in the ozone layer or the Government's inability to make it rain. A Minister for Drought (can you believe) was appointed who, after weeks of careful scientific analysis by his brilliant hand-picked staff, using the latest, state-of-the-art instrumentation, came out with the inspired statement that unless we all cut our water consumption there would have to be rationing. Eventually the rains came again . . . and everyone complained. Wretched weather!!

Peanuts for All

The big news from abroad this year was the death of that old tyrant Chairman Mao, and the election of a peanut farmer from Georgia as the new President of the United States (and why ever not?). Rhodesia was struggling to keep its boot firmly on the reluctant black rebels, while further down in South Africa the pot was boiling over with rioting and looting throughout the black townships (and we had our own race riot at the Notting Hill Carnival). Everyone seemed to be fighting everyone else (as usual) in the Middle East, while Isabel Peron, President of Argentina, was chucked out, giving the dreadfully overrated Lloyd-Webber and Rice yet another plot for a dreadfully overrated musical (*Evita*).

Meanwhile

January: One of the few millionaires not to lose their shirts in the worst year ever for bankruptcy was the crime writer Agatha Christie. She just died (aged 85).

February: Balletic ice-skater John Currie won the Olympic Gold Medal at Innsbruck. He managed, for the first time in history, to make skating into almost an art form (but not quite).

March: Arthur, the fab feline star of the Kattomeat (inspired name!) commercials, died. He had been scooping his supper straight from the tin, with his paw, for over ten years (who can't do that?). The poor pussy didn't make a penny, however, as he was owned lock, stock and whiskers by Spillers Pet Foods.

• More death. L. S. Lowry, the famous and much-acclaimed artist (and former rent collector), who couldn't paint to save his life – died.

May: All over London one could see graffiti proclaiming the innocence of George Davis, a taxi driver, jailed for armed robbery. Eventually the courts gave in under the enormous public pressure and released him. A couple of years later George was back inside again . . . for armed robbery. Egg on face? Not much!

June: A milestone in the culinary history of our fine country. McDonalds, the only meal you can eat without teeth (I should be in advertising), arrived (uninvited) from the States.

July: Obsequious little David Steel, son of a Presbyterian minister, leapt into poor Jeremy Thorpe's trousers (figuratively speaking), to lead the Liberal Party.
• Those horrid, blue three-wheeler invalid cars, that acted like huge fingers pointing out the disabled, were phased out. They were

apparently so dangerous that there was a good chance that if you were given one you'd like as not end up in a worse state than before.

September: Percy Shaw, the man who'd invented cat's eyes, closed his own for the last time. Apparently he'd had the idea when he'd seen a cat's eyes light up as he pedalled home from the pub on his bike (no! not the cat!). Most people just see pink elephants.

October: If it wasn't bad enough losing your husband, poor Mrs Mao was compared to 'dog dung' (Pekinese no doubt) and jailed, with her Gang of Four, for allegedly trying to overthrow the Chinese Government. It really hadn't been her year.

November: All the girls at Girton, the female Cambridge college, were found to be 'expecting' . . . men. The decision was taken to open its doors to the unfairer sex the following year.

December: The first of the punk bands, The Sex Pistols, invented by the great Malcolm McLaren, ran riot on a TV news review programme. Bill Grundy, the presenter, obviously trying to be hip, challenged them to repeat the 'F' word. This opened a tirade that the poor old 'viewers at home' had never before experienced. God knows what poor Bill expected.

1977

Jubilee Fever
Time to jolly up the British people's flagging self-esteem. Good Queen Elizabeth II had now held down the top job (albeit damn well paid) for 20 years, and her Silver Jubilee parade proved that there was still a forelock-tugging nation lurking behind their front doors, dying to wave a flag at something. No one could deny that those shiny old gilded coaches, driven by men in dreadful second-hand outfits, and pulled by big white royal horses, could still give the British punter a sense (misguided or not) of loyalty and patriotism that no politician could even dream of.

Lucky Jim Has An Idea
Jim Callaghan, the Prime Minister, must have dreamed he could do the same for himself. His nightmare term of Labour Government was still going down the electoral plug-hole, losing loads of by-elections, including two at the heart of cloth-cap-land – Walsall and Workington. The Government was back walking the tight-rope, with a majority of only one, and even that was looking a bit precarious. It was time for them to sweet-talk the Liberal Party as Ted Heath had tried some years ago to save his own (considerable) bacon. Remember? He, though, had got his face slapped for his trouble (see page 140).

This time David Steel was top Liberal and, luckily for Jim, young McDave would have sold his grandmother just to sniff even a tiny bit of power. The Lib/Lab pact was the first deal of its kind ever seen and Steel, no doubt, saw it as a way of eventually getting through the electoral reforms that would bring him and his Liberal lads and lassies in with a fighting chance.

Unfortunately (tee hee) it had exactly the opposite effect, as ardent Liberal supporters thought that sneaky Steel had sold out everything they stood for. So, at the next by-election, they let him

155

know just what a tacky thing they thought he'd done by voting elsewhere. Callaghan, of course, didn't give a damn; he'd bought himself just enough time for the economy to come round, wiping out a Tory 'No Confidence' motion which, sure as hell, would have seen him and his party back down at the Job Centre.

Oil Aboard

The economy, which had really hit the deck in 1976, was just beginning to twitch again, thanks largely to all that lovely, black North Sea Oil. But the situation still looked impossible, with nearly 1.5 million on the dole and production practically static.

Luckily the $ was in a worse state than the punch drunk £, which was looking, believe it or not, a lot less peaky than usual.

Work or Walk

Those perishing strikes had become a ball and chain round any real chance of Britain's economic recovery. On 15th March, the exasperated bosses of British Leyland, the mammoth state car and truck firm, finally flipped their lids (or bonnets) and told three thousand striking toolmakers that if they didn't get their idle backsides right back to work that instant they'd be sacked – no ifs or butts. Jim Callaghan backed them all the way, telling the strikers that there would be no more state cash to paper over the damage they were doing. By now, we had all fully realised that foreign car makers were champing at the bit to flood the country with their motors, and that these strikers were playing right into their hands. I wonder what they'd have said if they'd known that eighteen years later the whole company would be flogged to the Krauts (BMW).

Echoes of Adolph

One of the nastiest things to come out of the mid 70s was the rise of the National Front Party – a bunch of racist morons who, for some inexplicable reason, thought that they alone were the race chosen to inhabit Britain (shaved heads, lager bellies and covered in spots and tattoos). A pitched battle against the police occurred in Lewisham (home of pitched battles) who used their cosy new

SHAVEN HEAD

NO BRAIN

HATE

TATTOOS

RINGS

SPOTS

UNION JACK TEE SHIRT

How to spot a patriotic Brit

Ulster-tested riot shields for the first time.

School for Skivers
Scruffy Shirley Williams, the leftie Labour Education Secretary who made even her fellow politicians look stylish, had been largely responsible for the death of the grammar schools. She now had to eat humble pie and admit the failure of her latest wheeze to imprison kids, desperate to quit her new comprehensive schools, for an extra year after the age of fifteen.

Skateboard Summer
So what could all those kids do on leaving school? Simple – they went on the dole – and then on the skateboard. This was the year that every pavement, pathway, or drive was jam-packed with kids riding (or falling off) those funny little, American inspired, plywood planks-with-wheels-on.

Cricket-a-Go-Go
A loud, disagreeable Australian, who resembled a robber with a stocking over his face, Kerry Packer, came over to our country, like the devil incarnate, to buy the very souls of our best cricketers. He wanted them to play exhibition tests on telly wearing the most gaudy outfits, advertising everything from cars (foreign) to cat food. Like the sport or not, this simply wasn't cricket. The gentle sport of gentlemen was turned into showbiz overnight.

Punk Gets Pop

For years kids had searched for something that would be *really* guaranteed to drive their nearest and dearest to the therapist. The punk movement was perfect. Looks-wise, it had started on the streets (like all crazes) but, like day follows night, eventually it became a kind of half-baked fashion movement adapted by the clever(ish) designer Vivienne Westwood.

Fashion-wise, true punks were a dirty, delicious disaster area: ripped bondage clothing; spiky, greasy, parrot-coloured hair; studs and rings through the most unimaginable (and painful) parts of the body (yes – there too!!); and tattoos proclaiming obscenities across their foreheads or necks. Punks simply didn't give a monkey's what anybody thought and even competed with each other to see who could look the most hideous. Punkism only began to wither when certain smartened up and diluted items of their dress (like tartan bondage trousers) started to appear in high street gentlemen's outfitters in places like Tunbridge Wells and Bath.

Music-wise (if you can use that word), the 'credit' for the birth of the totally anarchic punk rock must really go to The Sex Pistols and their manager/guru Malcolm MacLaren. This horribly brilliant band started to crop up, like a contagious disease, around some of the seedier London clubs. 'We're not into music, we're into chaos' they proclaimed.

The most interesting aspect of punk was that it came from the kids, was for the kids and was largely controlled by the kids. It was a way of showing two filthy fingers to an establishment that had let them down so badly.

Meanwhile

January: No wonder Woy Jenkins resigned from the Cabinet. He'd obviously had the nod that he was to become the much higher paid President of the EEC in Brussels.

February: We might have guessed that the nice Mr Amin, head of Uganda, would turn into a despotic murderer. His most outrageous act was to have the Archbishop of Uganda murdered. Even his long-gone hero, Adolf, never tried things like that.

May: Nigel Short, who now looks like an ad for 'Man at C&A', was once a normal child. Well, if you call being, at eleven, the youngest ever competitor in a national chess championship normal.

August: The undisputed King of Rock and Roll, Elvis Presley, died from a drugs overdose at his deliciously tasteless home, Gracelands, in Memphis. If anyone still believes that money and fame automatically brings happiness, take a look at the state of 'Elvis the Pelvis' just before he went to rock and roll heaven.

Footnote: His 9 year old daughter Lisa Marie seemed relatively unmoved when told she was now a billionaire.

September: Freddie Laker astounded the world (and the other airlines) by offering cut-price flights to New York for £59 – and he even managed to make a profit.

Hit of the Year: 'Don't Cry For Me, Argentina' (ominous or what?)

1978

Bring Back Hadrian

So far, I haven't mentioned the fact that the Scots and Welsh, noticing that Britain was rapidly becoming the 'sick man of Europe', were revolting, claiming they were fed up with being simply an English colony. The clamour for devolution (self-government) was becoming deafening. If England wanted, as some bright political commentator put it, 'to embark on a journey from being a developed to an undeveloped country' then bully for them, but why should Scotland and Wales be dragged down with 'em?

Actually, much more to the point, the canny (and tight) Scots were miffed that the black gold (North Sea oil), was not pouring into *their* country from *their* sea-bed. Why, for Robbie Burns' sake, should they have to share it with the rest of us? Had the Scottish Nationalists read their history books, however, they'd have realised that they'd actually been given their precious home rule way back in 1913. Why else did they have their own McLaw system, own McChurch, own McNewspapers and even their own McTelly. McStrewth!

The Welsh were slightly different. Nobody could see Wales operating on its own economically (what if the bottom fell out of the leek and harp businesses?), so there had to be another reason for their wanting devolution. It seems, in retrospect, that they were more concerned about the loss of their language (I'd have thought that having places called Llanfairpwllgwyngyllgogerychwyrndrobwll-llantysiliogogogoch was something to be well avoided); and also the occupation of dinky little cottages by the English as weekend homes.

The Welsh pre-devolution solution to these problems was:

a. As soon as any foreign visitor (particularly English) were to ask them anything, they would suddenly not understand a word and switch to speaking their own, totally unintelligible, lingo.

b. To burn all the holiday cottages down (which seems more of an Irish solution). As their objection was the fact that the poor locals could no longer afford the inflated prices, then their actions simply meant there was nothing left to buy anyway.

Very nice Dai, shame it's my parent's new house!

This whole devolution business came to a well-silly head when Cornwall suddenly jumped up and said that it also wanted to free itself from the rest of Britain (and nationalise the pasty industry, no doubt). Anyway, how's about home rule for Wandsworth, where I live? What happened? Read on.

Poor Old Jim

Though just about everyone liked Jim Callaghan, his go at prime ministering was turning out to be fairly depressing. If Wilson had been a failure, then poor Jim seemed to be making matters worse. It has been said that every decision he made, either before or since becoming PM, had, in retrospect, turned out to be wrong – failing to devalue the £ in 1964, letting all the Asians in from Kenya in 1969, and trying to hang on to power too long in the vain hope of doing some pay deal with the unions who, thanks to crawly Wilson, had the Labour Government well and truly tucked up.

Although it was not as bad as the situation in 30s Germany (when Hitler took over), the time was ripe for a complete change and a real macho leader. David Steel, who was anything but stupid (or macho) realised that the Lib/Lab pact had no chance (and more to the point nor had he) so promptly yanked his Liberals out. So who on earth would this new leader be? No prizes for guessing . . . please read on.

Abroad
Time for a look across the waters. Who was doing what to whom in 1978?
1. The Ugandans were fighting the Tanzanians.
2. The Israelis were fighting the Palestinians (as usual).
3. Rhodesian rebels were fighting Ian Smith.
4. The Ethiopians were fighting the Somalians.
5. The Russians were helping the Ethiopian army to fight the Ethiopian Government.
6. The Iranians (ex-Persians) were getting ready to fight their leader, the Shah.
7. The Argentinians were fighting The Dutch . . . in the World Cup Final.

The Royals?
Following all the fabulous fun of the Royal Jubilee, and the birth of the first of a new generation of kids for us all to support (Princess Anne's nipper – Pete), our Royal Family began to settle down. The Queen, now a granny, only really had *that* sister to worry about. Princess Margaret now alarmed everyone by lurching perilously close to marrying Roddy Llewellyn, a sort of up-market playboy like his brother Dai – the sort always seen outside London nightclubs or with debby bimbos (dimbos?) called Henrietta, Camilla or Lucinda. Luckily, Roddy thought better of the match, so poor Margaret went back to her booze and fags.

Medical Madness
British doctors, scientists and quacks stunned the world. A gynaecologist from Oldham successfully planted the very first 'test tube babies' into their grateful mums; while at St Bartholomew's in London, doctors started using leeches again (in 1837 the hospital

got through 96,300) to suck blood out of unsightly bruises. Yukk!!

Even weirder, Ivor Rice from St Austell, resigned to going blind, took the advice of 70 year old Julie Owen of Kent, who claimed that regular bee stings (from her regular bees) would bring back his sight. He was so impressed with the result that he soon got up to ten stings a day. Pass the bees, honey.

Weirder Still! Embryonic mice, frozen over five years before, were scuttling around their cages after a nice warm bath. Scientists now reckoned it was totally possible to conceive a human nipper, freeze the poor little foetus, then actually have it whenever you wanted.

Meanwhile

January: Margaret Thatcher stated the obvious, in a slimy statement to gain popularity, when she said that many Britons 'fear being "swamped" by people with a different culture.' I wonder if she really meant that last word.

March: Foley Boxing Club were looking for someone to have a scrap with their new heavyweight star, Paul McDonald. All they came up with was a young 16 year old who was just leaving approved school. Unfortunately, the boy – a certain Frank Bruno – didn't have the right ABA (Amateur Boxing Association) cards so could only spar. Fortunately for Paul McDonald though. Know what I mean, 'Arry?

April: Our politicians' egos certainly got the better of them when they allowed proceedings in the House of Commons to be broadcast on the radio. Britain was shocked when it heard the behaviour and often sad level of debate of those it had elected.

May: Silent comedy? The hardly-cold corpse of Charlie Chaplin, which had two months earlier been nicked from his Swiss grave, was now found buried ten miles away. Perhaps old Charlie might have got the joke. Nobody else could.

June: Guy the gorilla, London Zoo's biggest attraction, had a bad time at the dentist. The 32 year old, 27 stone ape never woke up from the anaesthetic. I bet he would have done if he'd known they were going to stuff him.

• Absolutely no connection, but Jeremy Thorpe, the ex-Liberal leader, was interviewed by detectives investigating a plot to kill gay model Norman Scott. He was later charged in December.

August: Job vacant . . . Pope. Good news – after only four ballots, albino Cardinal Luciani was elected Pope Jean-Paul I.

September: Who said God looked after his own? After only 33 days of poping, Jean-Paul I, was found dead. (Yet another ad in the *Vatican Times*.) His replacement, Karil Wojtyla (a Pole) was named, rather unoriginally, Jean-Paul II (I think I'd have wanted something completely different). Still, at least you could get your tongue round it.

• Be careful when waiting for buses at Waterloo Bridge! Mr Georgi Markov, a Bulgarian defector, was jabbed in the leg by a poisoned umbrella. He died four days later. I suppose he'd have been all right if it had been raining. Murderers hate getting wet.

November: One of the problems with being a member of Reverend Jim Jones' religious sect, The People's Temple, was that you had to kill yourself. 913 devotees drank Kool Aid with just a little hint of cyanide (to give it that extra kick) and were found piled up at their hideaway in Guyana. Anyone could have told them soft drinks (and crack-pot religions) were bad for them.

1979

Winter of Discontent

The few long, miserable months which spanned 1978 and 1979 became known as the 'Winter of Discontent'. The on-going scrap between the Government and the unions had finally descended to an out-and-out brawl, with the unions doing everything in their power to beat the pay ceilings put on them by poor 'now-not-so-lucky' Jim Callaghan and his boys. Food and petrol supplies were up the creek owing to lorry drivers' go-slows, huge mounds of rubbish lay piled up in the streets and, in Liverpool, dead people lay piled up in the mortuaries impatiently waiting to be dug in. The pesky pickets didn't even stop at harassing hospitals and practically decided who they'd let in to get better.

This could well have been the most unpopular that any Government had ever become and, as Labour plummeted down in public opinion, in true see-saw fashion, the Tories rocketed up.

Devolution Dives

Remember all that fuss about self-government last year? After numerous debates in the Commons, loads of demonstrations and protests, both the Welsh and the Scots peoples were asked what *they* thought in a referendum. The Welsh, bless 'em, turned it down overwhelmingly, while the Scots who, we'd all been led to believe, hated being ruled by Sassenachs, hardly turned out to vote, so no conclusion could be come to.

Here Comes Margaret

At the back end of March, poor old Jim Callaghan lost the first vote of confidence for 55 years which meant there had to be an election as soon as possible. There was, and in early May, after the greatest political swing since the war, a certain Mrs Margaret Thatcher, wife, mother and superstar, became queen of all she surveyed – the first British Prime Ministress ever.

The Labour Party was completely shattered and, in order to get some kind of opposition together, the poor losers were forced to dip into the bran tub and have a re-selection of MPs. Britain had a new government, a new PM and, best of all, a new target of fun – Mr Denis Thatcher – who took on the role (in the silly papers) of the poor little red-nosed husband dominated by the big fat lady in the seaside postcards.

The biggest joke of all came when the unions, realising they'd slain the rather shabby goose (the Labour Government) that had laid, for so long, the golden eggs, agreed to a sleazy pact with the new Tory Government. Maybe they'd spotted the steely, I'm taking no nonsense, glint in the eye of 'her that must be obeyed'!

Blown To Bits

It certainly didn't pay to be a hardliner regarding Northern Ireland (or a close friend of Margaret Thatcher). The man with the daftest name in politics, Conservative Airey Neave, was blown up in the House of Commons car park. Later in the year, we were all once more shocked to the core when dear old Earl Mountbatten (Prince Philip's uncle) caught more than he bargained for when his fishing boat was ripped to smithereens by an IRA bomb off the Irish coast.

Irate Iran

Just as the situation in Iran had got to bursting point, on 16th January, the Shah, realising the natives weren't joking, hightailed it off to Egypt. His downfall had been engineered by the Ayatollah Khomeini who was himself in exile in Paris. Elated Iranians jumped up and down (as only they can) with joy, while women stuck flowers down the barrel of tanks which only the day before were trying to crush the demonstrations.

Someone asked the Shah, as he was leaving, how long he reckoned he was going to be away. The Shah said he wasn't sure, but one look round at the extremely cross, fanatical and screaming Iranians would have told him to take at least a toothbrush and a change of clothes.

Later in the year, the masses took the unprecedented action of storming the American Embassy in Teheran (see Things You Simply Don't Do). Screaming anti-American slogans, the mob took nearly 100 embassy staff hostage. America had always supported the ex-Shah so this action seemed to them like serious fighting talk.

Meanwhile

February: Sid Vicious, the member of the Sex Pistols who made the other punks seem like Cliff Richard, went most certainly down to the hot place when he died of a heroin overdose in New York.

April: Pictures taken from the US spacecraft, Voyager 1, revealed that the planet Jupiter has rings round it like Saturn. At the same time, earthbound astronomers discovered rings round Uranus too. ● Totally unconnected, Norman Scott, the male model 'linked' with ex-liberal leader Jeremy Thorpe, claimed in court that he'd been seduced twice by the politician at his mum's home. I've heard of liberal behaviour, but this was ridiculous. A month later poor Jeremy was found innocent of plotting murder and acquitted.

June: John Wayne (the Duke), the most famous film cowboy of all time, went to ride the great range in the sky when he died on the 11th. Outside his film career, Wayne was as right wing and red-necked as Genghis Khan, seeing the Vietnam War as the last great exhibition of American might.

August: Sebastian Coe became the very first athlete to hold three world records – the mile, the 800 and 1500 metres – at the same time. His ability to move fast, and keep looking behind him, could well be useful for his current job – Sebastian is now a Tory MP.

September: A very horrid murderer, nicknamed the 'Yorkshire Ripper', claimed his round dozen when he killed 20 year old Barbara Leach. Unlike most of his other victims (who were prostitutes) young Barbara was at Bradford University. ● Pope John Paul II flew to Ireland to beg all his Catholic fans to stop killing the other lot. As his plane flew over, many devout Irishmen stopped fighting and dropped to their knees in worship. When he'd gone, the 250,000 people who'd gone to see him went home and carried on exactly as they had before.

October: A new report from the Church of England proved that they were still split over whether to treat homosexuals as normal Christians or unreformed sinners. Their woolly thinking really came to light when they pronounced that gay sex was only all right if the partners *really* loved each other (and didn't do *it* with anyone else). Did this mean that 'straight' people could do whatever, to whoever, whenever they liked, as long as it was with someone of the opposite sex?

December: We all had a giggle when it was disclosed to a shocked House of Commons that the Queen's personal aristocratic art advisor had been, on his days off, a spy for the Russians. Sir Anthony Blunt turned out to be the infamous 'fourth man' in the Burgess, Maclean and Philby affair (see page 32). Naughty old Anthony had his not-very-hard-earned knighthood taken away. Apparently the Government had known about him since 1964 but they'd given him immunity in exchange for not spilling the beans. Nobody seems to know why Mrs Thatcher decided to shop him now.

Gosh Mr. Blunt, You know so much about Russian Art.

1980

Russian Revelations

A couple of days before the end of 1979, just as Mrs Thatcher was putting up the blue curtains in Number Ten, a shiver went up the spine of anyone who wasn't Russian. The news had broken that the Soviet Union, who had been far too quiet for far too long, had invaded Afghanistan. They certainly don't do things by half, those Ruskies; in only a few days they had 80,000 remarkably old-fashioned looking troops, armed to the teeth, pushing their considerable weight around. Afghanistan's President Hafizullah Amin (what is it about that name?) and his family were promptly executed by the KGB 'for crimes against the Afghan people'. You'd have thought the poor blighter, being a Communist, would have at least been politically correct as far as the Russians were concerned, but he obviously wasn't the right sort of communist, and the Kremlin claimed that its forces were 'requested to render urgent political, moral, military and economic assistance'. That's the Ruskies for you – all heart!

Poland Next?

The free world then waited with freshly baited breath when, after months of demos and strikes, Polish workers were, surprisingly, given loads of concessions by their Russian overlords. Most people assumed that just as they'd done in Hungary, Czechoslovakia and most recently Afghanistan, the Soviets would soon uncross their fingers, get the tanks out and crush the living daylights out of them. This might have happened if they hadn't been so stretched, soldier-wise, in Afghanistan, or weren't seriously running out of brownie points, public opinion-wise, with the rest of the world. But, wait as we all did, the iron fist hovered. Polish workers were allowed free trade unions and a central organisation called Solidarity, 'designer' stickers for which (for some bizarre reason) started to appear in the rear windows of British cars whose owners thought they were being frightfully 'right on'. The hero of the strikers, a shipyard worker called Lech Walesa, became their leader and much, much later the President of Poland.

Last Colony Disappears
Ian Smith displayed a wobbly smile when the Union Jack was finally lowered in Rhodesia, Britain's last remaining colony. The gentle Robert Mugabe came back from detention (for opposing Smith) to become the first black Prime Minister of the freshly named state of Zimbabwe. At long last, the seats in parliament were 80 to 20 in favour of the blacks.

Carter Boobs in the Desert
President Carter of the USA, meanwhile, sent his extra-special, super-dooper Delta Force to rescue those US hostages taken by the Iranians (see page 167). It was a monumental, gold-plated, impossible-to-repeat cock-up. For a start they didn't even get there!

On arrival in the Iranian desert, where they'd stopped for coffee and sandwiches, the mighty American Air Force realised it didn't actually have enough helicopters working properly. Just as they were all turning their planes and choppers round to come home, one of the few helicopters which *was* working crashed into the fuel supply aircraft and the whole lot went up in a fireball. Eight men died in the wreckage caused by the explosion. The Ayatollah Khomeini, hardly suppressing his glee, said that if the Yanks tried anything like that again he'd do horrible things to their precious hostages.

The late John Wayne must have turned in his grave to see his mighty country wearing a bright red face, and poor President Carter, sensing the worst, probably rang home to order his staff to get the old peanut farm ready for his unavoidable return from political life.

Sure enough, in November, a soon-to-be-doddery, old, ex-cowboy-film star, Ronald Reagan, Governor of California (where else?), beat him easily to the draw in the presidential elections.

Meanwhile Back in Britain

Poor Margaret Thatcher wasn't having that easy a ride in the top job. Unemployment had reached 2 million (the highest since 1936) and inflation was running at an unheard of 20%. Industry reported that orders were down anything between 10-40% and that it was now costing us 22% more to produce 4% less.

After my brilliant and incisive economics lecture (see page 135), you will realise that this situation could not be described as good and, true to form, the unions, bless their cotton socks, blamed the Government and, vice versa, the Government blamed them.

Jim Goes

Towards the end of the year, dear old Jim Callaghan resigned as Leader of the Opposition in favour of Michael Foot, a funny, old-fashioned, left-wing intellectual, who looked as if he'd bought his clothes from a Labour Party fund-raising jumble sale. The Tories could hardly hide their joy at Labour's choice, as they saw Foot as someone they could easily tread on. Foot, aged 67, who'd been one of the Ban the Bomb's leaders (he practically invented the dress code), instantly threw his somewhat light weight behind the protest against the installation of American Cruise Missiles at Greenham Common in Berkshire.

Meanwhile

February: A new survey revealed that over 50% of British married women now worked – higher than any other European Country.

Now this could have meant that we're more liberated in this country or, more likely, that the British were falling so far behind in the pay league that women had no blinking choice.

March: The 'New Wave of British Heavy Metal' was beginning to fill all the rock clubs. One must admit it looked, to us old timers, exactly the same as everything we'd seen before. A bunch of skinny geezers with hair over their faces, wrestling with guitars (in pretend anguish), playing the same chords and riffs at a volume that made your ears bleed.

• One of the foremost bands, Def Leppard, didn't appear to suffer at all when their drummer lost one of his arms. Actually, I reckon his style of drumming could have been equally as effective with no arms at all.

May: Alfred Hitchcock, the best suspense film director ever, died on the 29th. His trade mark had been to appear fleetingly in all his films looking like a cross between Winston Churchill and a pink football.

June: Police discovered, in a crate bound for the Moroccan Embassy in London, 650 lbs of cannabis. Talk about taking coals to Newcastle.

• Sir Billy Butlin, the king of holiday camps, died on the 12th. The idea of offering indoor and outdoor facilities for inmates –

sorry – holidaymakers, on a tight budget, had come to him after spending a miserable, rainy holiday in Skegness (what other kinds are there?). As if it wasn't bad enough being hard up, the poor working class British had to suffer Butlin's Holiday Camps as well. ● Excuse me, can we have our boat back? The wreck of the *Titanic* was found 12,000 feet below the surface of the Atlantic.

July: Britain invented a brand new sport with a great international flavour. The game was called 'Hooliganism' and the beauty of it was that there were no rules. The players would simply follow their favourite football team to foreign matches, and act like animals (sorry that's animalist) on arrival. In Turin, tear gas was useful on British fans (the finest hooligans in the world) but, unfortunately, the authorities scored an own goal when the wind changed direction and knocked out the players instead.

August: Good news! John Lennon's long awaited comeback lurched a step closer when Geffen Records signed him and Elton John.

December: Bad news! John Lennon's long-awaited comeback took an irreversible step backwards when a guy came up to him outside his hotel in New York and shot him dead.

Hit of the Year: 'Don't Stand So Close To Me' by the Police (should have been John Lennon!).

My, My, It's Lady Di

Britain had another new game to rival football hooliganism and Monopoly. It was called 'Guess who Prince Charles is going to Marry'. It seemed that every day a new aristocratic young wench would be dragged through the gutter press as a potential Queen of England. Poor old Charlie, it must be said, would have had to have been a super-stud to have got through all that lot and, actually, if the truth be told, might have been happier remaining a bachelor. It

I hear he only likes virgins

ROYAL AUDITIONS – QUEUE HERE.

was, therefore, with some considerable relief that it was announced on the 24th February that he was going to marry a pretty, butter-wouldn't-melt-in-her-mouth, super-posh 19 year old called Lady Diana Spencer, daughter of Earl Spencer (who'd once been his mum's equerry). As A N Wilson rather cruelly put it, in his brilliant and illuminating *Rise and Fall of the House of Windsor*, Prince Charles, just about the most eligible bachelor in the world, had chosen a bride, in the same way as the guy who leaves buying his presents to the last minute and rushes round on Christmas Eve picking up what's left. Little did he, she or we know that in a few years' time, shy Di would become more famous and press-worthy than all the other Royals put together.

Needless to say, all those old coaches were dragged out and dusted down, the big grey horses were tied to the fronts of them, the men in the silly hats sat on them, and the flagging Union Jack industry went into overtime so that the long-suffering British public would again have something to wave.

Brixton Blows Up
There was, however, one group of the community that, given half a chance, would have waved far more than flags at the royal pair. On 4th April, Brixton, a South London suburb, exploded in an orgy of burning, looting and violence the like of which had never before been seen in this country. Before you could say 'Bob Marley', every black teenager had exploded and set off on a terrifying rampage 'as a protest against police harassment'.

Rioting soon became craze of the month throughout most major towns in Britain. Everyone blamed everyone else, but it soon became obvious that the whole thing no longer had anything to do with blacks, police methods, lack of teenage prospects, or the terribly high price of drugs. It was just an excuse for young, bored kids to go berserk and do all the things that they'd longed to do while standing around, bored out of their wits on street corners. The riots, therefore, were a phenomenon which disappeared, like ice lollies in a sauna, as quickly as they had arrived.

Gang of Four
On the British political scene something occurred that made people who thought the two major parties were as useless and predictable as each other, sit up and pay attention. A 'gang' of four senior members of the Labour Party were given the elbow for forming a 'Council for Social Democracy', which was a posh name for a new clique fed up with the party's silly extremism. The four – Shirley Williams, Dr David Owen, 'Woy' Jenkins and William Rodgers – formed their own little party called the Social

Democrats, and all of the 'middle of the roaders', after the initial excitement had died down, waited (and waited, and w . . a . . i . . t . . e . . d), to hear their policies.

Thatcher Digs In

Just as the Labour Party were going further left, Maggie (now totally in charge) was definitely going further right. For a start, she had announced plants to sell off all the nationalised industries starting with British Aerospace. This was like a slap in the face with a wet kipper to the poor old Labour chaps for whom nationalisation was central to their beliefs. They also knew that once she'd done it, it would be practically impossible to reverse the process if they ever got back. In other words . . . they were about to be well and truly shafted.

Ripper Found

The now famous Yorkshire Ripper – a lorry driver called Peter Sutcliffe – confessed to killing and mutilating 13 women. He claimed he'd done them in because he was round the bend but the jury didn't think so (can carving up women who you've never seen before be perfectly natural behaviour?). When sentenced to life, Sutcliffe (who looked as normal as you or me) was totally impassive, though his poor wife, Sonia, seemed a little put out when she realised what he'd been up to on his nights out.

A Pop at a Pope

Why is it that only the nice people get shot at? On 15th May, an armed Turkish nutter leapt out of the crowd and shot the Pope four times (bad move if you want to get to heaven) as he was on multitude-blessing duty. I don't know if John Paul II was wearing his papal bullet-proof robe (well – he mit're been!) but either way, he survived the attack. It later turned out that the very undelightful Turkish gentleman who was known as 'Grey Wolf' was part of a much larger communist plot.

A month earlier, a disc jockey had tried to assassinate dear old President Reagan outside the O K Corral (sorry, it was really a hotel in Washington). Ex-film gunslinger Reagan was lucky to be heading for hospital rather than Boot Hill, but when the surgeons were preparing to dig the bullet out, he was still able to quip 'I hope you guys are Republicans', which really ain't bad for a decrepit old world leader.

On 30th June, the Queen fell off her horse when six shots were fired during the Trooping of the Colour. The shots turned out to be only blanks, but I don't suppose the horse (or the Queen) knew that.

Poles Poleaxed
It had to happen. Like day follows night, the long-awaited clampdown on Solidarity, the free trade union movement in Poland, by the Soviet-led authorities, ended in the arrest of 14,000 trade unionists including their hero leader Lech Walesa. A Military Council of National Salvation was set up, which was just a neat name for an organisation designed to put all the unionists and dissidents back in their boxes.

Meanwhile

January: A shudder went through the readers of *The Times* and *The Sunday Times* when it was bought by the owner of *The Sun* –

Australian Rupert Murdoch. Still, it could have been worse. At least he hasn't made us gawp at up-market, half-naked ladies on page 3 (yet).

February: Torvill and Dean, the squeaky-clean young ice dancers from Nottingham, won the European Ice Skating Championship. The best thing about it was that the championship had been in Russian hands for 12 years. The worst thing was that they were to make this naff 'ballroom-dancing-on-ice' even *more* popular.

March: The Sony Walkman, the first portable tape player, had taken the world by storm. At last kids could ruin their hearing without mum and dad knowing anything about it. Now a new band called Heaven 17 produced an album called *Music for Stowaways* specially for it.

April: Steve Davis, the red-headed snooker player, who looks like one of those faded plaster dummies in old-fashioned gentlemen's outfitters, won the World Championship at the age of 23. Later a production company tried to make him into a TV chat show host, but poor Steve snookered them well and truly by turning out to be even more boring than he looked.

May: Ken Livingstone – the man who sounds as if he's got a couple of the newts he breeds stuck up his nose – became the new leader of the Greater London Council. Despite being criticised for giving grants to organisations like 'Gay, Elderly, Ethnic Minorities Against Cruelty To Deaf, Incontinent Whales', he did become a firm favourite amongst Londoners.

July: Trouble broke out in Southall (now a suburb of Delhi) when a delightfully named skinhead band, The 4 Skins, were booked to appear in this predominantly Asian community. The skinhead supporters, who shared one brain cell (sometimes) and were known to be right of Margaret Thatcher (and racist with it) set fire to the hall that their band was playing in. Now that's what I call bright!

August: Moira Stewart, bless her, became Britain's first black newsreader.

September: Marcus Serjeant, the 17 year old lad who'd shot blanks at the Queen in June, got five years in prison. Daft really, if he'd done it to anyone else he probably wouldn't have been arrested. I wonder what he'd have got if he'd used real ammo. Probably a bedsitter in the tower!

October: A report came out stating that one in eight children lived in a one parent family. I wonder where the other poor little perishers lived. Out in the shed maybe.

November: British Leyland announced that they were to develop a new car with the Japanese motorcycle company, Honda. The scheme was called Project X and the car, I believe, ended up with only two wheels.

December: Two extremely nice Iranians were blown up when a bomb they were carrying through Marble Arch in London unsportingly went off.

Album of the Year: *Flesh and Blood* by Roxy Music.

1982

Thatcher V The Unions

There was simply no doubt in Maggie's mind that she'd been chosen by God (a family friend) to head the Tory Party and, therefore, the country, because she was the only politician ballsy enough to tell the unions where to get off. There would be no 'beer and sandwiches' meetings round at Number Ten, like the old Labour days; and there would certainly be no attempt to sweet-talk the union barons.

Maggie was not intimidated by the unions and to show she meant business she employed Norman Tebbit (a known union basher), who had the menacing manner and chilly charm of a Chingford (where he was from) undertaker, to head the Department of Employment. Together, they outlawed secondary strikes and strengthened the rights of individuals against closed shops (companies that weren't allowed to employ non-union labour). They also gave employers more clout to sack lousy employees without the unions breathing heavily down their necks, and made it far more likely that those unions would have to dig deep and pay compensation for all the trouble they caused.

Having said all this, however, the economic situation was playing right into Maggie's sweaty palm. With a shrinking market, lower orders, factory closures, mass redundancies, vast reductions of membership and nasty Norm standing over them, the unions were hardly in any position to push their weight around or call any shots. They were (whether you like it or not) never to have the same power again.

Falklands Fury

Meanwhile, miles away from Britain, an event occurred that was to have consequences that no one could ever have foreseen. Way out in the ocean, near to the bottom bit of Argentina, Britain had a tiny, far flung, football-pitch-sized colony called the Falkland Islands. A mere 1800 inbred people lived on this rather gloomy little outcrop with a few inbred grubby sheep.

On 31st March, a group of Argentine scrap-metal dealers landed on one of the islands (South Georgia) and raised the Argentine flag. Cheeky! but not world-shattering. On 2nd April, 12,500 Argentinians invaded without any warning, overwhelming (with no loss of life) the handful of sleepy Royal Marines, who'd picked the short straw and were guarding the islands (see easy but dead boring jobs). It appeared that the cruel military junta who were running Argentina, thought it would be a real laugh to nick back 'their' property before the islanders could have a party to celebrate their 150 years of occupation.

A huge fuss broke out, ending with Britain breaking off diplomatic relations with Argentina (big deal) and the United Nations asking the Argentinians, nicely, to withdraw (even bigger deal).

Maggie Goes Mad
Her that must be obeyed (Grand Führer Thatcher) went potty, seeing the invasion as a direct personal challenge, and with

Can't we find anything smaller to attack?

questionable, to say the least, attempts to find a non-violent solution, including the rejection of US General Haig's peace plan, she prepared a load of warships to be led by the aircraft carriers Hermes and Invincible. They set off at full steam on 8th April on their 8,000 mile journey. Many of us in Britain wondered what all the fuss was about. It certainly didn't seem worth one soldier, sailor or airman even getting a nosebleed over these dreary little sheep-nibbled islands.

All the troops loved it, of course (in the beginning). They at last had a chance to play proper soldiers and shoot their guns *for real*. And they did – much to the joy of the gutter press who descended to the very depths of the cesspit in their so-called news reporting.

As the death toll started climbing, however, world opinion started to look across at Britain and wonder:

a. Weren't we beginning to enjoy all this a little too much?
and

b. Wasn't it all a pathetic, sword-brandishing attempt to show
that we were still a big tough nation?

Rubbish we told ourselves. All was going fine. The Argies (as the tabloids called them) were dying like flies, all our fab equipment was working a treat and Margaret Thatcher, our brave leader, could deservedly strut around like Churchill and Hitler rolled into one.

Then, on 4th May, our HMS Sheffield was sunk by one of the Argentinian missiles (supplied by our chums the French) and Britain blubbed like a playground bully that had finally been stood up to. Suddenly, against all the odds, the surprisingly brill and brave Argentinian pilots started carving up (and sinking) our boats. Unbelievable cock-ups were caused by our almost totally inept field commanders, who scurried around blaming each other like public school sneaks, and whole battalions of our troops were found to be unfit to even manage an average route march. To cut a long and extremely distasteful story short, however, Britain did gradually start to make corned beef (literally) of the pathetically under-trained, under-equipped (and under-age) Argentinian army. On the 14th July, they surrendered having lost 650 brave young men. We lost 250 of our, equally brave, lads.

The 'war' was won, Margaret Thatcher was a hero, her job was saved, and she had proved once again that no one ever messes with her or the British. Well, that was the theory anyway. More than that, we'd finally managed to beat someone, all by ourselves, without the help of those clever-dick Americans.

History might well disagree, however, as some military experts believe Maggie was damn lucky. If we'd been up against even a half-decent army, or if some of the Commie big boys had joined in, it might well have been a very different story.

Postscript: Only four years later, Argentina beat Britain in the Quarter Finals of the World Cup. Does that, or does it not, say it all!?!?

Meanwhile

January: Oh dear, oh dear. Maggie faced severe criticism at the news that unemployment had reached the all time record of 3 million. Norman Tebbit, unbelievably, blamed the weather.

February: Sir Freddie Laker, who'd brought Britain the cut-price air fare, had to watch in horror as his huge airline took a nosedive and crashed. The recession, rising interest rates, and the decline in the value of the £ against the $ were blamed.

• De Lorean cars, produced in Ireland, backed by £17.5 million of our best British money, also went up the Swannee. John De Lorean, flash ex-boss of General Motors in America, thought he could make a killing with his rather vulgar-looking new sports car. Unfortunately, too many people agreed with me. For years, the US courts tried to pin everything from cocaine dealing to embezzlement on poor John, but to no avail. Interesting to note: if he hadn't gone under, he could have been our last surviving motor manufacturer.

June: *Question.* What's pink and hangs under our London bridges?
Answer. Italian bankers.

On 19th June, Roberto Calvi was found hanging under

Blackfriars Bridge. Nobody was quite sure how he got there.

• Lady Diana gave birth to her first heir to the throne. When Daddy was asked what they were going to call the little chap, Charles said rather distractedly 'You'll have to ask my wife, we're having a bit of an argument about that.' The first of many, dare I suggest.

How does one know what they eat?

August: The IRA really blew it public opinion-wise. Not content with simply wiping out soldiers, they blew up a detachment of the Blues and Royals (horse guards), and later the band of the Royal Green Jackets. All-in-all, eight soldiers were killed, but much, much worse, in the eyes of the British public . . . seven horses.

October: Prince (randy) Andrew had to cut short one of his all-expenses-paid holidays in Mustique, a Caribbean island, because the girl he was with was attracting too much attention. Apparently 'actress' Koo Stark had appeared nearly starkers in a bluish movie. Koo!! I think she sounded a lot better than the usual Sloane Rangers he pulled.

September: One of the most distasteful crimes ever seen in Britain was solved. Police found the trousers of Sir Geoffrey Howe, a

185

Cabinet Minister, stolen from a train while he was asleep. I've heard of pickpockets, but this was ridiculous.

December: 20,000 women held hands to encircle the Greenham Common Nuclear Weapons Base at Greenham Common. The nuclear missiles, about which they were protesting, eventually left in their own good time.

1983

Thatcher Reigns Supreme
All those who *didn't* see Mrs Thatcher as their saviour were gutted at the Tories' resounding victory at the General Election. But it *was* her victory, which ever way you looked at it, and the other parties knew from the start that all their little Davids (e.g. Owen and Steele) could not even touch the Tories' Goliathess.

The shabby Labour Party, led by the crusty (but soft-centred) Michael Foot, was practically wiped out in the South, while the new 'Alliance', this time between Steel's Liberals and the Gang of Four's sadly disappointing new Social Democratic party, only got 23 seats out of a possible 650.

Obviously the recipe for resounding political success in our rather sad little country (which had once bullied the world) was to get it into a war, and then to win that war resoundingly (first making sure the enemy had absolutely no chance of winning). There is no doubt, whatsoever, that 'victory' over the shaky Argentinian junta gave Maggie almost Hitlerian status amongst the vast (and growing) right of the electorate.

'Woy' Jenkins, realising he was flogging a dead ideal with the

Social Democrats, quit in the next few days, along with Labour 'leader' Michael Foot who resigned as PM and went back to his duffle coat and Hampstead supper-table intellectuals (though no one really noticed he'd gone). His place was taken by a jolly, red-haired, freckly 'boyo' from Wales called Neil Kinnock who, vigorous as he was, looked about as likely to be Prime Minister as Basil Brush (sorry, that's foxist).

Meanwhile, suave and handsome Dr Owen took over from Jenkins as head of the SDP and was then not heard of again for ages. He (and the rest of the Gang of Four) had, without any help from others, totally trashed their political careers by failing to come up with the cast-iron policies we'd all been waiting for. David Steel, after yet another broken 'love affair', with David Owen this time, crawled back into his little Liberal basket in Scotland and carried on dreaming.

Young Upwardly Mobile Professionals

We'd seen the birth of Sloane Rangers, punks, Hooray Henrys, hippies etc. etc. but now it was time for a completely new phenomenon. The 'yuppies' (see heading above) were a new mutation, and were beginning to make themselves felt in Britain – especially in the South, and especially in London. Due to Maggie's monetarist policies, credit had become very much the buzz word, and with it came the possibility to live wildly beyond one's means without ever (seemingly) needing to account for it. Suddenly every other car seemed to be a BMW or Porsche; wine and champagne bars spread like socially transmitted diseases; over-priced gymnasiums heaved with sweaty estate agents while house and flat prices went soaring through their roofs and kissing all and sundry on both cheeks became the 'in' thing at every opportunity.

Young people with less qualifications than Daffy Duck began making fortunes in the city – dealing in stocks, futures or simply money – all at a time when manufacturing, oddly enough, was in decline. The yuppies did all the things that in the past only 'old money' had done: attending summer balls and point-to-points, wearing brown trilbies and those awful snot-coloured waxed green jackets and buying cottages in France (while writing patronising books about them). To these fabulous Thatcher's Children, Maggie and her Chancellor, the profoundly greasy Nigel Lawson, were like gods. At last they'd made it possible to make paper fortunes, to buy whatever you wanted (whether you had the cash or not) without having to get your hands remotely dirty. Okay the chances were that their nerves would be shot away by the time they were thirty, but who cared? There were always plenty more where they came from. If you needed any more proof that the world was going screwy, the winner of 'Mastermind', that torture chamber for brainiacs, in 1983 was a certain Christopher Hughes – a (wait for it) London tube train driver.

Telly With Cornflakes

Another new phenomenon was the introduction of television the moment you opened your eyes. Obscenely jolly presenters, wearing too heavy make-up to cover the circles under their own eyes, fronted programmes, from naff mock living rooms that were about as inane as the newspapers they were replacing. Britain was beginning to suffer from too much news and current affairs. Indeed, you only had to fart in an unusual way and some precocious rookie reporter would be knocking at your front door for an interview.

The world seemed to be changing at an alarming rate. Suddenly, the safety police made you wear seat belts in your own car, which they then proceeded to incapacitate by strapping a horrid yellow clamp on one of its wheels if you were parked in the wrong place. Even if your car wasn't clamped, there was a fair chance the IRA would shove a bomb under it as they did outside Harrods in December 1988. If you did manage to get moving, then it was possible that the police would pull you over, drag you out and then shoot you, as they did only a stone's throw from Harrods, to a young guy called Stephen Waldorf whom they'd mistaken for someone else.

Don't worry Dave – his tax is out of date.

Cowboy Capers

Science fiction came a little closer when that old celluloid cowhand, Ronnie Reagan, announced a futuristic non-offensive missile shield called Star Wars right across the States to keep out the 'Evil Empire' (three guesses who they were?). Needless to say, the Russians did find it offensive, more or less claiming that it simply wasn't fair fighting (quite right). Mind you, they were fine ones to talk about fairness. In September, Russian fighters shot down a Korean airliner 'by accident', killing 269 passengers – and they didn't even say sorry. They did, however, claim that the plane had been spying over Siberia. Nice one, Russia. You often get a couple of hundred people going on spying holidays over barren wastelands.

Meanwhile

February: Who says civil servants are boring? Denis Nilsen was arrested on 11th February when police discovered two human heads, some flesh and a hand in his back garden in Hornsey, a suburb of London. Later the remains of 14 other bodies (all male) were found in and around the house. Nilsen was later found, strangely enough, to be homosexual. I must admit, it doesn't seem to me a very nice way to treat your boyfriends.

April: Britain's biggest robbery ever occurred when gunmen prised £7 million from a Security Express van.

May: Cliff Richard, the Dorian Grey (or should I say Heathcliff) of the pop world, celebrated 25 years in the business. Anyone else would have had the grace to retire but not our Cliff. Can you imagine him prancing around into his sixties? Good grief!

July: Mrs Victoria Gillick broke down after a High Court Judge refused to rule that it was illegal for a doctor to supply girls of under 16 with contraceptive pills without their mum's and dad's say so. Mrs Gillick didn't appear to believe in contraception herself as she had 10 nippers of her own!

September: The Social Democratic Party leader, David Owen, wasn't that thrilled with his limp little liaison with the Liberals. His party swore they'd have nothing to do with them for at least five years.

October: Smarmy Cecil Parkinson, who looks like everybody's idea of an upmarket lounge lizard, was fired from the Tory cabinet – much to everyone's delight. He'd been caught with his pinstripes well and truly round his ankles when it was discovered he'd just jilted his former secretary who was expecting his baby. As we've all learned, however, lying and cheating never really does you permanent harm in politics. He was later made a peer by his old mate Maggie.

December: Mehmet Ali Agca, the tetchy Turk who'd tried to kill the Pope, met the great man in his prison cell. Pope John was visiting the prison as a Christmas treat and even left a little gift for Mehmet. I bet it wasn't a cake with a file in it.

1984

Big Brother is Watching You

It was kind of spooky to note that, in the year that was the subject of George Orwell's famous book *1984* (written in 1948), 'Big Brother', a kind of world government that he predicted would one day rule our lives, seemed perilously close.

Firstly, Thatcher's Government, heavily breathed on by the Yanks, took the unprecedented step of banning unions at GCHQ, the secret government communications headquarters at Cheltenham, offering each of the employees £1000 to keep their traps shut. The Government said that they'd been forced to do it because the union movement had seen GCHQ as a weak link, as everything they handled was so damned sensitive. The unions could have, therefore, if they'd so desired, blackmailed the Tory Government into higher wage claims.

Secondly, a junior clerk at the Ministry of Defence split to the *Guardian* newspaper about the arrival of American Cruise Missiles at the Greenham Common base, and went swiftly to prison (without passing GO) for her trouble, highlighting the conflict between security and a country's right to know what the hell is going on.

Thirdly, our much boasted about 'special relationship' with America was shown to be the crock of horse-manure that it really was. Everyone over here suspected that instead of being the 'you scratch my back, I'll scratch yours' deal that Maggie and Ronnie were supposed to enjoy, the old Yankee thespian was manipulating her like a glove puppet. The question then became, who was controlling Reagan? Several incidents took place over the next few years that made us wonder whether we, or even those that spoke for us, had any real say over our destiny.

Trouble Down T'Pit

Arthur Scargill, that ferret-like champion (and president) of the moaning miners, saw union strength as the key to the building of a society fit for the working man. Thatcher, the pit-bull champion of the right, saw the unions as the main reason why the economy was rapidly disappearing down the post war plughole (and two fingers to the working man). She'd backed down three times from closing pits owing to little Arthur's threats – but not this time.

The '84 miners' strike, called to see who really had the biggest stick, started on 15th March. All the men-turned-yobbos that weren't underground, travelled the country preventing anyone else doing likewise. What they failed to grasp was that, due to cheap oil from the east, practically free gas and oil from our own North

Sea, smokeless zones in cities and 'nuclear' electricity, the demand for coal was becoming about the same as a drink of water to a drowning man.

On the miners' side – if, as in the past, essential industries had put their tools down, the Government would have found it difficult to send the troops in to keep things going because by 1984 the technology was becoming too sophisticated for soldiers to operate (and that ain't that sophisticated). Also, coal supplies were reckoned to be good for another 300 years, whereas the 'free' oil and gas would probably run out in 30 years or so.

Despite all this, Scargill didn't dare to have a national ballot and put it and himself to the test as he knew damn well he wouldn't get the majority he needed, so he decided to stick with the violence and bullying that had served him so well (and seemed so much more fun).

WIFE, KIDS AND ARTHUR SCARGILL'S EGO TO SUPPORT!

Bad Timing

Anyway, talk about a stupid time to have a fuel strike. The beginning of spring, and the imminent warm weather, is not exactly brilliant if you want to hold a country to ransom for coal, especially if the reserve coal supplies are as high as Scargill's ego.

By May, the nastiness started in earnest. The normal shirt-pulling scraps on the picket lines became much more violent, and then a couple of strikers dropped a huge slab of concrete off a bridge in South Wales. It landed, 'coincidentally', on a passing cab taking some miners to work, so killing the driver. Then Scargill, using a false name (Ferdie Ferret?), shot over to Paris to meet one of the frightful Libyan Leader, Colonel Gaddafi's, right-hand men. He had gone there, it was alleged, to get money and, unbelievably, guns, to fight the good fight. Gaddafi later claimed to have given the cheeky chap £163,000, which Scargill allegedly used to pay off his personal mortgage.

The strike seemed to go on forever, and many of the miners, who hadn't been exactly dying to strike in the first place, went through hardships the like of which hadn't been seen since the 30s. They then, grudgingly, began drifting back to work.

Maggie Digs In

Thatcher, and *her* new puppet American Ian MacGregor, Chairman of the Coal Board, who came only second to Noel Edmonds in subtlety, just sat back on her throne, knowing full well that Scargill's hypnotic (and despotic) hold over his fellow miners simply couldn't last. Anyway, any character assassination could be left to the man himself.

The writing was well on the wall by December when his boys, realising they were backing a loser, began traipsing back underground with their spades between their legs. Thatcher had 'won' another battle and her revolution was now fully secure. The battle with the union (any union) was over for years to come.

Meanwhile

January: Top pop group, at the beginning of the year, was Culture Club, which was led by half-man, half-pantomime dame (and half-wit) Boy George.

February: Borevill – sorry – Torvill and Dean beat the Ruskies to the Olympic Gold Medal for the recently included 'sport' of ice dancing. Hands up for Olympic Flower Arranging – it's just as naff!

April: Fatherly love? I don't think so. Marvin Gaye, one of the fabbest of the old style soul singers, was shot dead by his dad (an ex-church minister) over an argument about insurance. You can bet it wasn't life insurance.

June: Talk about milking the applause. Eric Morecambe, one of our funniest and most loved entertainers, died of a heart attack having taken six curtain calls at the Tewkesbury Theatre. His sad little straight man, Ernie Wise, later implied that Eric had held him back career-wise. Sure Ern, just as Batman held Robin back!

• Another sad departure, that of Sir John Betjeman, the teddy bear like Poet Laureate, occurred this month. His great skill had been to make us review, with affection, all those mundane, tasteless things that we'd always taken for granted.

July: There's a welcome at McDonald's, unless you happen to be waiting at the San Ysidro branch, California. Oliver Huberty (such a jolly name) strode into the restaurant and fired indiscriminately, killing 20 and injuring 16 men, women and children. C'mon Ollie, the Chicken McNuggets weren't *that* bad!!

September: The world expert on all things architectural, Prince Charles, compared the new extension of the National Gallery to 'a monstrous carbuncle on the face of a well-loved friend'. I wonder who got to the mirror first, Princess Di or Mrs Camilla Parker-Bowles?

October: The cowardly IRA hit the bull's-eye when, on 12th October, they blew up the Grand Hotel in Brighton, where the Cabinet was staying while attending the Tory Party Conference. One MP died and more than 30 were injured, including the normally unruffable Norman Tebbit. Maggie was, as usual, unhurt – one of the advantages of being an Iron Lady.

November: There were two female Prime Ministers in the world at the beginning of the month, but by the end Mrs Thatcher was alone. Indira Gandhi, Prime Minister of India, was assassinated by her bodyguards (bad choice, I'd have said) as she walked in the garden of her New Delhi house (well, old New Delhi house). The night before, she'd said to a reporter 'If I die today, every drop of my blood will invigorate the nation.' Seems like her bodyguards took her at her word.

December: Everyone in Britain had watched helplessly as millions of starving Ethiopians perished on our tellys every night. Bob Geldof, him of The Boomtown Rats, shocked our mean politicians by getting off his backside and actually doing something. His single 'Don't They Know It's Christmas', though awful, was recorded with some of the pop greats, provided loads of much-needed money to help the drought-wrecked country. Friends of all people, Grand Empress Thatcher, refused to drop the £500,000 VAT bill due on the record's profits, probably as revenge for being shown up so badly.

1985

The Poorly Pound

There couldn't have been a better time for the Labour Party to launch their strongest attack on Margaret Thatcher as the Tories had left practically an open goal. The economy was as unpredictable as a royal marriage and only those fast-burning city wise guys could really understand (and profit from) what was going down. Unemployment was soaring, manufacturing was plunging, the stock market was booming, but the £ had plummeted so low against the $ that (for the first time ever) they were nearly the same value. This had the nasty side-effect of a Britain rapidly filling with awful department-store dressed American tourists, who were buying up just about everything that wasn't screwed down (let's face it, they'd already had our London Bridge).

Poor Neil Kinnock, however, had turned out to be no match for the magnificent Margaret in Parliament. Instead of witty repartee, he just went redder and louder. Indeed, the last person even to begin to make her look foolish had been Jim Callaghan who, like Wilson, had disappeared almost without trace.

Loonies

Neil had his own problems, however, dealing with what came to be known as the Loony Left, whose golden boy seemed to be 'Red' Ken Livingstone. When the howl went up on the announcement that the Labour-led Greater London Council was to be scrapped by the Government, Kinnock must have secretly heaved a sigh of relief, as their 'leftie' antics had been getting too much hilarious tabloid coverage. Ken's GLC had supported and financed everything from gay and lesbian groups to peace movements and ethnic tenant associations. Following his lead, many other local governments started employing one another's officers until it all became one huge job for the boys – in other words, a lucrative carve-up by the extreme left.

Livingstone had become the male equivalent of tabloid-sized Samantha Fox (a blond bimbo currently famous for her huge b . . . rain) as he could also always be relied on to fill column inches ridiculing the Royals, admiring the IRA, and mocking monetarism by giving away nigh on £9 billion to the daftest of causes while in power (£250,000 of which was allegedly spent on his farewell party). But by now the looniness had spread. Haringey was giving courses on homosexuality to school kids, comparing Hitler's policies to Thatcher's union reforms, and ordering everyone to drink only Nicaraguan coffee. Lewisham voted £64,000 towards financing complaints against the police, and Hackney gave up its cosy little town-twinning arrangements with France and West Germany in favour of the Soviet Union.

Across the rest of the country the labour left were not only loonified but pretty sinister too. In Liverpool, a group called 'Militant Tendency', who were about as left as you can go before meeting up with the far right, had become almost a branch of the Communists, and were getting a stranglehold on the city council led by John Hamilton and his horribly flash deputy Derek Hatton (who was already receiving £10,000 year for a 17-hour week from another labour council). They were throwing around so much dosh that everyone in Liverpool (provided they were lesbian, black, one-parent or communist) thought every day was Christmas and praised them greatly. It was not only infuriating to Thatcher's Government but jolly embarrassing to Neil Kinnock. In the end, the corruption within 'Militant' became so blatant that the easy-going Kinnock had to pull his Welsh finger out and wage war on them, which pushed his ratings quite high for the first time ever. But the damage was done. The Loony Left had put paid to the Labour Party being taken seriously for years and years to come. Instead of a two-party system, it was now a one-party system and almost a one-woman system. Thatcher was as near as you could get to being a fully paid up dictator.

Gorby Mania

Unbelievably, news came from Russia that the next supreme head of the 'Evil Empire' (USSR) was a rather jolly-looking sort, called Mikhail Gorbachev, who had a birthmark that looked suspiciously like a map of America on his forehead. His wife, Raisa, seemed positively normal and nice, unlike most other Soviet leaders' wives, who had looked like Les Dawson's (God rest his soul) ugly sisters.

Only a few months earlier, Reagan, who'd been the butt of just about every joke in America and Britain, nevertheless romped home with a resounding victory to take a second term as President of the United States of America. A new game was set with Gorby and Ronnie as the two main contestants and the increasingly cocky Mrs Thatcher fully believing that she was the third.

198

Britain's Hooligans win 41-0

On 29th May, Britain's reputation abroad hit the decks when our own home-grown British football hooligans went on the rampage during the Juventus-Liverpool match, causing a riot which crushed to death 41 and injured 350 Italian and Belgian supporters. Football haters and fans alike were not that displeased when the Football Association banned English teams from playing abroad until further notice.

Music Mania

It's now the middle of the 80s and time to see what's going down on the music scene – man! From America, we had the ear-splitting country rock band ZZ Top, a group consisting of two long white beards with three men attached. Also, they sent us the androgynous (but brilliant) Prince, who looked like just about everything that your mother wouldn't like to meet. Bruce Springsteen, who'd perfected the greasy-truck-driver-with-the-mean-guitar look, was selling more records than anyone else, while the soon-to-be-weird Michael Jackson, for some obscure reason bought ATV Music, whose jewel in its crown was the rights to all the earlier (and better) Beatles songs. He paid £34 million which, one day, could have come in very useful (see page 247).

England's Wham, consisting of the pretty George Micheldopulous (Michael to you) and Andrew Ridgely (who?), became the first group to go to China. They claimed it was a goodwill trip, but I bet the potential un-got-to 200 million record buyers could just conceivably have had something to do with it. Unfortunately the poor Chinese, who for donkey's years had been forced to live on a diet of whiney, screechy patriotic songs,

a. Couldn't make head or tail of their music, and

b. Didn't find the two lads nearly as yummy as the girls back here did.

Wham were sharing the UK charts with the 'Why-am-I-so-gloomy-and-so-rich' Phil Collins, the 'Which-of-us-is-getting-the-most-limelight' Eurythmics, and the 'Does-being-outrageous-really-mean-that-I-can't-have-hair' Elton John.

Meanwhile

January: Sir Clive Sinclair, the computer wizard, who was everyone's idea of a boffin, proved that even geniuses have to have a day off. The silly scientist brought out an electric car, called the C5, which resembled a surgical boot with wheels on. If you want to travel around at 5 m.p.h. looking a total prat, before having your head cleaved from your body by an overtaking milk float, then this, dear readers, was the motor for you. Two months later production was 'suspended'.

February: Terry Waite, resembling R. Hood's huge best mate 'Little John', had the job of doing all the dirty work for the Archbishop of Canterbury. As his 'Special Envoy', Terry had the unenviable task of going round the most dangerous places in the world trying to sweet-talk nasty people into giving him our political hostages back. On 8th Feb., he did manage to get four released from Libya. So far so good!

April: The Government announced plans to ban all alcohol from football stadiums. Now I might be a bit dim, but wouldn't there be a faint danger of them getting totally sloshed *before* the match?

May: Roy Plomley, the immensely stuffy, but rather dear, host of radio's 'Desert Island Discs', that strangely English symbol of 'making it', went to his great island in the sky. I wonder if they put a copy of *The Bible, The Complete Works of Shakespeare*, and his chosen luxury (a radio?) in his casket with him?

July: Mangy Bob Geldof did it again. His vast Live Aid concert at Wembley, starring the cream of rock music, raised a staggering £40 million to help the hungry Ethiopians. Geldof was, all but, made a saint by the embarrassed Establishment. Mind you, you'd have to be a saint to be married to Paula Yates.

September: Up and up he goes. Jeffrey Archer, darling of those people who only read one book a year (smothered in suntan oil), was made Deputy Chairman of the Tory Party, a decision as unlikely as one of his plots.
• Laura Ashley, queen of safe, twee, suburban decoration and wimpy women's clothing, fell down the stairs to her death. Anyone, however, who thought we'd seen the last of those long flowery frocks and sissy chintzy curtains was sadly disappointed.

October: Just as the AIDS scare was reaching its zenith, the news came that the ultra-smooth film star, Rock Hudson, had just died from it. People were most shocked by the possible implication that this 'rock'-like symbol of machismo had never really fancied all the beautiful women he'd starred with. What a waste!

November: Maggie Thatcher and the Irish Prime Minister, Dr Garret Fitzgerald, signed what was regarded as the monumental Anglo-Irish Agreement. It gave the Irish Republic a proper saying in the running of Northern Ireland. Needless to say, it had as much impact as a rabid mouse in a football stadium.

1986

Westland Wonders

In January, the whole country was given ringside seats to a pitched battle within the Tory Cabinet. It was all over a once rather prestigious, but now sinking, helicopter manufacturer called Westland, who the flamboyant Michael Heseltine (Defence Secretary) wanted to save by selling to a sort of European helicopter consortium (Eurochopper?). His rival in the Government, swarthy Trade and Industry Secretary, Leon Brittan, admitted leaking to the press a government law officer's letter criticising the way Heseltine did his job. Brittan, who loved the Yanks and free enterprise, thought Sikorsky the US helicopter giant should put some of their cash into Westland, and had leaked this letter to make Heseltine look an incompetent twerp, so blowing any chance of a European deal.

Hot-head Heseltine had resigned a couple of days earlier, after charging out of a Cabinet Meeting in a fit of pique, when his boss Maggie had ticked him off by saying that in future all his public utterances should be vetted by her. Many of his Cabinet colleagues thought Heseltine's sudden disappearance meant that he'd been caught short and had gone for another leak but when, hours later, he hadn't returned, their pennies dropped as well! Heseltine was soon to become the darling of the back benchers, being the first person to dare to stand up to her-that-must-be-obeyed.

The whole smutty little affair backfired on Mrs T. when she tried to deny knowing anything about the famous first leak. Everyone, fans or not, then realised that her way of doing things needed severe watching.

Kinnock had yet another open goal when he got up to make his 'let's-trash-Thatcher-and-all-she-stands-for' speech in the Commons, but the ball dribbled to a stop before reaching the goal mouth and Maggie got out of the whole debate virtually unscathed.

All this was much enjoyed from the touchline by old Edward Heath who, never having recovered from being deposed by a 'mere' woman, seemed to have a personal vendetta against poor little Margaret.

Russian Roulette

Anyone who was the tiniest bit bothered about the way we got our nuclear power, shuddered when they heard of the fire at the Chernobyl nuclear power station in the Ukraine region of the USSR. Not without good reason. An American satellite, which just 'happened' to be flying overhead wearing its binoculars, noted that the station had literally blown its top off. A cloud of cancer-causing, tree-withering, milk-curdling horribleness had leaked right over Scandinavia and even threatened Northern Europe. Almost amusingly, the number of American tourists due to 'do' Europe mysteriously dropped, as they obviously thought we were all glowing and buzzing.

I wonder how they'll market radio-active milk?

America Blunders

The United States was getting into a right pickle internationally. There'd been a bit of a ding-dong between US and Libyan jets over the Mediterranean, but when America launched a full scale surprise attack on Libya, setting off from Britain (to save petrol), everyone accused them, and us, of war-mongering (who us? Never). Maggie was also accused of being simply the stool-pigeon of the Americans, having no say in what they did or didn't do.

On top of this, someone spilt the beans and claimed that the cash made by the Yanks from selling arms to Iran (dodgy in the first place) had been used to finance the Contra rebels fighting the leftie government in Nicaragua. The 'Irangate scandal', as it was called, nearly threw Reagan from the saddle. A horribly slick, all-American colonel, Oliver (Ollie) North, took most of the rap (lightly, on the back of the hand) when he admitted doing an 'arms for hostages' deal with the Iranians, using our dear, but somewhat naive, Terry Waite, as an innocent pawn. Reagan was later forced to admit that he knew all about it. By this time, however, the American people, who hadn't forgotten Nixon and rather expected lying and deception in high places let him off with a caution.

Condoms Galore

The Government launched its biggest ever health campaign in November, to try to stop the ravages of the AIDS virus from swamping Britain. Most at risk seemed to be male gays, bisexuals and needle-pricked druggies, but experts confidently expected Acquired Immune Deficiency Syndrome (AIDS) to huff and puff at the rest of us until it blew our defences down. The message was 'stick to one partner, use condoms, and if you have to take drugs, don't share your needles'.

Meanwhile

January: Mrs Thatcher and President Mitterand of France simply couldn't wait to meet each other underground. The Channel Tunnel project, which had started and stopped like a seaside donkey, was finally to go ahead. But when?
• The American Challenger space shuttle went up in smoke – literally – when it blew to pieces seconds after take off. All seven of the crew were tragically blown to kingdom come. Back to the drawing board.

February: One of the dangers of letting your Prime Minister out for a walk by his or herself is that people might really show what they think of them. Olof Palme, PM of Sweden, was strolling home from the movies when a man jumped out of the shadows and shot him dead. I bet our Mrs Thatcher would've frightened any attacker off!

April: Some people choose terrible partners. Poor pregnant Anne-Marie Murphy was stopped by customs as she was about to board a plane to Tel Aviv, and found to be carrying a 10lb bomb in the bottom of her bag. It was timed to go off over London while she and her 360 fellow passengers were ordering their first drinks (Molotov cocktails?). Nezar Hindawi, her Jordanian boyfriend, who'd promised to meet her in Tel Aviv later, was arrested in London, and charged with planting the bomb on the hapless girl. I believe Anne-Marie later called the romance off. Some people are so unforgiving.

Here you are darling. Just a little something for the journey.

• I hope Clint Eastwood said a bit more than he did in his movies when he became Mayor of Carmel, California. He was paid $200 a month. Hardly a fistful of dollars.

May: Super-cricketer Ian Botham was banned from first class cricket for smoking dope. Strangely enough, they didn't seem to mind him being a loud-mouthed yob.

June: Baa baa black sheep, have you any wool? Well Cumbrian lambs might have been all right for that, but you couldn't eat the little bleaters. They'd been contaminated by that horrid Chernobyl cloud.

July: Friend of the Africans (remember the VAT demand (see page 196), Margaret Thatcher, restated her opposition to sanctions against South Africa, because 'it would hurt the blacks most'. Mind you, Maggie, they did have far, far less to lose than your white chums.

August: Drag out those Royal coaches, it's time to wave those rather tattered flags and stir up a bit of patriotism. This time it was for the wedding of the loud, freckly, red-head (sounds like Neil Kinnock) Sarah Ferguson who was getting hitched to Prince Andrew. Had all the guests realised what was going to happen to this love match, they'd have bought their wedding presents sale or return.
• Henry Moore, the sculptor, who put his whole into his holes, died on 14th August. Many reckon he was to sculpture what Picasso was to painting. Others think he was to sculpture what Shakespeare was to plumbing.

October: The long awaited Big Bang, a nickname given to the turning over of the London Stock Exchange to computers on 27th October, turned out to be a damp squib when the whole system went down after an hour. (It was all right later, however, when they'd changed the plug.)

• Jeffrey Archer resigned as Deputy Chairman of the Conservatives when it was alleged that he had tried to finance a prostitute's quickly arranged foreign holiday to avoid a scandal. He said that he had never met the girl, but thought it a good idea to give her money to go away.

November: It was a sad month for movie fans. The great Hollywood heart-throb Archibald Leach died. Archibald Leach? I hear you cry. Sorry, he was slightly better known by his stage name Cary Grant.

December: Just as sadly missed, SuperMac, Harold Macmillan, died aged 92. We all looked wistfully back to a time when you could look up to a Prime Minister as a father figure (but not mother figure!).

1987

Waite-ing in Beirut

Brave Terry Waite, the Archbishop of Canterbury's Special (if a bit too trusting) Envoy was over in war-torn Beirut trying to save foreign hostages held by the extremely nice 'Party of God', whose boss was that extremely nice Ayatollah Khomeini. One day the huge man dismissed his guards, saying that some extremely nice men he'd met were taking him to see the hostages. Many might have thought it was like going into a lion's cage and asking the lions to look the other way, but not our Terry. His shining belief in

his fellow man positively glittered as he left with his 'guides'.
Needless to say, he disappeared without trace.

Enterprise Goes Under

One of the great tragedies at sea happened on 6th March when
the car ferry *Herald of Free Enterprise*, carrying hundreds of
passengers, literally up-ended just off the coast of Zeebrugge
(Belgium). It was like a nightmare remake of that film *The
Poseidon Adventure* with passengers trapped underwater in the
gradually sinking hull. Over 200 men, women and children died
the most frightful death in the near-freezing water. It turned out
that the Dover-bound ferry had suffered the same fate as the one
mentioned all those years before off the Irish coast (see page 40):
some silly idiot had forgotten to close the huge doors that let the
cars and – given half a chance – water in.

Thatcher Goes Walkabout

Meanwhile, Maggie put on her warm underwear and ventured to
Moscow to discuss disarmament with new-boy Gorbachev. The
Russians, always fond of a dictator, seemed relatively pleased to see
her, and some even kissed her on the cheek (the cheek!). In a
supermarket she bought, for no explicable reason, a tin of
pilchards and a loaf (probably because it was all they had).

Didn't someone else once do something with loaves and fish?

208

In June, her Iron Ladyship was re-elected for a staggering, history-making third term. All the opposition parties, crushed by the result, either blamed each other or the weather.

Property Madness

One of the reasons for her High and Mightiness's runaway victory was still based on the fact that if you *had* money or property, the Tories made sure you got even more (albeit on paper). House prices were still going through the roof and, if you had a reasonable sized house, especially if it was in the South, you could lounge around, safe in the knowledge that it would be earning you almost as much as if you worked.

To give you some idea of how silly it got, a Mrs Grace Newbold offered £36,000 for a converted shed measuring 5ft 6ins by 11ft in Knightsbridge. If that wasn't bad enough, it was decorated throughout with Laura Ashley wallpaper.

Sex and Nippers

The most amazing chain of events started on 29th June when Dr Marietta Higgs, a local paediatrician (and nosy parker) in Cleveland, announced that hundreds of kids were being 'tampered with' by their mummies and daddies. Over 200 children were promptly whipped away from their homes and put into care. The whole business got so out of hand that parents even became frightened of bathing their children in case they were done for indecency. The stupid woman was later found to be as wrong as all the claims she'd made but the damage, unfortunately, had already been done.

England Gets Windy

On 16th October, a light breeze turned into a wind. Then the wind turned into a bit of a gale. As it increased, TV viewers rang Michael Fish the TV weatherman (the one who dresses like a 70s office boy), to see if it was going to get any worse. He looked at his bit of seaweed and laughingly told them not to worry. That night 110 m.p.h. winds ripped through Southern England causing the worst damage this century. Trees fell like British Test wickets, especially in Sevenoaks (now 'One-oak', after the demise of the other six).

Stocks Hit the Deck

Another worst for the century! And it simply *had* to happen. On 19th October (Black Monday), £50 billion was wiped off the value of publicly quoted companies. It was like a tower of cards tumbling as all the smart city boys scrambled over each other, trying not to lose their shirts (and red braces), let alone their Porsches and smart docklands flats. It was the end of a Thatcher inspired 'bull' market that had seen shares shoot up three and a half times over the previous three years. The sight of grown men weeping as they watched their VDU screens tell them that the game called 'Get Rich Quick' was up, was enough to make even the bravest of onlookers . . . laugh his head off!

This was just the beginning of the next all-too-predictable decline in the nation's fortunes, soon to be labelled the Recession.

Good News

After a year of horrible news, a hint of better things to come happened on 8th December when Ronnie and Gorby (without Her Maggie-sty) signed the first-ever treaty to start sending their nuclear weapons to the breaker's yard. Everyone remarked how well the old cowboy and Comrade Map-head seemed to get on. Reagan could only remember one bit of Russian – 'Doverai no proverai' which meant 'Trust but verify'. Later Gorbachev was to look patronisingly at the poor old yank and mutter witheringly 'You repeat that at every meeting.'

Meanwhile

January: The term 'political correctness' hadn't even been born but poor old Noddy suffered from it anyway. MacDonald's Publishers daftly admitted, after a hammering from whinging nothing-better-to-do critics, that Noddy's world (by Enid Blyton) was ageist, racist and sexist. All the golliwogs instantly got their cards, and Big Ears was severely reprimanded for spending so much time alone in bed with little Noddy.

February: Andy Warhol, the wacky, misunderstood American sleaze-merchant and painter, died during an operation. Warhol who looked, unlike Big Ears, to be everyone's idea of a child molester, was the first person to make us study an everyday object (like a soup can) and give it the same respect as a famous academic painting. His haunting prediction 'in the future everyone will be famous for fifteen minutes' seems almost inevitable given the gutter press's insatiable appetite for every aspect of our personal lives.

Oh Julian lovey! You've eaten the art!

March: The huge British band Frankie Goes To Hollywood did exactly that – and Paris and Rome and Scunthorpe. The extremely camp group went in separate directions (in more ways than one), after having their own fifteen minutes of fame. They were hardly to be seen again.

May: Now there's vandalism and vandalism. British Telecom, in its infinite wisdom, went on an orgy of destruction. They removed a major feature of our national heritage when, to beat the soon-to-be-upon-us conservation laws, they tore down hundreds of our filthy, urine-smelling, never-working, always-occupied, red telephone boxes. They replaced them with always clean, always efficient, but totally soulless plastic booths.

July: Oxford University refused for the second time to give Her Extreme Cleverness Margaret Thatcher the honorary degree she so richly deserved. Funny really they seem to give everyone else one.

September: At least Andy Warhol was honest when he took the art market for a ride. Vincent Van Gogh, who'd sold his stuff for a couple of drinks and a cheese roll, would have laughed his other ear off if he'd been at the Christie's auction when his *Sunflowers* painting (£8.99 at Boots) sold for £24 million.

October: The whole weight of modern American science was put behind a no-holds-barred search for the Loch Ness Monster. After scanning the whole pond with Sonar they came up with nothing. Isn't it weird, the more people *don't* see the damn thing, the more they believe it's there. Beats me!

November: Lester Piggot, the jockey who looks like a Steven Spielberg make-up department's reject, was jailed for three years for failing to pay over £3 million tax.

December: Quote of the year by novelist Martin Amis:
'How do we prevent the use of nuclear weapons? By threatening to use nuclear weapons. And we can't get rid of the nuclear weapons *because* of the nuclear weapons.'

1988

War and Peace

1988 was an odd year for the British. While the rest of the world was putting away their slings and arrows of discontent, the tiff in our own back yard (Northern Ireland) seemed to be getting worse. Reagan and Gorbachev, although visually as unlikely chums as Kermit and Miss Piggy, seemed to be getting almost indecently matey and were falling over to sign each other's bits of paper. The long, drawn-out Iran Iraq war, which nobody over here seemed to give a damn about (I wonder why?) was finally running out of steam (and bullets) and the 20 year old 'quiet war', to decide who was going to control Angola and Namibia, also appeared to be grinding to a halt.

In May, the Ruskies left Afghanistan, realising they were pi . . . urinating into the wind. They just couldn't crush the spirit of the people (or the rebels). Even the embryonic rumble between the States and those nice Iranians, resulting in the bombing of Iranian oil platforms and the shooting down of one of their airbuses, came to a shaky peace when both sides realised the whole business was getting out of hand.

Leaders Leave

One major, and one *very* minor, leader resigned. Wrinkly Ronald Reagan (President of the USA), who had recently (and stupidly) let it slip that all his decisions were based on the advice of his spidery wife Nancy's astrologer, left the White House. Then David Steele (leader of anything he could get his hands on), finally got the message after 12 years that the country would rather have the likes of clever-dick Jeffrey Archer or smoothy adulterer Cecil Parkinson in power than him. He'd simply run out of people to try and jump into bed (politically-speaking) with.

More Grub for Africa

If you'd gone out on the streets today (5th Feb) you'd have been sure of a big surprise. No, it wasn't the Teddy Bear's Picnic, it was even more childish. Normally normal people, like bank clerks and policemen, could be observed wearing stick-on red clown noses to celebrate Comic Relief – another wizard wheeze to get money out of the British for African aid.

Impersonating a police officer eh?

Happy Birthday Mandela

Cynical people might have wondered, when yet another huge concert, this time for the birthday of imprisoned Nelson Mandela and the Anti-Apartheid Movement, took place at Wembley, where all this would end, and who and what these concerts were really for? They might conceivably have thought the whole business was yet another world-wide, ego-massaging showcase for ageing rock stars like Midge Ure, Boy George, Paul Young, Joe Cocker, and the Bee Gees (who needed more than a concert to save them) to name but a few. Or they might have thought that it gave an opportunity, in a couple of fame-filled, self-indulgent hours to show how 'right-on' they all were – even the ones that hadn't even heard of old Mandela before.

Actually when you get down to it, who gives a damn? It was all in a good cause.

No Aid for AIDS

It is interesting to note, however, that when the Action Against Aids organisers tried to jump on the bandwagon later in the year, our 'caring' rock stars weren't that interested.

Was AIDS no longer trendy?

Maggie Goes to the Poles

Over in Poland, our own tireless champion of the rights of the working man, Maggie Thatcher, congratulated Lech Walesa and his merry men on their struggles for freedom and union recognition. Many people, back home, wondered if they were hearing right. Surely this couldn't be the same Margaret Thatcher that had crusaded almost single-handedly for years to snap the back of the unions in Britain?

Her timing as usual, was immaculate, as the deepest rumblings ever heard in the modern world were coming from the Soviet Union. Estonia had joined a growing bunch of states ruled by Big Brother to demand that they go it alone. This was like a slap in the face for poor Mr Nice-Guy Mikhail Gorbachev, who wanted to have all the regions run directly from Moscow.

In fact, at the end of the year, he gave the whole world a huge Christmas present when he announced that he was to chop the number of Soviet troops by 500,000. Having said that, however, it wasn't that fab a gesture. For a start, they simply couldn't afford all their soldiers (the Soviet Union was practically bust) and secondly, large as that number might seem, it only represented 10% of the whole army.

Designer Drugs

Not much has been said so far about the huge revolution in the highly profitable illegal drugs industry that had plagued (and stoned) the youth of Britain for years.

When this book began, in the mid 40s, only rather arty people were known to smoke marijuana and, with a few upper-class exceptions, the use of cocaine and heroin was still only really connected with medicine. This was mostly the case until the early

60s when the earthy rhythm and blues cult hit the teenage clubs and pubs. A lot of the early bands came out of art schools, where they'd been puffing away like steam trains for years, but it was the Rolling Stones' drug trial that brought the whole business out into the open.

Acid (LSD)

It was in the hippie period that young people, mostly from the middle classes, started to 'turn on and tune in' in much greater numbers. LSD (D-lysergic acid diethylamide) came from the States (as did most things) and became freely available. LSD was the drug that enabled the participant to fly, swim or make love to anything from an egg whisk to a daffodil, all in the comfort of his or her own psychodelic bean-bag.

Cocaine

The eighties saw us copying (from the dear old States again) the use of smart designer drugs like cocaine, which soon came after the cheese and biscuits at ultra fashionable advertising or media type dinner parties.

Ecstasy

Ecstasy became synonymous with that other 80s phenomenon, the 'rave'. Enterprising whizz kids hired (illegally) ginormous spaces like warehouses or even open fields and then circulated by word of mouth that a vast party would take place on a secret date. Trillions of teenagers would (and still do) jig up and down non-stop to the point of exhaustion, to ear-crunching, repetitive Acid House music, fortified by ecstasy 'tabs' easily available from local dealers. These were the first parties where alcohol consumption was practically non existent (the two don't mix). The jury's still out, however, over the harmful effects of this relatively new drug.

Crack
The last and nastiest of the new drugs crept in from the States where in some cities it was literally reaching plague proportions. 'Crack', a derivative of cocaine was, and is, the perfect drug if you want to kill yourself just that little bit quicker, being almost instantly addictive and, better (or worse) than that . . . cheap.

Meanwhile

March: Prince Charles appeared to be more than piste-off when he and his party skied off-piste in Switzerland, and were caught by an avalanche. Tragically, one of his friends was killed in the accident.

June: Mike Gatting, Captain of the English cricket team, was fired for 'irresponsible' off-field behaviour. People muttered that sadly cricket, the sport of gentlemen, was becoming as populated with yobs as its rather common younger brother, football.

August: Bad year if you happened to be a seal. A horrid mystery disease was sealing the fate of thousands of the poor dears round Britain.

September: The 'speed' attained by black American sprinter Ben Johnson, at the Olympics in the 100 metre final, turned out to have been taken *before* the race. He and eight other athletes were disqualified for taking illegal drugs.

October: The Turin Shroud, one of the Catholic Church's most sacred relics, because it was supposed to hold an imprint of Jesus' head, was found to be a fake. Strangely enough, the old shroud-man looked rather like a cross between Father Christmas and Jimmy Hill (the football guru).

November: There seemed to be a little trouble brewing in sleepy old Yugoslavia. The Serbs, it appeared, were rather anxious to be independent. Oh well, we thought, it would probably blow over.

December: For some time, another woman Tory Politician, Edwina Currie, had been making a bit of a prat of herself with unsolicited foot-in-the-mouth statements. This time, she suggested that most British eggs were infected with the killer disease salmonella; just what you needed to hear as you were about to tuck into your soft boiled egg (with soldiers). Overnight, the egg business was smashed. Chickens throughout the country were clucking annoyed at having been 'laid off'.

1989

Fresh Salman

The year opened with the most extraordinary event. Salman Rushdie, a hugely talented writer (so we've been told), released a book called *The Satanic Verses* which caused more hullabaloo than anything ever published before (including *Noddy in Toyland*). In the book he, according to those very nice Iranians, took the mickey out of Islam, the *Koran* (their bible) and their prophet which, in the great scheme of things, wasn't the brightest move he ever made.

That very nice Ayatollah Khomeini declared to the world that poor Salman, who was only trying to make a £ or two, was now under a permanent sentence of death and offered a million bucks to the first person to kill him. His very nice Moslem supporters then went absolutely crazy, burning the books and threatening anyone who had had anything to do with *The Satanic Verses* (mostly the poor staff at Penguin Books). He then threatened death to England and America, which we all, on both sides of the pond, found a little unreasonable.

Since then, the poor author of the now bestselling book has been in permanent hiding from the few very nice hit squads

Terribly sorry Miss Rushdie. Your cheque to the plastic surgeon seams to have bounced.

219

chasing around trying to find him. Salman Rushdie has, therefore, lived in literally hundreds of different places and has a permanent bodyguard (paid for by us) to keep a look out for anyone unusual coming to his various front doors offering poisoned apples (like the wicked queen in *Snow White*).

In June the Ayatollah died and all those Iranians forgot about Salman Rushdie (but only for ten minutes).

The Wind of Change

The huge rusty Iron Curtain was amazingly beginning to creak open, and the stench of stale air was gushing out. The Communist world was bursting out of its faded, far too restrictive, worn-out work clothes. The whole brave experiment that Mr Lenin had started in 1917 simply hadn't worked. Young people in Moscow, Peking or Warsaw had given the Communist ideal the big thumbs down and now simply wanted, for better or worse, to put on their Levis and Reeboks, strap on their Walkmen and ease down to the shopping mall for a Big Mac and a large Coke. They were simply fed up to the back teeth of having a Big Brother breathing down their necks telling them what they should do or think. In China, unfortunately, it all happened too soon and hundreds of revolting students were massacred in Tiananmen Square, Peking, on the orders of the wrinkly authorities, who were terrified of democratic elections.

No Wall for Humpty

Perhaps the ugliest and most symbolic manifestation of Communist oppression came tumbling down in November, never to be put back together again. The 28 mile long Berlin Wall, which for so long had kept the German people apart, was pulled apart, brick by bloody brick. The Cold War was over. All that remained to be asked was – now what?

And Back in Britain?

The hugest joke was that, certainly in this country, the very thing that all those poor Eastern bloc persons dreamed of, freedom through capitalism, was turning out to be just a different tune played on the same flat piano. Unless you were so loaded that the economy didn't really affect you (and there were still quite a few of those left), your average British man in the street was feeling pretty disillusioned. Just about all the aspects of his pre-Thatcher life which gave him security against hard times, be it through the health service, education for his kids, or the social services, were simply falling apart through lack of finance. The house that he'd worked so hard for was now, for practically the first time in history, reducing in value. Worse he might even have been encouraged (thanks to Thatcher and her monetarist policies) to borrow more and more to the point that he now might owe more than it was worth. Crime and violence were reaching new heights, especially among the young, whose prospects of work after school were becoming as likely as winning the World Cup.

On top of all this, Maggie's henchmen were starting to stab each other in the back, as they realised what a dog's breakfast they were making of running the country. While they all squabbled, however, careful observation uncovered a rather funny little grey man with a set lipless grin on his face, lurking in the background, hanging on to the hem of his leader's skirt. No prizes will be given for guessing his name.

Tunnel Vision
The Channel Tunnel, to which we were all indifferent, was now well under way and, as long as the English and French diggers

didn't miss each other – making one, instead of two, tunnels – they could reckon on joining up in a couple of years' time. The problem then became how, and by what route, the punters at this end and 'les punters' at the other, were going to get to the tunnel. The French, typically, got on with the job right away, while we were (and still are now) arguing about whose houses the damn train line was going to run under.

Meanwhile

February: Angels go underground. The latest import from the States were the Guardian Angels, a group of New York vigilantes who, not content with making life difficult for their own subway muggers and rapists, decided to come over and make life a misery for ours.

March: Heavyweight World Champion Mike Tyson, the nearest thing to a pit-bull terrier on human legs, came over and savaged our dear, but ever so slightly slow, Frank Bruno, who had stupidly challenged him. Frank then went back to panto where the worst thing you could be hit by was a custard pie. Behind you Frank!
• Later in the year, as a result of a new fashion among yobs to have dogs that could do their throat-tearing for them, the American pit-bull terrier was banned (and then put down – tee hee!) or, in Tyson's case, sent to prison for rape.

April: Madonna, that ridiculous caricature of the modern woman, was fired by Pepsi Cola who were about to use her for a £5 million promotion, due to pressure from the church. The ad was to show a black Christ weeping tears of blood after being kissed by the singer. Ah well, that's the way it must get some people.

May: A funny little Briton, Jackie Mann, who looked like Biggles' granddad, was abducted in Beirut. That's nothing! Everyone was *still* looking for poor old Terry (it won't be a long) Waite.

July: Ken Dodd, the buck-toothed comedian who resembled a Spitting Image reject, was acquitted of defrauding the Inland Revenue. Shame really, many people were rather looking forward to crazy Ken and all his daft Diddy Men being off the scene for a few years.

September: Crawly Archbishop of Canterbury, Robert Runcie, thought he'd get tons of heaven points, when he offered the Pope Supreme Primacy, in other words an acknowledgement that he was 'top dog' in the religious stakes. The Pope thought it was quite a gas, but loads of Protestants said that our Archbishop had got no right to give away the top job to a blinking Catholic.

October: Hungary became the next country to show two fingers to their Soviet 'masters' when it announced the birth of a new Hungarian Republic. The ruling Communist Party, seeing the way things were going, quickly changed its name to the Socialist Party and promised unheard-of, free elections.
• Two months later, Czechoslovakia followed, digging out and cheering their old hero Dubček who'd been so humiliated 20 years earlier by the Soviets.

November: A brilliant, fabulous, never-to-be-forgotten, Red Letter Day (23rd) for all those people that didn't think that Maggie was quite as marvellous as *she* did. Sir Anthony Meyer (nicknamed 'Sir Nobody'), a mere backbencher, shocked the press when he became the first Tory ever to stand up and say he could do the job a darned sight better than his boss.

December: Wow! What a year. It ended with the execution of the appalling Rumanian dictator Nicolae Ceauşescu and his Mrs on Christmas Day (that'll be one they don't forget). Out with them went the whole of the Communist Party in favour of the brand new National Salvation Front. The Commies were now tumbling like ninepins.

1990

Thatcher Wobbles

The dream that was Thatcherism was now turning into a nightmare. For a start, Britain had imported £20.31 billion quid's worth of goods more than she had managed to flog abroad. The mortgage rates had soared to new heights (15.4%), which meant that loads of poor devils who'd borrowed up to the hilt, encouraged by the building societies and Maggie, were now being chucked out of their homes because they couldn't make the repayments. Inflation rose to 10.9%, ambulance drivers were on strike and, not totally Maggie's fault, all our cows went round the bend with the weird 'Mad Cow' disease that made them wag their stupid heads from side to side.

Can humans catch that cow disease?

Maggie was also getting a terrible ragging for her personal pet 'poll tax' which, although representative of her 'if-you-ain't-making-it-tough-luck' politics, was proving to be almost too unfair a stunt for even the Tories to pull. What the poll tax did was to replace the old rates, which were levied according to the size and value of the property you lived in, with a flat rate simply geared to the individual inhabitant. To put things a little clearer, every *individual* had to pay poll tax but the amount she or he paid varied from area to area. It meant that the Duke of Westminster, who probably has more money than Michael Jackson, the Queen and me put together, could end up paying the same as an old age pensioner living in Hackney. Pretty fair eh! The extremely well off, of course, thought it was fab, but those in the middle and right at the bottom were not so sure.

Wimpy Labour

Now, your chance, Labour! If an opposition party couldn't capitalise on all this garbage, then they really should have packed their bags and gone home. Labour couldn't, and didn't!

Neil Kinnock proved he had the killer instinct of a damp sheep by totally failing to hit Maggie where it hurt most (deep in the ego) and his ramshackle flock of what often seemed like refugees from a church hall debating society, were light years away from anything that could conceivably be considered a future government (unless it was of Toytown). One of the only guys with any fire in his belly was a no-nonsense, say-what-you-think, damn-the-consequences MP called Dennis Skinner, nicknamed the Beast of Bolsover. He reminded us of some of those long-lost, old style, cloth-capped, committed socialists who used to put ideals before their obsession with personal advancement. Had there been a few more like the Beast, things might have been a lot different.

Thatcher Beaten

This discontent came to a head when Sir Geoffrey Howe (him of the silly hair), who'd resigned from Maggie's Bratpack a week earlier, realising that nobody else, especially from the other side, was going to put paid to her, suddenly turned on his mistress and savaged her like an untrained fox hound. When others in the anti-Thatcher Tory camp smelt blood they all began tearing at her until she could no longer stand (as leader).

The new Prime Minister, can you believe, was that funny little background-grey man, with the voice and presence of Mr Bean's dim brother – John Major. About the only thing remotely interesting about him was the fact that his dad had been a circus acrobat, a really useful background for someone with the top job in politics. Everyone thought he'd also be torn to pieces by the opposition but, continuing the circus analogy, it turned out to be like putting a novice lion tamer into a cage of . . . bunny rabbits.

Thatcher was gone. Whether we liked her or not (answers on a postcard), in ten years she'd become as famous as any Prime Minister in history. She'd dragged us out of one recession and, after de-nationalising many of our major industries and smashing the unions, had left us in a worse one. Small businessmen, who'd followed her like the Israelites followed Moses into the Red Sea, were abandoned like drowning kittens.

Maggie had been a passionate nationalist, showing an *un*healthy disrespect for foreigners, and blamed the likes of mega-European Nigel Lawson for wrecking her dreams of being Empress of 'Great

Britain the Great' again. Most of all, many believed she'd become the champion of all those nice people who live in nice houses (well out of the inner cities) who reckoned that if people weren't successful, it was their own bloody fault.

On a different level, she had taken on almost queen-like status and indeed many royal reporters have since said that our Queen, who apparently couldn't bear the grocer's upstart daughter (and disagreed with her on most things) saw her Royal self vying with Maggie for top woman status amongst her loyal (ish) subjects.

But to those of us, however, who were sick of being patronised in that oily, you-know-it's-all-for-your-own-good voice, designed to make us feel like retarded children, it was goodbye and good riddance. Now we had this new, enigmatic, strong, brave and handsome leader to make things better again. Superman? No, John Major.

Yippee! It's War Again

In August Iraq, led by the kindly-looking but murderous Saddam Hussein, rolled over into poor little oil-rich Kuwait and took the country by storm because, it was claimed, they had nicked £2.4 billion quids' worth of their oil. Those selfless protectors of the world (and their own huge oil interests), the United States, hardly drew breath, before dispatching the largest force ever seen into Saudi Arabia to stop Saddam going any further. Anything-but-stupid Hussein speed up the peace treaty with those very nice Iranians (what's a million lives amongst friends?) and prepared to fight the mighty but (to all Iraqis) evil West.

Sides soon started to be taken and before long the Palestinians joined the Iraqis. Britain simply couldn't wait to send troops alongside of 'our best mates' the Yanks, and even France sided with us, sending another 4000 men to Saudi. The UN surprised us all by giving the Allies permission to go in and liberate Kuwait, and then President Bush surprised us all (even more) by offering to pow-wow with Hussein before going in with guns blazing. The world chess board was now set up, all that was needed was for someone to make the first move.

Meanwhile

February: Good news. Nelson Mandela was freed at last from prison in Cape Town. Bad news, he was met by Winnie his Mrs who'd been up to all sorts of mischief while he'd been inside. As we all know, Nelson Mandela went on to witness the end of apartheid, the first free elections and his own inauguration as president.

March: A couple of weeks after the mind-numbing vote of the Central Committee of the Soviet Communist Party to abandon the Commie's guaranteed monopoly on power, thousands of Soviet citizens, the bit well and truly between their teeth, hit the streets demanding more and more reforms. The West looked on dumbfounded.

April: British customs officials seized loads of lengths of, what were labelled, petroleum piping bound for Iraq. Big deal I expect you think. It turned out that if you were able to put all the bits together, they would form something strangely resembling a huge gun, capable of firing gigantic nuclear shells hundreds of miles. Somebody, somewhere had a lot of explaining to do (and still has!).

Anyone seen Jack?

May: Just to prove that Mad Cow Disease (see page 224) couldn't be passed on to us, Agriculture Minister John Gummer, who strangely resembled a mad human, made his daughter eat a £1.60 hamburger (along with himself). Little Cordelia seemed fine, but was reported to make occasional, strange moo-ing noises whilst waving her little head about.

June: The Government unveiled its proposed 'hard ecu', which was apparently the first step towards a single European currency. Over the next few years, the poor British public were to be subjected to a deluge of unutterably boring reporting on the subject, involving something called the Maastricht Treaty. If you want to know more, you'll have to buy another book, as I can't understand a word of it. Maggie, you might have guessed, was totally against losing our £, but no one really listened to her as she was well on the skids by now.

July: A horrid new tabloid phenomenon in the form of a rather witless footballer, called Paul Gascoigne, became a regular feature of the gruesome, gutter press. Geordie 'Gazza' (as he was stylishly nicknamed) came to almost film-star status after blubbing his eyes out in the middle of a World Cup game on telly. Pathetic!

August: Irish Brian Keenan, one of the Beirut hostages, was freed, looking absolutely awful, after 1,597 days in captivity. First question he was asked was whether he'd seen our Terry (Waite) lately?

September: Yet another war with France. This time over, can you believe? Juvenile sheep! French farmers were getting their pantalons in a twist over the amount of British lambs being sold over there. Over 400 of the little dears were torched after being hijacked in France. Luckily, although it was poor compensation for them, they were dead already. The fires were reportedly put out with industrial quantities of mint sauce.

October: For the first time since the war, Germany became one big powerful country again, when East and West joined up. From now on all the rest of the world had to look out for was funny men with little black moustaches.

December: We all thought it would never happen. English and French tunnellers celebrated, with champagne on their side and plain water on ours (which says it all), when they finally met in the middle.

Quote of the Year: 'It's a funny old world' – Margaret Thatcher (ex-Prime Minister).

1991

Instant War
Well, he wouldn't listen would he? Saddam Hussein continued to taunt the mighty Americans (and little us) until Bush (and then Major) had had enough. On 17th January Baghdad didn't know what had hit it when operation Desert Storm was launched. The brilliant 'invisible' American Stealth Bomber avoided Iraq's radar, tiptoed up to the city and sent one of its 'smart' bombers literally through the Baghdad streets like a flying carpet, ignoring all speed limits and traffic lights, until it reached the telecommunications centre which it blew to pieces.

Faced with 700,000 Americans and backup forces from another 30 countries, the mighty Iraqi army seemed somewhat weedified and after a month during which 97,000 air attacks pounded Iraq, killing 50,000 and wounding another 100,000 soldiers (let alone civilians), a saddened Saddam ran away. Kuwait was now free and America could light its big cigar again. Its oil interests were safe.

Masterful Major

Britain lost only sixteen soldiers, nine of which were killed by mistake by the gun happy Yanks. At home, the British man-in-the-armchair soldier seemed rather disappointed that this smashing TV war (which was never going to affect him) was over. Little John Major couldn't believe his luck at having been on the right side of a war in an otherwise underwhelming year. Unfortunately poor John didn't get the same adulation that 'super-hero' Maggie had received for her pet war. Judging by his almost continuous robotic grin, however, Major seemed to rather like being Prime Minister and didn't notice that most of his 'subjects' thought him a bit of a wally.

Maastricht Moves On

Wally or not, at the end of the year Major finally signed the highly controversial (and deeply boring) Maastricht Treaty, setting 1999 as the date for a single currency throughout Europe, and extending the powers of both the European Commission and European Parliament. Needless to say, Major claimed it as a victory for Britain, while the Opposition said he'd condemned us to the 'slow-lane' in a two-tier Europe. Any slower and we'd be in the lay-by I'd have thought.

The Party's Over

The events in Russia were turning into a music-hall farce. The hardline Communists had finally had enough of President of all the Soviet Republics, Gorbachev's, reforms and overthrew him in a real Mikhail Mousevich coup, putting him under house arrest at his country residence. His former rival, caricature Russian and extreme reformer Boris Yeltsin, the new President of Russia, now rallied to his call for help. Yeltsin had also been held under a sort of house arrest while all this to-ing and fro-ing and coup-ing was going on but he now returned to Moscow, where he stood on a tank (the sort with a gun) outside the Russian Parliament and demanded the return of his old enemy Gorbachev, calling himself the champion of democracy.

The coup fell to bits and Gorbachev returned to Moscow in triumph. Unfortunately Yeltsin had smelt the faint but heady aroma of absolute power and realised that if he played his cards right (by making Gorby look stupid) he could get to be top man himself. Yeltsin then shocked the western world by actually suspending the Russian Communist Party.

Here in Britain, we couldn't believe what we were hearing. After years of pussy-footing around the huge Russian bear for fear of what he might do if we made him cross, the decrepit old beast suddenly keeled over. The Soviet Union was disintegrating before our very eyes.

In December, Gorbachev resigned as the first (and last) President of the whole of the Soviet Union, having presided over probably the most amazing seven years of Soviet history. Unfortunately, all his power had come from the Communist Party and when it was disbanded it had simply cleared the path for bolshy Boris. As Gorbachev spoke, the red flag was lowered for ever over the Kremlin. Just to put the boot in, Yeltsin later accused 'his new chum' Gorbachev of bringing the Soviet Union to dictatorship. The Russians had finally perfected the knife-in-the-back school of politics.

The Bouncing Czech

In the middle of the night of 5th November, one of the major figures in British business and public life, Robert Maxwell, mysteriously plopped off his fab yacht parked somewhere off the Canary Islands. The exuberant, outspoken, rags to riches tycoon had become a household name by owning a string of businesses and publications headed by the *Daily Mirror*.

His immensely fat naked body was mistaken for a whale (great white) when spotted floating nearby, but nobody had a clue whether he'd simply gone for a midnight dip or had tried to do himself in.

It eventually emerged that Maxwell had been swindling his own newspaper's pension fund holders to the tune of £400 million. This plunder had been used to stave off creditors trying to get some of the £1.5 billion he owed. Suddenly, like rats leaving a sinking yacht, all his erstwhile crawly friends said that they'd always hated him. The whole Maxwell story and the mystery of his death soon became open house for every comedian and satirical magazine.

Gullible's Travels

Only the hardest of us could fail to have glistening eyes at the news that the brave, but somewhat gullible, Terry Waite, who by this time must have run well out of travellers cheques, had been released. His jaunt up the road to meet some English hostages in Beirut had lasted five years, most of which he'd spent chained to a wall in a windowless cell (I bet they don't mention that in the travel brochures!). By the time he got back, the Archbish. that he'd been doing all the Special Envoying for, had actually retired and had to be dragged out of mothballs himself. I would have thought the now *Lord* Runcie, should have taken his back wages (plus overtime) to meet him, to make up for sending him on such a daft and dangerous mission.

Waite, released with American Tom Sutherland, was the last of the British hostages to leave Lebanon.

Yugoslavia in Trouble

Sleepy Yugoslavia seemed to be getting itself into all sorts of bother while the rest of the world looked on helplessly. The trouble was that Yugoslavia was really a holding name for six republics: Slovenia, Croatia, Serbia, Bosnia Hercegovina, Montenegro and Macedonia, all of which had a deep distrust and even hatred of one another, owing to their different racial and religious origins. If this weren't bad enough, it had long been the case that throughout Yugoslavia the townspeople had no time for the countryfolk and vice versa.

Only a leader with the power of Marshal Tito had been able to keep all these factions apart and paper over the cracks in the hugely divided country. Tito, who had always managed to keep his communist regime free from Russian dominatin, had run, what almost had to be, a police state until his death in 1980.

In 1991, all the states outside Serbia and Montenegro declared themselves independent as they were well fed up with growing Serbian domination. The top Serb, the warmongering Slobodan Milosevic, hoping to be boss of the whole lot, wouldn't have it and declared their actions illegal. The blood started to flow when he sent the Yugoslavian army (largely Serbian) to sort the Croats out. Terms like 'ethnic cleansing' were used as Serbian soldiers started throwing Croatians out of their homes in order that they could be occupied by them and theirs. But this was just the beginning.

Meanwhile

January: In an inspired piece of clairvoyancy, John Major announced that on no account would the poll tax ever be abolished.
• Why do the British always get everything wrong? 10,000 NHS beds were made ready for the injured in the Gulf War. As it happened, however, the injured could have had loads of beds –

each. Great isn't it! The only sure way to get an NHS bed these days is to go and get shot up thousands of miles away, in a war that's got nothing to do with you in the first place.

February: A rude, crude, sexist (but jolly funny) magazine called *Viz*, pitched to appeal to a readership with a mental capacity of a dim dormouse, became the publishing success of the decade. Strangely enough, retailers, who would normally shy away from such degrading material (acting as our moral guardians), seemed to stock it without a whimper. I don't suppose that could have anything to do with the loot they were making.

March: The poll tax that John (why-does-everyone-have-a-go-at-me?) Major said would be with us for ever . . . suddenly wasn't. It had taken the Government this long to think up an even unfairer way of grabbing our money – the community tax.

April: London Zoo let it be known that they might have to close due to lack of funding. Loads of animals were seen lurking around Job Centres trying to get work in circuses.

May: A Mars a day helps you work, rest and . . . zoom into orbit with a rocket strapped to your backside. Helen Sharman, who had worked in the famous chocolate factory, became Britain's very first woman to go into orbit. She beat 13,000 rivals to fly with the Russian Soyez TM-12 spacecraft.

June: Five homosexual couples were married in Trafalgar Square at a huge Gay Rights demo. Poor Nelson must have blushed when he saw what was going on and remembered asking Hardy to kiss him!

August: *Terminator 2: Judgement Day* had its premier in London. It featured a half-man, half-robot character played by the half-man, half-gristle Arnold Schwarzenegger – a former Mr Universe. If his brain's half as developed as his body he might even make President of America? Let's face it, Ronnie did.

September: Women were finally allowed into the all-male inner sanctum of The Magic Circle, the professional body for conjurors and illusionists. Their membership multiplied with alarming speed (one of the advantages of being sawn in half every five minutes).

October: Another woman with that magic touch (and who many would have willingly volunteered to saw in half) was Maggie Thatcher. Having brought us to a major (and Major) recession, she ended up writing about how she did it, flogging the sad tale for £2.5 million. And they say there's justice!

November: How odd, that at a time when church attendance was receding like Paul Daniel's hairline, the most popular boys' names were Matthew, James, Joshua, Joseph and Luke. Names like Rebecca, Hannah and Rachel well outscored previous royal favourites like Elizabeth, Margaret, Diana and Anne. Oddly enough nobody wanted to call their kid Fergie!

December: The Queen, on her Christmas broadcast, hinted she'd no intention of abdicating. Purely coincidentally, a new telly was ordered on Boxing Day for Highgrove, Prince Charles's house. I understand his was mysteriously smashed.

Quote of the Year: 'The great, the jewel and the mother of battles has begun.' Saddam Hussein

1992

Annus Horribilis

On 23rd November 1992, our gracious Queen Elizabeth (God save her), at a banquet to celebrate 40 years on the throne, told us all that she'd had an *annus horribilis* (Latin for bad bottom?). She certainly wasn't kidding, and as most of us royal watchers realised, she wasn't really just talking about the last year, but a complete decade. A decade that had seen the whole standing of the 'Firm' (Royal Family) tumble at such a rate that one might be forgiven for wondering whether they'd found some sort of public *bad*-relations company to get them out of the whole blooming monarchy business.

Personality Plus

Many people believe that the rot started when the younger members of the Windsors, a rather boring family, of rather average intelligence (bang goes my knighthood!), discovered the media and in particular telly. Many of us then began to lose interest in them because, in their individual crusades for publicity, they let us know how uninteresting they actually were. By demystifying themselves to such an extent, they almost begged the question: what are we actually for?

Most of us lesser mortals would, secretly, be happier to see our Kings, Queens and their offspring wearing their crowns and robes every day, wafting about being royal. The last thing we need is to see them slithering down to our level either by choice or by accident. Certainly these staggeringly banal shows like 'It's a Royal Knockout', or even those quirkily funny 'at home with the Queen' documentaries, have done their elite image no good whatsoever.

Prince Charles

Prince Charles was (and is) causing more concern than most. He is known to think himself a bit of an intellectual (because all those toadying mates have told him so) but in fact often seems to be out to prove the old saying that a little knowledge is a dangerous thing. His speech at the GATT agricultural talks in November 1992, for example, when he went completely against Her Majesty's Government's line, left everyone (including the Government) wondering how much damage he might do when (or if) he got the 'big job'. Or there was the time he pitched up in a flash plane, on a bleak, windswept Hebridean island, to make a TV documentary with sleek Selina Scott, only to criticise the natives for leaving their picturesque, but freezing, turf-roofed hovels in favour of snug windproof bungalows.

I say Selina - could you ask their opinion on modern architecture?

Till Death Us Do Part

One of the very few functions left for the Royal Family was to set us poor weak and immoral subjects a good example. In March, however, the Queen's favourite, Andrew, split with the fearful fun-girl Fergie, leaving her in their gross £5 million 'ranch' (nicknamed Southfork) that we'd all so kindly built them. Two months later, she was photographed in the South of France, topless (not that pretty a sight) having her freckly toes sucked (even less pretty a sight) by her Texan 'financial advisor'.

In June, Princess Anne finally got shot of her horsy, Hooray Henry husband Mark Phillips and was soon observed canoodling with some other man in uniform.

Then, surprise, surprise, in December Charles and Di announced their long-awaited separation amidst a plethora of self-leaked rumours about their naughty connections. The country, amazed by the ending of their 'fairy-tale' romance, was initially divided between those who felt sorry for the poor princess with the shy, 'who me?' smile, and those who didn't.

When it came right down to it, what experts were now pondering was, what would happen if dippy Diana, in a fit of royal pique, decided to take her sons and heirs (to the throne) to live abroad? They feared it could well represent the end of the Firm – and even the end of the monarchy.

But How Much Did They Cost?

The horribly ungrateful British also chose 1992 to get a magnifying glass focused on the income of the Royals. Apart from all the millions we were giving HRH to buy her groceries, she actually enjoyed one of the most valuable art collections in the world, was custodian of Buck House, Balmoral, Windsor Castle and Sandringham, and owned two studs full of the very best racehorses (they don't come cheap!) and bucketfuls of priceless jewels. On top of this she had all the Royal parks, the State coaches and horses, a few stretched Rollers, her own Royal ship and even her own train (which was always on time). And on top of *all* that lot, when she went on her international walkabouts, the astronomical bills for her, her family, their staff, her ladies in waiting, equerries and miscellaneous hangers-on (not including the corgis), were sent to the Foreign Office and eventually on to us.

Even though we British were limping through the hardest of hard times, the Royals, in their infinite humility, never hesitated in flaunting their wealth and fab lifestyles. In fact, it was only when the pressure of recession-made resentment got to boiling point, that the Queen 'suggested' she paid tax like the rest of us, even though, with the help of the best accountants in the world, she would, no doubt, 'write off' most of it.

Major Makes It Again
Top of the lacklustre charts, John Major and his tedious Tory team shocked us all by winning another General Election. It wasn't so much a question of how the battle was won but, rather, how it was lost. Neil Kinnock finally realised that if he couldn't beat the weedy Major, he'd never beat anyone, and Paddy Ashdown, leader of the Liberal Democrats, also acknowledged that he'd failed to make any impact whatsoever on what had been a totally disillusioned electorate.

By July, Labour had a new leader in John Smith, a slightly intense Scot, who looked more like your average local building society manager than a future PM. The poor chap had in front of him the most enormous task of reviving a party, not only broken by defeat, but bereft of Tory-conquering ideas.

Mining the Pits
For once, a protest march actually did some positive good. John Major and his gang had to bottle out of government plans to terminate 31 coal pits (and 30,000 miners), when thousands of the desperate diggers and across-the-board consumers took to the London streets on 21st October. The government realised that, although they had no intention of changing their plans, they'd have to be a bit more sneaky about it.

Bosnia Boils Over
What had seemed to the British like another armchair war, in a country that was never going to mean more to us than a few cheap Yugoslavian holidays, suddenly took on an horrific new aspect,

when news came of Serbian 'death camps' in Bosnia and the rape of some 40,000 Muslim women and children. Echoes of Nazi Germany sent shivers down the spines of all that could remember the last war when terms like 'ethnic cleansing' were used freely. What had seemed like a relatively simple feud had, almost overnight, developed into the most complex collision of the Serbs and the Croats, the Croats and the Moslems and the Moslems and the Serbs. By the end of 1992, over 1.5 million people had lost their homes. The bottled-up hatred going back hundreds of years was finally uncorked. This conflict certainly wasn't going to be another short sharp scrap like the Gulf War, despite the efforts of David (now Lord) Owen who, with Cyrus Vance (from the States) had been given the job of trying to sort out the mess.

Meanwhile

January: Alison Halford, Britain's most senior policewoman, was fired for being caught romping starkers in a swimming pool with a male officer (perhaps they were looking for his truncheon).

February: Fine, upstanding, military man of integrity Paddy Ashdown, leader of the Liberal Democrats, joined the long list of senior politicians caught cheating on their wives. No worries Paddy, everyone (in the House of Commons) does it these days.

March: Prince Charles now turned out to be the world authority on – wait for it – cheese, when he addressed a meeting in France. He was ranting on about EEC 'bacterially correct' manufacturing methods.

April: You either liked him or not. Benny Hill, the extremely vulgar and sexist comedian, who was one of our more embarrassing exports to the States, died. Feminists did not attend the funeral.

May: Oh dear, now the cold war was over, and the Ruskies were our mates, poor MI5 were left with empty desks and nobody to spy on. They therefore turned their attention to the IRA.

June: 'Names' – rich people who'd been milking huge profits from investing in Lloyds Insurance underwriting syndicates – suddenly faced debts of over £2 billion. It must be admitted that many people cried crocodile tears at seeing all these fat cats getting stitched up. Let's face it lads and ladies, you win some, you lose some.

July: Just as the recession was reaching dizzy heights, MPs, always sensitive to their public's plight, gave themselves a 40% expenses rise. They'd obviously been taking a leaf out of the Queen's book.

August: In case you're wondering how things were getting on in Northern Ireland, they had just celebrated their 3000th victim. And what was being done about these horrendous troubles – zilch!

September: Another MP intent on following royal lines, the Heritage Secretary, Kermit look-alike David (Minister for Fun) Mellor was caught with his socks (amongst other things) down, when a newspaper reported his affair with a young (short-sighted?)

actress. He too was having his toes sucked, though there wasn't a woman in the land who would have traded places. He later resigned over his friendship with a Palestine Liberation Organisation official's daughter, Mona Bauwens, who traded self-publicity for a free holiday for him and his long-suffering family.

November: Clean-cut, though not (allegedly) clean-living, Bill Clinton, from Little Rock Arkansas, became the new President of the USA at 46. More importantly, Hillary Clinton became First Lady.
• Just to round off 1992 nicely for the Queen, Windsor, her favourite castle, caught fire and was severely damaged. The poor dear was seen wandering through the charred wreckage in headscarf and wellies, probably wondering what she'd done wrong to deserve such a year (and whether we, her long-suffering subjects, were going to make her pay the castle menders).

1993

Open Sesame
The year opened with our meanie Queenie, who'd just been let off paying massive inheritance tax, still losing sleep over whether we were going to ask her to put her hand in her own voluminous pocket to pay the amount needed to patch up her charred and uninsured castle. She then came up with a brainwave. Why not open a teeny-weeny bit of Buck House to the public and charge the punters £8 a head to look round it? This, needless to say, appealed to the tight-fisted Firm as it meant that they could make their subjects pay twice for 'their' palace (the first payment being

through taxes). It was a bit like the Government Ltd (extremely) selling us back our own nationalised industries by privatising them.

You wouldn't have been exactly killed in the rush, however, and the whole thing turned out to be a bit of a financial flop, which again must have made the poor dear wonder if she was losing her grip.

Major in Major Trouble

Poor old John Major was by now having his own *annus horribilis*, with just about everyone in Parliament (and the press, and the telly, and the radio, and the pubs, and the . . . well, everyone!) slagging him off. Despite telling us reassuringly, in that voice borrowed off an adenoidal Croydon train spotter, that the recession was now over we, the Great British, saw absolutely no evidence of it. Unemployment amongst the young, even if they'd decided upon going to university instead of joy riding and/or drug dealing, was the worst that could ever be remembered. Even those East End barrow boys had been forced out of their jobs in the Stock Exchange and were having to use their Porsches (now not worth much more than a few pounds of carrots) to deliver a few pounds of carrots to the street markets where they'd originally come from. Most of all, you didn't need to be the Governor of the Bank of England to work out that, through taxation, the rich were most certainly getting richer, while us mere mortals were most certainly not.

Norman Lamont, the Chancellor of the Exchequer (the one that looked like the villain in a Charlie Chaplin movie) took the rap for the hopeless mismanagement of the economy by the Tory Government. Major, realising that he was just as responsible as his friend and supporter, called Lamont in, and promptly . . . fired him. Lamont was replaced by the greasy Kenneth Clarke, who turned out to be a dodgy choice when he later admitted to being poised to grab the premiership should Major receive his own personal knife in the back.

The Tory majority had now dropped to 20 and John Major could at last claim, in all humility, to be the most unpopular Prime Minister since records began, even though he, for the life of him, couldn't understand why.

It was a time when, just as we were realising what a sad bunch our Royals were, Tory ministers were getting caught out left, right and centre owing to their fingers (and toes) being found in just about everywhere they shouldn't be. Again it was open season for the opposition parties to shoot them down like tin ducks in a rifle range, but where were they? John Smith, who'd shown so much promise when he became leader of the Labour Party, didn't even seem to have a boot to put *in*, and as for Paddy Ashdown, he'd simply taken on the role of dear old David Steel, ranting and raving with the same charisma and effect as an angry budgie.

Chinks in Ireland

Little chinks of light began to shine under the bloody Northern Irish door. After just about the worst atrocity ever – the bombing of a perfectly run-of-the-mill shopping street in Warrington – disgust for the IRA finally seemed to reach them, and through various means they let it be known that they were willing to talk if the British Government were too. It was, however, remarked that one of the stumbling blocks might be that, if the violence did cease in the province, there'd be a lot of fiery paddies queuing up at the Job Centre looking on the 'Murderers Required' notice board.

No Light in Yugoslavia

Despite the valiant efforts of Owen and Vance on behalf of the European Community and the United Nations (which had actually made the situation worse) the civil war continued to spiral downwards. The 6000 United Nations troops were busting their guts to get food to the starving people in Bosnia-Hercegovina (where most of the fighting was now concentrated) but were often like piggy in the middle, being fired on from all sides.

Politicians from other parts of Europe, and indeed the world, still resisted involving the lives of their own troops, in a battle which had nothing to do with them (and, unlike Kuwait, had no oil!). So much for the grand statements of the EC and the UN who had promised to protect all European countries. When it got right down to it, they seemed to have absolutely no foreign policy whatsoever regarding poor old war-torn Yugoslavia.

Video Nasties

Continuing on the aggression theme, violent video films and even those mindless video games went on trial when two little lads were brought to book for the most disgusting murder probably ever seen. Toddler James Bulger had been dragged away from a shopping mall (usually a pleasant experience) and savagely bludgeoned to death by two kids only a handful of years older than himself. Men, women and children gasped in horror as the story emerged. The very media that caught them, video (in the form of a concealed camera), was later accused of inciting these mini-monsters to do this savage crime.

Smacko-Jacko

The year ended with the most extraordinary allegations against the perfectly ordinary, run-of-the-mill multi-millionaire, Michael Jackson, who liked to play with his chimpanzee in his own deserted funfair, or perform in his spooky private theatre surrounded by sick, bedridden kids. It was claimed that the black-eyed, ashen-faced, twitchy singer, with the talking voice of a sub-normal three year old, had had many children to stay in his weird 'ranch' for anything but the purest of reasons.

Meanwhile

January: Probably the most famous ballet dancer in the world, Rudolf Nureyev, who defected to Britain in 1961, died on the 17th of AIDs. He'd danced his last *Swan Lake*. Now, sadly, it was his Swan Song.

May: Not for Bill Clinton a short-back-and-sides at the local barber's. Oh no, man-of-the-people Bill had his personal hairdresser chop his personal locks aboard his personal plane *Airforce One*. The hairdo cost £130 (a mere snip), but the real expense was entailed by keeping Los Angeles Airport closed for over 40 minutes while his plane sat on the runway.

June: Sleaze lives. Poor John Major reeled at having to announce the resignation of one of his mates, Michael (Michael Mates), junior minister for Northern Ireland, over alleged connections with fugitive tycoon Asil Nadir. It all had to do with how the Tories obtained their secret funds.
• On the 15th, Graham Hill's boy, Damon, finally cracked his first Formula 1 Grand Prix in Hungary. Three cheers, I say.

July: Rolls Royce opened their first showroom in Moscow. Is *that* what progress means?

August: In America, Briton Mark Nyman won the World Scrabble Championship with the 30 point scoring word 'WET'. I think he must have been pretty wet to enter it.

September: Florida's brilliant for your hols providing you don't get murdered. British tourist Gary Colley was shot dead in his car in front of his girlfriend – the ninth tourist that year.
• Israel and the Palestine Liberation Organization finally recognized each other. I should think so too, they'd been looking at each other through their gunsights for long enough.

November: Don't go to sleep while your wife's awake – especially if she's mad. American John Wayne Bobbit woke up (rather suddenly) to find his wife chopping off his penis, which she then thoughtlessly threw away. He was cleared of the marital sexual assault (rape) which she had accused him of, and later she was cleared of malicious wounding, because she was found to be insane. It turned out all right in the end as, due to the dexterity of his surgeons, Bobbit went off to star in porno movies. Only in America!

December: Talking of penises (or is that peni?) the obelisk in the Place de la Concorde, Paris, was dressed in a 22 metre condom to mark World AIDs Day. I wonder if the manufacturers had had much call for that size before?
• Princess Di announced to a tense world that she was retiring from public life. Oh yes, and I hereby announce I'm going into a monastery.

1994

Back to What?
Dear home-loving 'I'm-just-one-of-you', John Major spent January trying to save his awesome 'back to basics' campaign, designed to bring back 'old-fashioned family values' (everyone sitting round a

cheery fireside and discussing the weather). Poor old John was fighting an uphill battle. With half his lads playing away-matches from the marriage front (and worse – being found out), and the other half doing extremely odd things not involving women at all, I bet he wished he'd never opened his mouth in the first place. He'd already lost a couple of ministers through 'improprieties' and then, not a month after his plea to the country, it was revealed in the *News of the Screws* (sorry – *World*) that Sir Peter Harding, Chief of the Defence Staff, had been 'on board' Bienvenida Buck (the well-known printing error), ex-wife of a navy minister. So much for the government's family values.

Oh Mrs Porter

I wonder if cheating would have been included in John's clean sweep. If so that rich dame – Dame Shirley Porter – would have been in the Hoover bag pronto. Naughty Shirley was accused of being responsible for a 'disgraceful and unauthorized' £21 million vote-rigging scandal. It was rather neat (if you *are* a cheat). She allegedly set about selling off council houses in

eight key seats, confident in the knowledge that the only punters with any dosh would, more than likely, be Tories.

Rover Goes Walkies

Major must have been having his own *annus horribilis*. The last British-owned car manufacturer (apart from Reliant Robin) – Rover – announced that it was to be bought by BMW, a German company. The biggest joke is that all the yuppies who bought their flash foreign motors in the late eighties and early nineties were now falling over themselves to flog the damn things.

Sarajevo Remembers

It didn't seem possible that, only ten years earlier, the Yugoslavian town slap in the middle of the war zone had been host to the Olympic Games. The wrecked stadium was a sad reminder as NATO threatened (at last) to give the Serbian cowards who were bombing the once-beautiful city, a taste of their own medicine. As with all cowards, the Serbs collapsed under greater strength and withdrew their gun emplacements, just as NATO warplanes were preparing for take-off.

House of Horrors

I always imagine Gloucester as such a nice place – lots of tea shoppes and blue-haired old ladies chatting on street corners. In March, police charged a rather ordinary looking builder, Frederick West, with the horrible murders of eight women, including his own daughter, some of whom were buried in the cellar of his house. The soon to be nicknamed 'Nightmare on Cromwell Street' eerily turned out to be a family business (back to basics?) when his good ladywife Rosemary was later charged with helping him with his hobby.

Chunnel Vision

Napoleon would giggle in his grave if he heard that the Channel Tunnel, which he started as a wizard wheeze to attack the English, had only just opened. The Queen (by this time probably looking for a discreet means of escape) opened the damn thing on the 6th of May. Not bad! It had only taken 150 odd years.

251

Nelson Becomes Boss

Named after Napoleon's bitter foe, Nelson Mandela, who spent 27 years in a South African jail, became the first black president of the whole of South Africa. 'Let there be justice for all,' he cried. Unfortunately the locals had had no experience of justice, so didn't know what it meant.

Rwanda Explodes

Just as one part of Africa *appeared* to be sorting itself out, the ancient feud between the Hutus and the Tutsis flared up again. It all caught fire when the president of Rwanda, Habyarimana, died when his plane crashed (believed shot down). Battles raged between the army (mostly from the majority Hutu tribe) and Tutsi rebels. By April the whole place was a bloodbath as the two tribes wreaked dreadful vengeance on each other. 500,000 were believed to have died.

Labour Loss

Just as the Labour Party thought it was on the right track with a new middle-of-the-road leader, he went and died. John Smith, 55, was to be regarded as the best Prime Minister Britain never had.

Labour Gain

Much to the disgust of the Labour lefties, Tony Blair became the youngest ever Labour Party leader on the 21st of July. The never-to-be-seen-not-smiling ex-public schoolboy pronounced triumphantly that he would not rest until his party was in its rightful place. Unfortunately, nobody was quite sure where exactly that was. Anyway, that was the good news. The bad news was that Super-Anorak, Paddy Ashdown, still desperately trying to get his Lib Dem party off the no-hopers bench, offered his services to New Labour. It was a bit like offering Damon Hill a caravan to pull in his next Grand Prix. Blair's ex-boss Neil Kinnock, meantime, landed a plum job as commissioner to the European Union, on a salary of a mere £140,000 a year. Nice to see socialism really working, eh?

Windsor's Bouncy Castle

Things never get better for the poor old Royals. Mo Mowlam, Shadow Heritage secretary, announced that if she had her way she'd turn Buck House and Windsor Castle over to the National Trust. Luckily she didn't quite see the Queen sitting in a booth taking the money for The Buck House of Heritage or Windsor World of Privilege. The Royals, she claimed, would pay to have a brand new palace, located somewhere like Milton Keynes (far more fitting to their role in modern Britain). Mobile home designers were asked to tender ideas.

Prince of Caring

Princess Diana (Squidgy) appeared to be caring for people whom maybe she shouldn't. Cavalry officer James Hewitt revealed the affair in October. Poor James was refused entry to his barracks when the regiment heard about the alleged indiscretion. That's what you get for attempting to 'enter' the royal family. A little later, poor Charles shed crocodile tears as he competed for sympathy regarding his loveless marriage. 'It's just like a Greek tragedy,' he moaned. Perhaps he should have talked more with his tragic Greek dad.

Ireland Bombs Out
Following the IRA's professed ceasefire in September, the three main Loyalist factions followed suit (3000 deaths too late in my opinion). The big question we all asked, however, was what were those poor chaps (on both sides) going to do on a Friday night if they couldn't shoot or blow people to bits? Just like kids in a playground they also announced that they would only stop if the other side did. 'It wasn't our fault, Miss – they started it.'

Lottery Fever
On Saturday 19th October seven people became millionaires and 24,999,993 didn't, because of the very first National Lottery draw, organized by a company called Camelot. It started maybe one of the most boring and seemingly endless 'news' stories of all time. Week after week we British are now subjected to the ordeal of watching totally inappropriate and greedy people winning huge amounts of money that each and every one of us would have far more use for. I, for instance, would give most of it away to more deserving causes like the Save Fergie's Finances Fund (and my name's Pinocchio!).

Meanwhile

January: The Queen fractured her wrist in an alleged riding accident. Reports that the Duchess of York had a severely bruised bottom were strenuously denied by the Palace.
• All charges were dropped against Michael Jackson regarding his alleged sexual jiggery-pokery with a small boy. The fact that $5 million changed hands out of court had nothing to do with it, I'm sure. I ask you, how would a perfectly healthy, normal and regular guy like our Michael become involved in that sort of thing? I also think it wicked to suggest than an amount like that can buy practically anything, including silence.

February: *Huge Breast Settlement:* Dow Corning, Bristol-Meyers, Squib and Baxter, America's largest breast implant manufacturer, had to pay $4.5 million compensation because their implants ruptured and leaked (causing said breasts to droop and presumably settle).

• A huge outcry (apart from me) proclaimed that Torvill and Dean, our Olympic skating champions, were robbed of a repeat victory at the Lillehammer Olympics when they came third. The unhappy couple retired the following week. Perhaps they should have chosen *The Party's Over* to skate to.

March: The finest snap of the Loch Ness monster was revealed to be a hoax. It turned out to be a toy submarine with a head and neck made from plastic wood. I thought it might have been a relative of Robert Maxwell.

• The skull of the earliest human being ever recorded was found in Ethiopia. He or she (no other identifying parts, unfortunately) was around 3.9 million years old. Shame really. If the old person had been British, he or she would have got 39,000 letters of congratulation from the Queen.

May: Poor Prime Minister Major announced that he found beggars offensive. He said that the benefit system (which you need a degree in gobbledegook to understand) meant nobody was *that* poor. Well, I bet those poor devils sleeping on the streets feel a lot better for knowing that, Johnnie.

June: The great playwright Dennis Potter who, in his last interview, blamed the tabloid press for the decline of standards in Britain, died on Tuesday 7th. 'And Good Riddance Sez the *Sun*!!!'

August: Forty privileged people fainted at a Buckingham Palace garden party, as did the rhinos at London Zoo. Any suggested connection between the two is simply offensive. It wasn't from boredom either – just the effects of the abnormal heatwave.

• Faye Dunaway sued Andrew Lloyd Webber (later hilariously a Lord), because she was sacked from the cast of musical *Sunset Boulevard*. He said she couldn't sing! When we see him in the House of Lords, we'll no doubt find out *he* can't speak.

September: The roll-on, roll-off ferry *Estonia*, turned out to be roll-over too. Following the failure of a cargo door, the huge ship listed to one side and sunk 300 feet into icy water. 900 were feared dead.

December: Opinion polls showed that support for John Major's government had sunk to its lowest level since gaining power: 8% of the people surveyed.

• Commonwealth gold medal athlete Diane Modahl was accused of having 42 times the normal level of male testosterone in her blood following a routine drugs test. She was banned from competition for four years. Before you start all the bearded lady jokes, she was acquitted on appeal in July 95.

1995

Grozny Groans

They might have abandoned Communism, but those Russian leaders have still got a long way to go when it comes to listening to the wants of their own people. The region of Chechnya didn't want to be Russian any more and declared itself an independent republic. 'Oh no you don't,' growled the great bear, and promptly deployed thousands of troops to teach 'em a lesson. The brave Chechen resistance fighters fought for their lives to defend the capital Grozny, but it was a classic David and Goliath situation, and in *real* life David seldom wins.

Calf Alert
You didn't have to be a veggie to be repelled by the heartless way that veal calves were shipped abroad in crates, and equally repelled by the way our government (which is supposed to do what we say) pussy-footed round the issue. February opened with Jill Phipps, an animal rights activist, being run over by a lorry that was trying to get a load of the poor little cowlets into Coventry Airport.

Barings Go Belly Up
One of London's oldest and poshest merchant banks went into a flat spin when it was discovered that one of their not-very-bright traders, the slightly slimy Nick Leeson, had been playing fast and loose on the Japanese futures market and, when the yen hit the fan, had done a runner. The naughty lad had lost 17 billion quid and had broken one of the unwritten rules of banking. It's OK to *make* fortunes by simply shifting decimal points and not actually producing a bloody thing, but woe betide you if it goes the other way. Tee hee, I say!!

Major Watches his Back

Four days after our illustrious Prime Minister resigned from his other job – Leader of the Conservative Party – in order to test whether his chums still liked him, a rather smarmy Pinocchio look-alike called John Redwood stood up and challenged him. Despite the fact that most of the Tories had been sniping at Major behind his back, when it came right down to it, the cowardly cabinet refused to go out on a limb. There was no chance they were going to vote for some new guy if there was the faintest chance of losing their jobs if it all went the other way. Poor Redwood had fallen into the worst trap known to man (or politician) – believing a word of what his colleagues told him. Major, of course, won hands down, while canny Michael Heseltine, well aware of which side his bread was buttered, became his deputy.

Condon Puts his Boot in It

Metropolitan Police Commissioner Sir Paul Condon, London's head bobby, put his police-issue boot firmly in his mouth when he reported that 80% of all street muggings were carried out by black people. Labour MP Bernie Grant, who just happened to be black, condemned the statement as 'a licence for racists'. Less reactionary people regarded Sir Paul's pronouncement as a bit like claiming that most policemen are fascists. Possibly true – but not particularly helpful.

Hugh Grant Puts his **** in It

On June 27th, Hugh Grant, the foppish star of *Four Weddings and a Funeral*, was fined $500 in a Los Angeles court for lewd conduct with a 'stranger' in the back of his car. Most people were rather surprised that he had it in him. Divine Brown, the recipient of Hugh Grant's 'affections', could hardly believe who she'd had in her.

France Puts a Bomb in It

Trust the French to go out of their way to be politically incorrect. Just when everyone else was bending over backwards to do the

259

right thing nuclear-wise (at least in the West), on the 5th of September they went and exploded a nuclear bomb that practically blasted the Muroroa Atoll out of the inappropriately named Pacific. The more the rest of the world protested, the more those pesky French revelled in getting up our noses. And just to rub it in, they exploded another – five times more powerful – on October 1st. *Sacré bleu!*

FIRST YOU SEE EET – THEN YOU DON'T!

The Big Sleaze

Oh dear, oh dear, those poor Tory MPs lost their hard-fought battle to keep secret the details of all their other sources of loot (especially as it was earned during the time when they should have been working *for us*). From November they would have to disclose details of all their outside consultancies. John Major was well gutted; largely because he'd personally campaigned on their behalf. It also got in the way of MPs receiving payment for advising private companies on parliamentary affairs. The Sleaze Factor, as MPs' secret dealings had been labelled, was at last being delved into and, quoting Corporal Jones of *Dad's Army*, 'They didn't like it up 'em.'

West Goes Down

The whole nasty West murder trial finally ended with Rosemary, Fred's wife, going to prison for the rest of her life. She'd been found guilty of helping her husband murder three of the girls in a manner too disgusting even for *me* to report. At least Rosemary will have some good company in Durham Jail. That's where they keep that nice Myra Hindley (see page 101). Rosemary's dear hubby Mr West hanged himself in prison rather than face trial (saving us from having to hear the gory details). It was about the only decent thing he ever did in his miserable, perverted life.

Head Dead
On December 9th the head teacher of a Maida Vale school was tragically stabbed to death by one of the assailants of a pupil he'd been trying to protect. A huge hue and cry went up to ban knives, even though many people pointed out that anything from a trombone to a frozen turkey could be a dangerous weapon if used with attitude. One also wonders if there would have been such a fuss if he'd been the school-crossing man. Cynical, *moi*?

Meanwhile

January: Camilla Parker Bowles, Prince Charles' rather lived-in, rather than live-in, 'bit on the side' announced her divorce from her husband. Prince Charles, of course (being one of the Royal family and used to gross hypocrisy) carried on as usual.

February: A new MG sports car was revealed by Rover in February. Great, the MGF was not only made by Germans (BMW), but looked much the same as all those dreadful 'sucked sweet' Japanese sports cars.
• 14-year-old Peter Kerry smashed the bad-things-to-do-to-your-parents record when he took his dad's credit cards and calmly flew off round the world. Oddly enough he used his dad's passport, which either meant that he looked much older than his years or his dad was a jockey.

March: New York police officer Carol Shaya-Castro was sacked for posing nude in *Playboy* (which paid her $100,000). Blimey, we'd pay that much to the majority of our female police officers to keep their clothes ON!

May: It was announced that there were plans to add a written bit to the driving test. How nice to know that all those dreadful drivers can at least drive OK on paper.

June: The flip side to the Cinderella story: OJ Simpson, accused of murdering his wife, was forced to try on a pair of blood-stained gloves found at the scene. The ex American-football star, who apparently has huge hands (all the better for murdering you with), tried to make out they didn't fit.
• Further proof that there is a God who looks after the deserving: Lee Taylor-Ryan went swiftly to jail for stealing cars but not before collecting £6.5 million on the Lottery (and not bothering to pass Go).

YOU WILL REMEMBER ME OUTSIDE, WON'T YOU SIR?

August: A 3000-year-old man was found (dead), preserved by the Siberian perma-frost (great for peas as well). He was covered from front to back with a tattoo of an elk, had long red braided hair, embroidered trousers, fur coat and matching boots. I should think he was probably murdered by the Siberian Bad Taste Police.
• The world seemed to be amazed when they heard the TV presenter Michael Barrymore announce he was gay. Well! Who'd have guessed? By the way, did you know a penguin's a sort of bird?

September: It was revealed that, in future, pigs' organs will be used in some transplants. Suffering sausages!

• Brian MacKinnon celebrated his 32nd birthday by going back to school. So what? The problem, as it turned out, was that the school in question was the one he had left when he was 17. 'I just wanted to see if I could do better the second time round,' said Brian, who, rather surprisingly, went undetected for ages. I'd have thought that his new school mates should have been the ones to have their heads (and eyes) examined.

October: Meat eaters throughout Britain had a little giggle when Linda McCartney, goody-goody wife of ex-Beatle Paul, had her super-healthy veggie burgers removed from sale, because of claims they contained too much fat.

November: Damien Hirst, suspected of suffering from mad-artist disease, won the coveted Turner Prize for his Friesian cow suspended in formaldehyde. 'A load of bullocks,' one observer was heard to whisper.

December: The government announced that the level of alcohol which can be considered to be safely consumed in a week is to be raised. Oh no, does that mean that I'll have to drink more to get drunk?

1996

Justice Triumphs
No one was very surprised when those poor misled Maxwell boys who'd made fortunes out of their horrible Dad (Big Max)'s dirty dealings were acquitted of fraud charges. How proud we all were that our wonderful legal system proved that they had absolutely no knowledge of what their own father and business colleague was getting up to. I'm convinced – for one.

Treble Standards

The great British public weren't that surprised either, when Harriet Harman, one of Tony Blair's right-hand women, sent her son to a rather posh school in Orpington rather than the local Southwark comprehensive. After all, her boss had sent his son to the dead smart Oratory, so why not? Out of the blue, Bernie Grant from the far left of the party supported her, saying that London's inner schools were atrocious (and it was all the Tories' fault). That's my kind of party: one whose principles can be bent any way you wish to prove a point.

Keeping your hand in

The IRA finally got bored with being pacifists. As I wondered back in 1994 (see page 254), what were all these trained killers going to do with their spare time – learn Riverdancing? Just to show that they could still kill and maim innocent people, they bombed Canary Wharf on February 10th and one of our red buses (is nothing sacred?) on the Aldwych a little later. OK,

the cease-fire was now over, but let's face it, it had always seemed too good to be true.

Great Scott

Remember all that business about that huge gun that wasn't a gun (see page 228), and the way that big business and government appeared to have their sticky hands in it? Three years later the Scott Enquiry published its findings in what should have been an unbiased report. The government had cleverly got to Sir Richard Scott first, leaning on him to water it down and present it in such a way as to make them all look squeaky clean. Even so there were still pretty damning statements, like the one about the Attorney

General, Nicholas Lyell: 'I do not accept that he was not personally at fault.' Nought out of ten for grammar, Sir Richard, but we know what you're saying.

Dunblane

The biggest and worstest story of the year broke on the 13th of March when a maniac gun freak, Thomas Hamilton, decided to take it out on a society that had rejected him, by walking calmly into an infant school and slaughtering 16 innocent little kids and their teacher. The media, God bless it, went into sickening overdrive, plummeting to new depths of invasive tastelessness. Everyone right up (or down) to the Royals competed in public shows of sympathy, until the good folk of Dunblane told them, in no uncertain terms, to leave them alone to their grief. By this time anyone with half a brain realized that there was absolutely no point allowing people to own guns, even if it did upset a few sad anoraks who got their rocks off shooting at paper targets. Actually, I say everyone but, guess what, the government went strangely silent. Nothing to do with having their own gun club under the House of Commons – I'm sure.

Mad Ministers Disease

At last our betters decided to let us in on the truth about cow meat and what it could actually do to us. On 21st March our leaders finally admitted the high possibility of a link between Mad Cow Disease and a smart new disease called Creutzfeldt-Jakob which had apparently been killing people for years. The only notable change was that beef went real cheap in the supermarkets (for about ten minutes). It was a bit like the AIDS scare: if you didn't actually know anyone (or any cow) with it, it didn't seem anything to really worry about. Anyway, it was a bit too late. Most of us had been eating the stuff – contaminated or otherwise – for years, so what was the point of worrying now?

German Uprising

On the 26th of June, Germany beat Britain in the Euro '96 soccer semi-finals. The match was won (or lost) on penalty shootouts, which I reckon wouldn't have been a bad way to settle the last war. Our fab British fans, having been praised for their good sportsmanship throughout the tournament, promptly went looking for anyone with a foreign accent to beat up.

Death Before Life?

Worst place to be a frozen embryo was Britain in July '97. For some reason the people in charge couldn't trace the 900 parents of some 3300 of the poor chilly babelets. It appeared that after five years, the weeny frozen five-year-olds must be destroyed (a bit like throwing away frozen beans when past their freezer date). The Vatican called it 'pre-natal massacre'. C'mon lads, what about all those starving, unwanted Third World babies?

Congratulations × 8

Talking of embryos, in August an extremely astute woman called Mandy Allwood discovered, after taking a fertility drug, that she had eight inside her (that's what happens if you don't read the label properly). She was extremely astute because she tried to turn the whole business into a media circus by employing that tasteful publicist Max Clifford and flogging her rather fascinating and heartrending story to the true defender of all that's good – *The News of the World*. Smart Mandy, naturally went on to better things. And the babies? Oh, they all died.

Life After Death?

Had the country gone embryo blinking mad? In October, the ominously named Diane Blood (sounds like a pirate's wife) was refused permission to use her dead husband's emission to help make the child they'd planned. Apparently the law says you can't use the sperm of anyone (frozen or not) without their written permission – even if they are dead. Who said the law was an ass? Arse more like! I know I'm not supposed to do this (jump ahead in to a different year, I mean) but it all came right in 1997, when she was allowed to take her dead hubby's sperm to Belgium (think of another good reason for going) to do the business there.

Riding High

1996 was the year for naughty school kids. Reports flooded in to the press of children who'd been terrorizing their teachers being banned from the classroom. It was a bit like the 'Man bites dog' story. The telly news featured a shower of irate, if somewhat monosyllabic, parents who, having not spent a minute thinking of their darling little 'uns' education (or their own), throwing the 'Why pick on them' switch. Worst of all was the Ridings School in Halifax where, in October, 60 little monsters were kicked out, much to the dismay of their mums and dads. Bring back the cane I say . . . but only for the parents!

Margaret and the Spice Girls

Like so many famous-for-15 minutes (I hope) pop groups, the delightful and politically mature Spice Girls reckoned correctly that their new-found adulation gave them the right to utter words of wisdom on all things. 'Margaret Thatcher is our inspiration,' they cried in December, even though many horribly cynical people believed someone else might just be working their mouths (like ventriloquists' dummies). Let's face it, everyone else under 25 goes along with that sentiment (not). One can only hope they go the same way as their mentor (but please make it quicker).

Meanwhile

January: Daphne Banks, 61, having been pronounced dead and dumped in a sealed tray in a hospital mortuary, was observed to

twitch and let out a snore. Good job she wasn't in the House of
Lords – no one would have noticed.

February: Joan Collins won her court battle with her publishers
Random House, who dared to suggest that the eminent woman of
letters' latest effort was not proper literature. I bet *my* publishers
would have no problem proving mine wasn't. Hang on a minute!
They *are* my publishers.
• Sperm count drops – shock horror! The semen from 500
Scottish volunteers was found to be of worse quality that those
born in the '50s – by 25%. No jokes about there being quite
enough Scotsmen already, please.

March: Tory MP Sir Nicholas Scott (yet another one) was fined
£900, and banned from driving for a year after trapping a toddler
in a pushchair between his car and another before calmly (if
somewhat irrationally) leaving the scene of the accident. He'd just
left a party (soon to be the Tory party). Odd really, it's very unlike
a politician to create a messy situation and then pretend he had
nothing to do with it.

May: Dustin Hoffman, while at the Cannes Film Festival, claimed that films are becoming too violent – yet another example of someone who's made his fortune and feels obliged to lecture others. *Marathon Man*, in which he starred, was one of the most violent films I've ever seen. Put your mouth where your money is, Dustin.

June: After the great 'smack' debate (the one about violence not drugs) Tony Blair admitted that he'd smacked his children when little. He did say he was sorry, however. Not half as sorry as they were, I bet.

July: Isn't it bloody marvellous! In a country where seriously sick people are being shunted round the country because of the shortage of hospital beds, and our schools are falling to pieces through hopeless underfunding, our politicians saw fit to vote themselves a ten grand pay rise. Would it be too cynical to suggest that the day they voted it in was one of the rare times the Commons was full?

August: After loads of speculation, the fairy tale marriage of the century spiralled down the great plughole of history. Prince Charles finally got shot of Di and vice versa. There was hardly a damp eye in the land – especially not Camilla's.

November: Questions were asked as to whether Paul Gascoigne should be removed from the England team for beating up his wife. Poor lad, they can't do that – it might make him cry. To be honest, I'd have booted him out for simply being a total prat, let alone an overgrown, lager-swilling bully. And I'd even have lent him my hankie.

1997

Kraut Alert

Talking of Germans (which we weren't), the whole of the country had a behind-the-hands giggle at the news that mighty Germany was now wading in economic poo (relatively speaking) with unemployment the highest in Europe. For years we British had had to watch in disbelief as we slowly slid down the pan, while they (along with the Japanese), soared on to an economic plain that we could only drool over. And for years we'd had to put up with their cocky Euro-Fuhrers telling us so patronizingly where we'd been going wrong. Notice I didn't mention the war!

Di's Frock Sensation

Princess Di, in a rush of generosity, decided to auction most of her past-their-prime (fashionwise) dresses for charity. *The Daily Express* in a rush of pure fact-finding investigative journalism (what?) claimed that she was keeping a large part of the money for herself (which she wasn't). I reckon that if anyone should have got a kickback it should have been the British taxpayer. We paid for the damned clobber in the first place.

Robin Hood Goes Underground

A new breed of protester has emerged over the last few years from the sit-it-out-and-see-what-they-do school of civil action. All those familiar old crusties who had set up camps in old coaches and ambulances, claiming the dole and demanding to be left to do their own thing (man!), much to the distress of local inhabitants, found a fab new game and an inspired *raison d'être*. They became Eco Protesters, scouring the country searching out plans for new roads and tearing their dreadlocked hair out over the trees that would be lost in the building process. As well as sitting in the threatened trees like vagrant vultures, they decided to live in holes.

AN ENGLISHMAN'S HOLE IS HIS CASTLE

In October 1996 a group of youths decided to 'dig in' to halt a dual carriageway being built between Exeter and Honiton. Their leader and spokesman, a brilliant, incisive bloke called Swampy, stayed in his own personal bijou and detached hole long after the others. 'My mum started with Ban the Bomb and later ended up at Greenham,' he stuttered, when he finally came blinking into the cold, grey January light.

'It's terrible, when they come here and cut down your home in front of you,' wailed profusely-pierced colleague, Hattie, an old-style tree dweller who'd just been dispossessed of a very nice two-up-no-down beech. 'This is not a war between them and us, it's about saving the environment.'

And my name's Woody Woodpecker, Hattie!

Who's Gonna Win?
The big buzz at the beginning of the year was whether pretty boy Tony Blair was going to topple the now-established Johnny Major and, much more important, if such a catastrophe did happen, whether the Spice Girls, our five young political gurus, would be forced to change sides. The election was set for May 1st. Would the Tories be finally shown the door after 17 years? Watch this space.

Same But Different

The whole election bun-fight gradually began to take the country over. The Tories carefully massaged the trade figures to make it look as if England, instead of being the sick dog of Europe, was actually king of the kennel, while also making sure that house prices, so long a yardstick of well-being with the property-owning classes, started to go up again. I say, chaps, perhaps the Tories knew what they were doing all along! Suddenly the opinion polls were telling different stories as, just like the old tortoise and hare yarn, tortoise Major started pulling back the enormous lead of the runaway favourite – hare Blair.

Blair, of course, was fully aware that the great, all-powerful British Middle Classes would vote to protect the money in their own personal pockets (just like they did last time), so he carefully softened his socialism and dowsed his politics in honey, making his policies much sweeter to swallow. As happens before any election, the major parties, terrified of sticking their necks out too far, appeared to move closer and closer together until, in the end, the choice for the floating punter seemed a bit of a toss-up.

Somewhere in the middle, like the proverbial piggy, poor old Paddy Pants Down's Lib Dem party staggered backwards and forwards, never quite sure on whose side it would be allowed to flop down. But the main teams were already picked, the whistle was about to be blown and eighteen years of Conservative rule were up for grabs.

General Election '97

Nobody could have foretold the titanic trouncing the Tories received on the fateful night of May 1st. As the results began to trickle in, words like 'landslide' were scrubbed out in favour of 'earthquake', 'wipe-out' or 'massacre'. One by one, all those Conservative MPs we'd loved to hate (well, some of us) were kicked through their constituency back doors. The likes of Edwina–bad egg–Currie, David–toe sucker–Mellor, Norman–what recession?–Lamont, Rhodes–punish 'em plenty–Boyson, Neil–super sleaze–Hamilton and finally, joy of all joys, the man who

272

looked more like his *Spitting Image* puppet than . . . his *Spitting Image* puppet, Defence Secretary and man most likely to succeed Major, the sublimely awful Michael Portillo. It was all too much for one night. Sort of like having all your birthdays at once.

All Over

'We have been comprehensively defeated,' sighed a pale (or should I say paler) Johnny Major, while his surviving colleagues, sensing his weakened condition, began snapping at his heels (behind his back of course), all with a well-practised eye on his job. Blair, equally shell-shocked, and now the youngest PM since 1812, with the largest majority for half a century, stood blinking in the spotlight with his faithful wife (and daughter of a has-been sitcom star) Cherie, no doubt wondering what he'd let himself in for. Imagine actually *trying* to become Prime Minister. I'd rather ask a fox if I could take its place in a hunt, or apply for the job as target in a shooting range.

Blimey, even Paddy had a good night. Nearly three times more Lib Dem MPs, which, although still not being that many (around 45), seemed to make the old chap deliriously happy. It must have been like finally catching a fish after his poor, wrinkled worm had been in the water for years (metaphorically speaking).

And What Now?

At last England had made up its mind and Scotland and Wales had made up their minds even more. The Tories had been told in no uncertain terms to get lost and a brand New Labour government with a sparkly new leader had the kind of majority that meant it could do exactly as it liked.

Princess Di – the Bitter End

On the night of 31st August, all the other news stories of 1997– even the decade – were totally eclipsed by a tragedy that occurred in Paris. Critics and fans alike were stunned by the news and circumstances of the death of the Princess of Wales and Dodi, the son of Mohamed Al Fayed. Everyone had their own version of what had caused the crash in that tunnel close to the Seine. It soon became the mystery of the century.

Di Mania

But it wasn't the accident that shocked we Royal watchers, it was the astounding reaction of the British public. From one sad little posy, placed outside the gates of Buck House, a mountain of flowers, which must have made a millionaire of every florist in the land, grew and grew till it spread right up to Kensington Palace.

Final Tribute

If for nothing else, Princess Diana will be remembered for her work amongst AIDS victims and even more for the almost unilateral ban on the use of landmines on 4th December, a cause which she had championed in the last few months of her life. (I say almost, because the two most important countries, USA and China, said no.)

Meanwhile

There's none so odd as religious folk. 39 members of the California Heaven's Gate sect decided to try to reach their heavenly home in March by committing mass suicide. They hoped that by killing themselves they'd get a free ride on a UFO.

Anyone who remembered the speech, at a Conservative Party Conference, given by a precocious teenager, William Hague, was gobsmacked when he was elected as the Tory leader in July. Great news for Labour supporters, however.

On 1st July Britain gave Hong Kong back to the Chinese. The

Chinese leader assured the residents that it would rule the island with 'prudence and responsibility', and then moved in 4,000 fully armed troops to prove it.

British Nannies are Best? Please Debate

19-year-old Louise Woodward was found guilty in November of violently shaking her American charge, little Matthew Eappen. She allegedly hit his head on the floor to stop him crying. It worked. The poor kid died from fatal brain damage.

1998

White House Follies

The story that kept us all on our toes for the best part of this year came, surprisingly, not from Posh and Beck's marriage plans, but from the naughty antics of Bill Clinton, President of the USA. The most powerful man in the world – bar none – was caught with his stars-and-stripes pants well and truly down, in the juiciest scandal ever – starring young White House intern, Monica Lewinsky.

Blair Blaah!

Tony Blair and his government were continuing to do rather well and to shove his ratings even higher he announced details of the contents of the much fabled Millennium Dome, a forthcoming treat for all his subjects at the dawning of a new century. As we all know now, it was to become a rip-roaring . . . disaster.

Baltic Battling

We in Britain continued to be stunned by the hatred that was exposed as the country formerly known as Yugoslavia continued to tear itself into ever smaller pieces in front of our very eyes. On 12th October NATO leaders took off their kid gloves and threatened to bomb the ethnically cleansing Serbs into submission.

Slippery Serbian supremo Milosovich finally agreed to behave himself and even allowed observers in to see that he did. He didn't.

Peace at Last?
In April, English and Irish politicians finally agreed on a peace settlement that looked as though it might put an end to Catholics and Protestants killing each other in Northern Ireland. Rather prematurely, Tony Blair referred to the settlement as a triumph of courage. 'The hand of history is upon us,' he crooned with satisfaction. A month later, in a referendum, Irishmen on both sides of the border backed the peace agreement, leaving a lot of professional terrorists wondering what they were going to do next. Was it really all over? Watch this space.

Old Spice
A great loss to the world of culture. Music lovers were shaken to the core at the announcement that Spice Girl Geri Halliwell (Ginger Spice) was to leave the rest of the girls.

Only Kidding
Surprise, surprise. On 5th August the worst outrage since the Northern Irish troubles began 31 years earlier occurred in Omagh High Street. 28 people were blown to bits by a Republican bomb. It was an appalling tragedy. Even the IRA spokesman Gerry Adams was moved to comment that it might not have been the best thing they could have done to further their cause.

Terribly Sorry
Sir Paul Condon, Commissioner of the Metropolitan Police, apologised on 1st October for the right mess his boys had made of finding the killers of Stephen Lawrence, the black teenager murdered at a bus stop by white racist youths. The lad's father would have none of it, claiming that the speech was merely a poorly handled PR job.

Beef Back
On 23rd November, after nearly three years, the European Union farm ministers decided to lift their ban on British beef that had followed the outbreak of the Mad Cow Disease. British farmers and

taxpayers, who'd lost over £4 billion, sighed with relief, though the cows seemed strangely unmoved. I don't suppose it matters much whether you're eaten or not when you're dead.

Lord Almighty!

The poor old Queen looked like she'd been forced to suck lemons at the State Opening of Parliament on 24th November. She had to announce, amid muffled cheers, that the right of hereditary Lords (her mates) to sit or vote in what they'd always thought was their own house was soon to be rescinded. Strangely enough, of the 759 lords at risk, only 18 favoured the Labour party. No wonder the Queen looked miffed...

Saddam Smashed

Nasty, cynical people might claim that Bill Clinton timed his massive air attack called 'Desert Fox' on Kuwait in order to take the pressure off his looming impeachment over the Lewinski affair. Either way, our boy Blair was right behind him. Countless Tomahawk cruise missiles whizzed from British Tornado fighters that had been waiting patiently on the American carrier Enterprise.

Meanwhile

January: Talk about egg on your face. William, the 17-year-old son of anti-cannabis campaigner and Home Secretary Jack Straw, was named in court. He'd been arrested for selling the stuff just before Christmas. Whoops!

February: 32-year-old circus worker Nigel Wesson was interviewed by a hospital orderly after having his left arm nibbled off by a tiger. Before going into the operating theatre he was asked if he was allergic to anything. 'Only tigers,' was his rather witty reply.

March: This year's Oscar ceremonies were dominated by the movie *Titanic* which won 11 awards. Unfortunately there wasn't one for gross over-sentimentality, otherwise it would certainly have had 12.

April: British singer George Michael was arrested for performing a 'lewd act' in a public loo in Hollywood. At least he wasn't our president.

May: 'Old Blue Eyes', Frank Sinatra, died on the 14th in Beverly Hills, aged 82. Many believed the Mafia mourned the loss more than most.

July: Good news for Derek Bentley who was hanged for the murder of a policeman back in 1953. On the 30th of this month his conviction was overturned by the Court of Appeal. Some cynics claimed it was 48 years too late.

September: Shock, horror. It was announced on the 5th that the wonder drug Viagra would not be available on our National Health Service. Instead tablets would cost at least £6 each. Thousands of middle-aged men went limp at the news.

October: 82-year-old General Augusto Pinochet, the former dictatorial leader of Chile, had his stay in London delayed indefinitely when he was arrested on charges of murder and torture back home. Practically his only friend over here was our own Maggie Thatcher.

December: That nice Peter Mandelson, the Trade and Industry Secretary, was forced to resign when it was discovered that he'd been lent £373,000 by good chum Geoffrey Robinson who was, rather appropriately, the Paymaster General.

1999

Euro Time
On midnight of the last day of 1998, the European Union kicked off the start of the euro as their new official currency. The franc, lira and deutschmark had a stay of execution for 3 years. Dear old Britain, as usual, dithered in the wings, unable to make up its mind.

Clinton Gets Off
It was obvious the American people didn't want their smutty but likeable president to go. The impeachment trial ended on 12th February with a complete acquittal. He hadn't, so they reckoned, told porkies after all.

Frankenstein Foods Ltd

Poor old Tony Blair nearly choked on his genetically modified breakfast, having proclaimed in public that tinkering around with foods was perfectly safe. When the press revealed that even human genes were being grafted into plants, producing 'Frankenstein foods', the good old general public would have no more of it. The government was forced to ban all commercially grown GM foods until further trials prove that we won't all be growing extra heads or limbs.

The Second Coming

A star shone over the capital on 5th March to guide the wise men of the press to a very special birth. Lo, a boy-child had been born. Not in a manger, but the Portland Hospital in London's West End. Mother Posh (Victoria Adams) and father Becks (David Beckham) became proud parents to young Brooklyn, so named because that's where he was conceived. Phew! I was lucky. On that basis, my parents could have called me Luton.

NATO Blasts Off

Well you can't say they weren't warned. NATO finally began strategic strikes against Serbia on Monday 29th March. Slobodan Milosovich had completely broken his word to the Albanian population of Kosovo and had instigated a major offensive to drive them from their homes. Thousands of refugees were already heading for nearby Macedonia to avoid being slaughtered. It was a war that Milosovich couldn't win.

On 3rd April NATO turned its attention to the Serbian capital of Belgrade. 8 well-directed cruise missiles turned the ministerial centre into a huge roaring bonfire, even outdoing the Germans' best efforts in 1941. Nato leaders then suggested that this was just a taster. There was far worse to come.

Dando Dead!

Popular TV star Jill Dando was gunned down outside her Fulham house on Monday 26th March. The 37-year-old was shot in the head in broad daylight, but no one saw a thing.

There Was a Princess Called Diana . . .
If you want to be poet laureate, write a gushy rhyme about Lady Diana Spencer. . . that's what Andrew Motion did. It all went sour, however, when his appointment on 18th May was derided by fellow poets, claiming it 'a disgrace, a scandal and an insult to the country's intelligence'.

We Give In
The Serb parliament put their hands up and accepted the peace plans from Russia and the European Union. The deal was that they stopped trying to ethnically cleanse Kosovo and that it would henceforth be occupied by NATO troops. Just to make sure they didn't cheat, the bombing was to continue until all the details were ironed out and agreed. On 13th June, NATO and Russian troops were greeted as saviours by the shell-shocked ethnic Albanians as they rolled into Kosovo.

Eclipse Eclipsed
Millions of people looked up to the sky on 11th August to watch the sun being obscured by the moon in the middle of the day. How? A total eclipse, the first since 1927, was due. Unfortunately it was a typically English Wednesday, so the whole thing was hidden by heavy cloud.

Railway Horror
The beginning of what was to become nearly the end for British Rail came on Tuesday 5th October when two commuter trains were involved in a head-on collision at Ladbroke Grove Station in West London. 30 people lost their lives in the fireball that engulfed the carriages.

Millennium Frenzy

You'd think it was the end of the world as we knew it. The back end of 1999 was completely taken over by talk of what we were going to do on the big night and how we were going to cope when everything with anything resembling a computer inside it would close down leaving the world in chaos and panic.

Meanwhile

Warning! Don't eat monkeys. Scientists announced on 31st January that the AIDS virus that has so far infected over 30 million people world-wide, probably came from hunters eating bad chimps.

Isn't she maaaaaarvelous! The Queen Mum entered her 100th year on 4th August.

Forget the Dome. The brilliant London Eye Ferris wheel, the tallest in the world, appeared by the Thames in October. It had hardly been up a month before it was covered by Green Peace protesters claiming it was a waste of money.

2000

As the clock struck twelve and we slid into a new millennium, we all waited for the total panic and confusion that would no doubt follow the collapse of all our computers. All that happened, was a massive sense of anti-climax. Almost symbolically, the promised 'River of Fire' firework extravaganza on the River Thames, failed to ignite, the London Eye wasn't ready to go round and anyone daft enough to visit the Dome realised there wasn't anything remotely worth seeing inside.

In and Out

On 7th January, the Tory MP Jonathan Aitkin was released from prison having served well under half his 18-month sentence. He'd been found guilty of lying while under oath about accepting bribes.

Water Water Everywhere

In March, horrendous stories hit the headlines of the flooding in Mozambique, south-east Africa. Millions were left homeless and 700 died. We in Britain were terribly sorry, naturally, but nonetheless thankful that nothing like that ever happens over here. Or does it? The year 2000 was to prove Britain's wettest for the last 400 and lowland areas flooded repeatedly causing misery for the poor people whose homes were ruined.

Good News, Bad News

Just as the situation in Yugoslavia seemed finally to be sorting itself out, due to the forced resignation of the hateful dictator Milosovich, the proverbial shit hit the fan once more in the Middle East. In October, the long standing tiff between the Palestinians and Israelis began again and hundreds were killed as a result.

Meanwhile

Somebody thought of a daft TV idea that involved locking up a bunch of desperately media-hungry wannabes, keeping the camera on them 24-hours a day and then asking them to kick each other out one at a time as they fell out of favour. *Big Brother* was the biggest TV hit to date, which I'm afraid says more about the British viewing public than just about anything else.

The England cricket team led by Nasser Hussain (from a fine old English family) won its first test series against Pakistan for 38 years in December.

A bad year ended worse when little Damilola Taylor, a 10-year-old Nigerian boy was stabbed and left to bleed to death in Peckham, a distressed area of London. It followed a trail of bullying that left youngsters in fear of losing their dinner money or worse – their mobile phones.

Isn't fashion wonderful. Fashion designer Hussein Chalayan produced a range of frocks out of spun sugar that would fall to bits as soon as you tapped them. Sweet but stupid.

On a lighter note, the TV hit of the year, *Who Wants to be a Millionaire*, led us all to despair when we realised we had to have intelligent friends. 'Phone a friend', '50-50, or 'ask the audience' became part of everyday speak.

CAN I HAVE MY BALL BACK?